SpringerBriefs in Finance

SpringerBriefs present concise summaries of cutting-edge research and practical applications across a wide spectrum of fields. Featuring compact volumes of 50 to 125 pages, the series covers a range of content from professional to academic. Typical topics might include: a timely report of state-of-the art analytical techniques, a bridge between new research results, as published in journal articles, and a contextual literature review, a snapshot of a hot or emerging topic, an in-depth case study or clinical example, and a presentation of core concepts that students must understand in order to make independent contributions. SpringerBriefs in Finance showcase emerging theory, empirical research, and practical application in corporate finance, banking, financial management, behavioral finance, financial markets, social and entrepreneurial finance, microfinance, and related fields, from a global author community. Briefs are characterized by fast, global electronic dissemination, standard publishing contracts, standardized manuscript preparation and formatting guidelines, and expedited production schedules.

Monica Violeta Achim • Robert W. McGee
Editors

Financial Crime in Romania

A Community Pulse Survey

Springer

Editors
Monica Violeta Achim
Economics and Business Administration
Babeş-Bolyai University
Cluj-Napoca, Romania

Robert W. McGee
Broadwell College of Business
and Economics
Fayetteville State University
Fayetteville, NC, USA

ISSN 2193-1720 ISSN 2193-1739 (electronic)
SpringerBriefs in Finance
ISBN 978-3-031-27882-2 ISBN 978-3-031-27883-9 (eBook)
https://doi.org/10.1007/978-3-031-27883-9

This Springer imprint is published by the registered company Springer Nature Switzerland AG
The registered company address is: Gewerbestrasse 11, 6330 Cham, Switzerland

Abstract

The aim of this book is to determine the financial crime community pulse in Romania. For this purpose, a survey questionnaire was distributed to 1856 respondents between May 27 and June 6, 2022.

The first objective of our book consists in finding the main patterns that characterize the Romanian community, related to the financial crime perception variables (the level of tax compliance, the level of tax morale reflected as the attitude of citizens toward accepting cheating on taxes, the perception of the corruption level in Romanian public institutions, the level of skills possessed by citizens to detect the risk of money laundering, and the attitude towards giving information to bank officers). We find that a majority of 64% of the citizens interviewed had a good or very good level of tax compliance, meaning that they have declared that they paid their taxes long before the last deadline (for discount benefits or not only for discount benefits). Regarding their tax morale, we found that a majority of 74% of the Romanian respondents had an active attitude *toward accepting cheating on taxes* (they usually or always receive their receipt and take it); about 13% of respondents have a proactive attitude (if they do not receive their receipt, they ask for it) while another 13% of respondents have a passive attitude (if they receive or do not receive their receipt, it doesn't matter). When it comes to corruption, a majority of 66% of Romanian citizens have declared that they perceived the level of Romanian corruption to be high or very high. Additionally, our results show that a majority of 70% of our citizens have low or very low skills to detect the risk of money laundering in a business; about 25% of those interviewed have medium skills, while only about 5% have high or very high skills for detecting suspicious transactions. About 68% of citizens have a good attitude toward being asked for information by bank officers, while about 32% have a medium or bad attitude (refuse or hardly provide required information to bank officers).

The second objective of the book is to investigate how the demographic aspects considered in the survey (age, gender, region of living, professional status, and education) are associated with the considered financial crime perception variables. In the majority of cases, the demographic variables were found to be significant determinants for the perception of financial crime, while age was found to have the most significant impact. The results are important for policy makers in order to adopt the proper policies that would reduce the level of financial crime in Romania.

JEL Classification H26; D73; G18

Keywords Corruption; Tax avoidance; Tax behavior; Gender; Age; AML skills; Education; Professional status; Pulse; Romania

Acknowledgments

This work was supported by a grant of the Romanian Ministry of Education and Research, CNCS-UEFISCDI, project number PN-III-P4-ID-PCE-2020-2174, within PNCDI III titled "Intelligent analysis and prediction of the economic and financial crime in a cyber-dominated and interconnected business world," conducted over the period 2021–2023.

Research conducted to explore contributing factors to the anti-money laundering (AML) landscape in Romania. The AML analysis has been sponsored by SAS Romania.

This study is part of the COST project CA19130 FinAI – Fintech and Artificial Intelligence in Finance – Towards a Transparent Financial Industry.

Contents

About the Authors

Monica Violeta Achim is full professor and doctoral supervisor in the field of Finance at the Faculty of Economics and Business Administration, Babeş-Bolyai University, Cluj-Napoca, Romania. With over 24 years of experience in academia, she has published, as author and co-author, over 150 scientific articles and 25 books. Her most recent reference work is the book *Economic and Financial Crime. Corruption, Shadow Economy and Money Laundering*, published by Springer. In 2020 she earned an Award for Excellence in Scientific Research at Babeş-Bolyai University, Faculty of Economics and Business Administration, Cluj-Napoca, Romania, in recognition of the results obtained in her research activity. She heads a big grant titled "Intelligent analysis and prediction of economic and financial crime in a cyber-dominated and interconnected business world," conducted over the period 2021–2023, financed from the Romanian Ministry of Education and Research, CNCS-UEFISCDI, project number PN-III-P4-ID-PCE-2020-2174 (www.fincrime.net).

Sorin Nicolae Borlea is professor and doctoral supervisor in the field of Finance at the University of Oradea and Vasile Goldiş University, and associate scientific researcher at the European Research Institute of Babeş-Bolyai University Cluj-Napoca. He has over 16 years of experience in the academic field and 30 years in the business environment. He has published over 90 scientific articles and 20 books. His most recent reference work is the co-authored book *Economic and Financial Crime: Corruption, Shadow Economy and Money Laundering*, published by Springer. In parallel with the academic field, he works in the business environment as financial auditor, accounting expert, tax consultant, and financial analyst, being strongly anchored in economic and financial crime issues in the files managed by the Court of Cluj-Napoca. He is well known in the business environment as a perfectionist, being ranked in the top 10 accounting experts in Cluj County (2017). He is a member of the project titled "Intelligent analysis and prediction of the economic and financial crime in a cyber-dominated and interconnected business world," conducted over the period 2021–2023, financed from the Romanian Ministry of Education and Research, CNCS-UEFISCDI, project number PN-III-P4-ID-PCE-2020-2174 (www.fincrime.net).

Mihai Gaicu holds a BSc and a MSc in Business Engineering from Solvay Brussels School and a specialized Master in Data Science, Big Data from the Free University of Brussels. He acquired experience over 2 years in the Banking sector and the IT industry, focusing on Financial Crime and Artificial Intelligence. He is a subject-matter expert in Anti-Money Laundering and currently working as a global solution advisor at SAS Institute. His role consists of collaborating with R&D and delivery teams to deploy industry best practices for AML solutions and helping financial institutions around the world to fight fraud and to meet regulatory compliance.

Codruța Mare is professor at the Department of Statistics-Forecasts-Mathematics and PhD coordinator in the field of Cybernetics and Statistics, Faculty of Economics and Business Administration, and the Scientific Director of the Interdisciplinary Centre for Data Science, Babeș-Bolyai University, Cluj-Napoca, Romania. She teaches several types of Statistics and Econometrics methods, from Descriptive Statistics to Economic Forecasting and Spatial Econometrics. She has expertise in consultancy and research projects conducted both for public institutions (The World Bank, European Commission, Romanian Ministry of Structural Funds, Cluj-Napoca City Hall, etc.) and for private companies, along with delivering training both in data analysis and visualization, in Romania and abroad. Results of her research were published in books and articles in prestigious international journals. She is a member of the project titled "Intelligent analysis and prediction of the economic and financial crime in a cyber-dominated and interconnected business world," conducted over the period 2021–2023, financed from the Romanian Ministry of Education and Research, CNCS-UEFISCDI, project number PN-III-P4-ID-PCE-2020-2174 (www.fincrime.net).

Robert W. McGee is business professor at Fayetteville State University, USA. He has earned 23 academic degrees, including 13 doctorates from universities in the United States and 4 European countries. He has published more than 60 books, including several novels, and more than 1000 articles, book chapters, conference papers, and working papers. Various studies have ranked him #1 in the world for both accounting ethics and business ethics scholarship. He is an attorney and CPA (retired) and has worked or lectured in more than 30 countries. He drafted the accounting law for Armenia and Bosnia and reviewed the accounting law for Mozambique. He was in charge of assisting the Finance Ministries of Armenia and Bosnia convert their countries to International Financial Reporting Standards. He is also a world champion in taekwondo, karate, kung fu, and tai chi (both Yang and Sun styles) and has won more than 900 gold medals.

Gabriela-Mihaela Mureșan holds a PhD in Finance and currently works as lecturer at the Department of Finance, Faculty of Economics and Business Administration Babeș-Bolyai University. She has published more than 20 research papers, 2 international books, 2 national books, and attended several international conferences. Her research interests are broadly focused in the field of insurance, financial analysis, and economic psychology. She is especially interested in human behavior, manipulation, money addiction, culture, happiness, ethics, corruption, fraud, corporate performance, bankruptcy, and creative accounting. She is member of the project titled "Intelligent analysis and prediction of the economic and financial crime in a cyber-dominated and interconnected business world," conducted over the period 2021–2023, financed from the Romanian Ministry of Education and Research, CNCS-UEFISCDI, project number PN-III-P4-ID-PCE-2020-2174 (www.fincrime.net).

Ioana Lavinia Safta has a degree in Economics, with a Master's degree in Audit and Control Accounting Management. She is currently a second-year PhD student in Finance, with an interest in economics, "The relationship between creative accounting and fraud, models for detecting the risk of fraud at the level of economic entities." She worked as assistant professor at the Department of Finance, Faculty of Economics and Business Administration, Babeş-Bolyai University in Cluj-Napoca. She gained over 3 years of experience in accounting, working as an accountant in a financial expertise and audit firm. She is the author/co-author of scientific articles in her studies area. Her research interests are focused on finance and accounting. Lately, she has given special attention on issues related to economic and financial crime. She is a member of the project titled "Intelligent analysis and prediction of economic and financial crime in a cyber-dominated and interconnected business world," conducted over the period 2021–2023, financed from the Romanian Ministry of Education and Research, CNCS-UEFISCDI, project number PN-III-P4-ID-PCE-2020-2174 (www.fincrime.net).

Mircea Constantin Şcheau holds a PhD in Public Order and National Security with a topic of interest for economic and security fields, "Cybercrime on financial transfers," who received the "Victor Slavescu Prize" awarded by the Romanian Academy. Author/co-author of 3 volumes and more than 40 scientific articles on management, law enforcement, critical infrastructure, information technology, and defense; lecturer at numerous international conferences and member, inter alia, of the "Policies and strategies in the European Union's single market" research group of the European Research Institute of Babeş-Bolyai University, Cluj-Napoca. He is a member of the project titled "Intelligent analysis and prediction of the economic and financial crime in a cyber-dominated and interconnected business world," conducted over the period 2021–2023, financed from the Romanian Ministry of Education and Research, CNCS-UEFISCDI, project number PN-III-P4-ID-PCE-2020-2174 (www.fincrime.net).

Viorela-Ligia Văidean is associate professor in the field of Finance at the Faculty of Economics and Business Administration, Babeş-Bolyai University, Cluj-Napoca. She obtained a Bachelor degree in Finance and Banking from Babeş-Bolyai University (BBU) Cluj-Napoca, Romania, in 2006, further graduating from a Master program in Corporate Finance and Insurances and another degree in Project Management and Evaluation. She successfully followed a full-time PhD program, obtaining her PhD in the Finance field, in 2010. In 2015 she graduated from a post-doctoral study program. She has worked as teaching assistant and then lecturer for the Finance Department within BBU Cluj-Napoca. She has also worked as an expert for different EU-financed projects and grants. She has published more than 40 research papers and attended several international conferences. She has been the author or co-author of 10 books and international book chapters. Her research interests cover the areas of Health Economics, Corporate Finance, Financial Management, Organized Crime, and Fiscal Policies. She is member of the project titled "Intelligent analysis and prediction of the economic and financial crime in a cyber-dominated and interconnected business world," conducted over the period 2021–2023, financed from the Romanian Ministry of Education and Research, CNCS-UEFISCDI, project number PN-III-P4-ID-PCE-2020-2174 (www.fincrime.net).

List of Figures

List of Tables

Chapter 1
Financial Crime: Introduction

Monica Violeta Achim, Robert W. McGee, and Mircea Constantin Şcheau

Abstract This chapter introduces the reader to the structure and content of the book, which reports the results of a large study of attitudes of the Romanian people toward corruption and a variety of ethically questionable financial activities. Demographic variables such as gender, age, education level, and geographic region are examined to determine whether different subgroups view these ethical issues differently.

Keywords Financial crime · Corruption · Cybercrime · Romania

It is not necessary to have a higher education in the field of fighting crime in order to understand that economic and financial crime has existed since ancient times, and that it has evolved and adapted to society. Starting from several thousand years ago when criminals forged certain coins, and going through the period of the Middle Ages when the first documented cases of tax fraud were registered, we reach the point where tax evasion goes hand in hand with other types of criminal actions. We may talk about insurance fraud, transport fraud, or fraud in the financial industry or in the car manufacturing industry, and we may especially talk about the reasons that allow these frauds to exist, i.e., corruption. It is difficult to conceive that criminal activity may be perpetuated without the complicity of those who should be adopting a trenchant position and of those who should form a common front to combat these actions that would be ultimately directed against themselves.

M. V. Achim (✉)
Faculty of Economics and Business Administration, Babeş-Bolyai University, Cluj-Napoca, Romania
e-mail: monica.achim@econ.ubbcluj.ro

R. W. McGee
Fayetteville State University, Fayetteville, NC, USA

M. C. Şcheau
European Research Institute, Babeş-Boyai University, Cluj-Napoca, Romania

M. V. Achim, R. W. McGee (eds.), *Financial Crime in Romania*, SpringerBriefs in Finance, https://doi.org/10.1007/978-3-031-27883-9_1

Financial crime and corruption are by no means new or modern concepts. We only witness a repositioning of crime, which is driven by technological evolution. Criminals and investigators adapt to new realities. The speed of information transmission increases. The way money is spent, stratified, and reintegrated follows the same rules of the past, with the supplementary note that their range of movement is much wider. We may even state, without being afraid of making any mistakes, that imagination has become the last frontier, and despite all the efforts made to combat economic and financial crimes, it remains a long-standing problem.

According to estimates from Global Financial Integrity (2020), the illicit financial flow (trade misinvoicing, smuggling, tax evasion, etc.) over the ten-year period of 2008–2017 amounts to US$ 8.7 trillion *worldwide*. Regarding corruption, recent data provided by Transparency International (2021) shows that despite some progress, the great majority of countries are still failing to tackle public sector corruption effectively. Therefore, the corrupting role of big money in political party financing and the undue influence it exerts on the political systems must be urgently addressed by governments (Transparency International, 2021). The study of Achim et al. (2021) validates that the northern countries, namely Denmark, Finland, Sweden, and the Netherlands, have the lowest level of corruption in the entire European Union, while the eastern European countries (Romania, Hungary, and Croatia) face the largest levels of corruption. Regarding the cost of corruption, Lagarde (2017) reveals that 2% of global gross domestic product is paid annually in bribes, amounting to about US$ 1.5–2 trillion per year around the world. Furthermore, the study by Medina and Schneider (2019) found that 19% of European countries' GDP is lost in the shadow economy, while the highest levels of shadow economy are found in Cyprus and Greece (25%) followed by Romania, Bulgaria, and Croatia (with 23%).

Crisis times create challenges for criminals to find new channels to engage in crime. For instance, the COVID-19 pandemic has led to a deterioration of working conditions and disruptions of financial markets, accentuating the need of companies to liquidate. Cyber scams, fraud, disinformation, and other cyber-enabled crimes would become a growth industry, as people under lockdown conditions tend to spend their time online (Global Initiative Against Transnational Organized Crime, 2020). In March 2020 the number of cybercrime events had increased about two times compared to the same month in 2018 (Hackmageddon, 2020). Under these conditions, the theft of banking data, followed by the compromise of savings accounts, fraud at some institutions and companies, or blocking access to information systems, increased pressure upon society. Both managers and policy decision makers need to become aware of these acts further on, so they need to know the economic and financial risks in order to be able to adopt an effective fight against these undesirable phenomena.

The present survey has *two main objectives*:

The first objective consists in finding the main patterns that characterize the Romanian community, such as the level of tax compliance, tax morale (attitude of citizens toward accepting cheating on taxes), the perceived corruption level in the Romanian public institutions, the level of skills possessed by citizens to detect the risk of money laundering, and the attitude customers have toward bankers who ask personal financial questions. Descriptive studies were conducted to uncover information about these issues.

The second objective of the study was to investigate how age, gender, region of living, professional status, and education may influence the level of tax compliance, the attitude of citizens toward accepting tax cheating, the perception of corruption levels in Romanian public institutions, the level of skills possessed by citizens to detect the risk of money laundering, and the attitude toward providing information to bank officers. A profile of the Romanian fraudster was also sketched. For this purpose, an empirical study was conducted to answer some of these questions.

In the Chap. 2, "Financial Crime: A Literature Review," we identified and discussed some of the research studies published so far that are relevant to our study. In the Chap. 3, "Bibliometric Analysis of Financial Crime Links Using Visual Maps," correlations were made between various criminal models and potential determining factors of the crime. The Chap. 5, "Methodology and Data" presents the methods that led to the formulation of the Results and Conclusions. The entire manuscript is documented and constructed in such a way as to complement past investigations and at the same time form the basis for future in-depth research.

References

Achim, M. V., Văidean, V. L., & Borlea, N. S. (2021). Does technology matter for combating economic and financial crime? A panel data study. *Technological and Economic Development of Economy, 27*(1), 223–261. https://doi.org/10.3846/tede.2021.13977

Global Financial Integrity. (2020). *Trade-related illicit financial flows in 135 developing countries: 2008–2017.*

Global Initiative Against Transnational Organized Crime. (2020, March). *Crime and contagion. The impact of a pandemic on organized crime.*

Hackmageddon. (2020). Available at https://www.hackmageddon.com/. Accessed 3 Mar 2022.

Lagarde, C. (2017, September 18). *Addressing corruption with clarity*. Brookings Institution.

Medina, L., & Schneider, F. (2019). *Shedding light on the shadow economy: A global database and the interaction with the official one*. Available at SSRN 3502028.

Transparency International. (2021). *Corruption Perception Index 2021.*

Monica Violeta Achim is full professor and doctoral supervisor in the field of finance at the Faculty of Economics and Business Administration, Babeş-Bolyai University, Cluj-Napoca, Romania. With over 24 years of experience in academia, she has authored and coauthored over 150 scientific articles and 25 books. Her most recent reference work is the book *Economic and Financial Crime: Corruption, Shadow Economy and Money Laundering*, published by Springer. In 2020 she received an Award for Excellence in Scientific Research at Babeş-Bolyai University, Faculty of Economics and Business Administration, Cluj-Napoca, Romania, in recognition of the results obtained in her research activity. She heads a big grant titled "Intelligent analysis and prediction of the economic and financial crime in a cyber-dominated and interconnected business world," conducted over the period 2021–2023, financed by the Romanian Ministry of Education and Research, CNCS – UEFISCDI, project number PN-III-P4-ID-PCE-2020-2174 (www.fincrime.net).

Robert W. McGee is a business professor at Fayetteville State University, USA. He holds 23 academic degrees, including 13 doctorates from universities in the USA and 4 European countries. He has authored more than 60 books, including several novels, and more than 1000 articles, book chapters, conference papers, and working papers. Various studies have ranked him No. 1 in the world for both accounting ethics and business ethics scholarship. He is an attorney and Certified Public Accountant (CPA) (retired) and has worked or lectured in more than 30 countries. He drafted the accounting law for Armenia and Bosnia and reviewed the accounting law for Mozambique. He was in charge of assisting the Finance Ministries of Armenia and Bosnia convert their countries to International Financial Reporting Standards. He is also a world champion in taekwondo, karate, kung fu, and tai chi (both Yang and Sun styles) and has won more than 900 gold medals.

Mircea Constantin Şcheau holds a PhD in Public Order and National Security with a topic of interest for economic and security fields, "Cybercrime on financial transfers." He received the "Victor Slavescu Prize" awarded by the Romanian Academy. He is the author/coauthor of three volumes, more than 40 scientific articles on management, law enforcement, critical infrastructure, information technology, and defense. He is a lecturer at numerous international conferences and member, inter alia, of the "Policies and strategies in the European Union's single market" research group of the European Research Institute of Babeş-Boyai University, Cluj-Napoca. He is a member of the project titled "Intelligent analysis and prediction of the economic and financial crime in a cyber-dominated and interconnected business world," conducted over the period 2021–2023, financed by the Romanian Ministry of Education and Research, CNCS – UEFISCDI, project number PN-III-P4-ID-PCE-2020-2174 (www.fincrime.net).

Chapter 2
Financial Crime: A Literature Review

Monica Violeta Achim, Sorin Nicolae Borlea, Robert W. McGee, Gabriela-Mihaela Mureşan, Ioana Lavinia Safta (Plesa), and Viorela-Ligia Văidean

Abstract This chapter reviews the literature on some of the subfields of economic and financial crime. Among the topics discussed are tax evasion, bribery, money laundering, and corruption in general. The determinants of financial crime are also identified. Several demographic variables are also examined to determine whether gender, age, education, income level, religion, geographic region, size of city, etc., are statistically significant. Nearly 150 studies are mentioned.

Keywords Financial crime · Culture · Romania · Tax evasion · Bribery · Fraud

The specialized literature identified many determinants of economic and financial crime. We may classify the factors taking into account their scope (worldwide, regional, macro, meso, micro, or individual) and their nature (economic, political, social, and cultural).

Included among the economic determinants of economic and financial crime are: *economic development* (Chelliah, 1971; Torgler, 2004; Torgler & Schneider, 2009; Achim & Borlea, 2020; Mara, 2021); *cash usage* (Medina & Schneider, 2018; Schneider & Buehn, 2016); *unemployment* (Medina & Schneider, 2018; Schneider & Buehn, 2016); *share of agriculture in total economy* (Medina & Schneider, 2018;

M. V. Achim · G.-M. Mureşan · I. L. Safta (Plesa) · V.-L. Văidean
Faculty of Economics and Business Administration, Babeş-Bolyai University, Cluj-Napoca, Romania

S. N. Borlea
Faculty of Economics, University of Oradea, Oradea, Romania

Faculty of Economics, Computer Science and Engineering, "Vasile Goldiş" Western University of Arad, Arad, Romania

European Research Institute, Babeş-Bolyai University, Cluj-Napoca, Romania

R. W. McGee (✉)
Fayetteville State University, Fayetteville, NC, USA

M. V. Achim, R. W. McGee (eds.), *Financial Crime in Romania*, SpringerBriefs in Finance, https://doi.org/10.1007/978-3-031-27883-9_2

Hassan & Schneider, 2016; Kelmson et al., 2019); *technical and scientific revolutions/digitalization* (Gaspareniene et al., 2016; Remeikiene et al., 2017; Satalkina & Steiner, 2020; Şcheau, 2018; Achim et al., 2021).

Political factors represent another category of important factors that create incentives for economic and financial crime. Here we may mention *institutional quality, rule of law, governance effectiveness, bureaucracy* (Kirchler, 2007; Johnson et al., 1997; Enste 2010; Williams & Shadid, 2016; Mara, 2021; Preobragenskaya & McGee, 2016); *preventive measures* (Williams, 2020); *probability of detecting risk* (McGee & Petrides, 2023a; Schneider & Buehn, 2016; Williams, 2020); and *tax burden* (Devereux & De Mooij, 2009; Dreher & Siemers, 2009; Dreher & Schneider, 2010, McGee, 2012; Schneider & Klinglmair, 2004; Torgler & Schneider, 2009; Masca & Pitea, 2021; Achim et al., 2018b, 2022; Yew et al., 2015). For example, fiscal policies may impact both corruption and the shadow economy. Achim et al. (2018b) found differential results comparing the influence of fiscal policy on the level of corruption based on the level of a country's development and the quality of its institutions. For developed countries, it was found that a low tax burden and high-quality institutions led to a lower level of corruption, while, for developing countries, low tax burden increased corruption because of low governance efficiency under which people may easily circumvent the law.

Achim et al. (2022) conducted a study of European Union countries for the period 2005–2018 that analyzed their Laffer Curves. They found evidence to support the existence of a U-shaped relationship between tax burden and the size of the shadow economy only in the case of direct taxes, while for indirect taxes and social contributions, an inverted U-shaped relationship was validated. In addition, different resilience thresholds were found for different components of taxes among the old and new European Union countries.

Respect for government (McGee & Benk, 2023a) and governmental institutions such as the police (McGee & Benk, 2023b) and the justice system (McGee & Benk, 2023c) was also correlated with attitudes toward the acceptability of both bribery (McGee & Benk, 2023a, b) and tax evasion (McGee & Shopovski, 2023a, b).

One recent study ranked 56 countries in terms of the perceived risk of taking or accepting a bribe (McGee & Petrides, 2023a). The study used a Likert Scale where 1 equals no risk at all and 10 equals a very high risk. The average value for Romania was 6.20, which caused it to rank No. 23 out of 56 countries. Taking or paying a bribe in Romania is found to be perceived as being slightly riskier than taking a bribe in Kenya, Nigeria, or Armenia, and slightly less risky than taking or paying a bribe in Bangladesh, the Philippines, or Singapore. Another study investigated whether some forms of bribery were worse than others (McGee & Petrides, 2023b).

Various recent studies go beyond explanations of a strictly economic nature in terms of identifying the causes of economic phenomena, paying increased attention to the analysis of *sociocultural* factors represented by tax morale, social norms (attitude), culture, religion, and happiness (Frey & Stutzer, 2012; Halla, 2010; Schneider & Klinglmair, 2004; Torgler & Schneider, 2009). There is an important strand of literature that investigates whether values, social norms, attitudes, *culture*, *lifestyle*, and *historical heritage* differ across countries and whether these differences have important effects on tax morale and tax compliance behavior. The intrinsic motivation to pay taxes varies across cultures (Achim & Borlea, 2020; McGee, 2023d). This explains why different levels of compliance are associated with different levels of tax morale (Alm & Torgler, 2006; Kirchler, 2007; Çule & Fulton, 2009; Cubillas et al., 2018; Alm & Torgler 2006; Kirchler, 2007; Kogler et al., 2013; McGee, 2012; Medina & Schneider, 2018; Schneider & Buehn, 2016).

Also related to cultural factors are studies that investigate the determinants of collecting receivables. Statistics show that trade receivables are collected faster in northern Europe than in southern Europe. The average period for collecting receivables in Europe has decreased from around 56 days in 2008 to 52 days in 2012, but the results differ from country to country. In northern Europe, the average period for collecting receivables is the lowest: Finland (27 days), Norway (34 days), Estonia (35 days), Sweden (35 days), Denmark (37 days). In southern Europe, this average duration is longer: Spain (97 days), Italy (96 days), Portugal (90 days), and Greece (80 days). These differences are based on cultural peculiarities of northern and southern Europe. (European Payment Index 2012, European Commission, 2012).

Referring to tax evasion in different countries, Torgler (2002), Kirchler (2007), and Kogler et al. (2013) identify *sociocultural factors* among the determinants of the level of tax compliance. The results identify a decrease in the level of tax compliance vertically, as it descends from the north to the south of Europe and horizontally, respectively from the west to the east of Europe, and sociocultural factors (mentioned above) are among the determinants for such a variation. In this view, Achim et al. (2019) investigated whether culture plays a role in the size of the shadow economy in the European countries over the period 2005–2015. They found that collectivism, femininity, a short-term orientation, restraint, and religiosity increased the size of the shadow economy, whereas greater happiness decreased it. Previous research of Achim et al. (2018a) found for European countries, analyzed for the period of 2008–2013, that happier people are more likely to act honestly, thus causing a decrease in the size of shadow economy. This result is valid for both old and new European Union countries.

Regarding the influence of culture, particularly examining the language spoken for economic transactions, studies conducted by Head (2003) and Helliwell (2000) found that "two countries that speak the same language will make two to three times more exchanges than if they would not share a common language." The same study estimated that the volume of transactions is about 65% higher if countries have a common border than if they do not have a common border. The existence of common borders can facilitate money laundering, especially when the money laundered is in cash (European Commission, ECOLEF, 2013, p. 40; Achim & Borlea, 2020, p. 196). In the same way, Brosio et al. (2002) investigated tax frauds in different regions of Italy and found that in the poorer regions from the south of Italy, tax fraud was significantly higher than in the richer northern regions.

Last but not least, there are *individual factors* such as: *gender* (McGee et al., 2006; McGee & Rossi, 2006, McGee 2012a), *age* (McGee et al., 2006; McGee, 2012b); *professional status* (McGee, 2012; McGee & Shopovski, 2023a, b); *education level* (McGee & Ross, 2014; McGee 2012c; Achim et al., 2020); *income level*

(McGee, 2012i), *social class* (McGee, 2012); *religious practice* (McGee, 2012d; Achim et al., 2019; Borlea et al., 2019); *religious denomination* (Bose, 2012; Cohn, 2012, 2012; Jalili, 2012; McGee 2012e, g, h, l; McGee & Smith, 2012; Tamari 1998), marital status (McGee, 2012f), academic major (McGee, 2012); *trust* (Achim et al., 2019; Kirchler, 2007); *ethnicity* (McGee, 2012); and *urban* vs. *rural status*, and *size of town* (McGee, 2012) that have an effect on tax morale. All these individual factors represent intrinsic motivations for cheating on taxes. In this view, a large study by Borlea et al. (2019) was conducted that included more than 148 countries. They found that power distance, trust in the legal system, happiness, and religion were the most important behavioral determinants of corruption, explaining about 50% of the level of corruption around the world.

McGee (2006) analyzed the three main views on the ethics of tax evasion that have been discussed in the literature over the past few centuries: is it never ethical, is it never unethical, or is it sometimes ethical! However, *why do people evade taxes*? In this regard, McGee found three general arguments that have justified tax evasion over the centuries: (1) a high level of corruption; (2) the lack of money, unfairness in the tax system, or excessively high tax rates; (3) philosophical, moral, or religious opposition. In a demographic study of 33 countries, McGee and Tyler (2006) found that citizens' attitudes are a key factor in the collection of taxes. Armenians evade taxes because there is the lack of a mechanism to collect taxes and also because they believe the government does not deserve their income (McGee, 1999).

One might assume that bribery is always unethical. However, that might not be the case (McGee, 2023a, b). For example, if someone bribes a prison guard to allow a political prisoner to escape, bribery might be a just act if the prisoner is not guilty of any wrongdoing. McGee and Block (2023) examine some cases where bribery might be morally acceptable, and separate bribery into two categories – helping-hand bribery and greedy-hand bribery. McGee (2023c) provides a summary of the Rothbard-Block theory of bribery (McGee, 2023c), which basically takes the position that bribery may not be unethical if no one's rights are violated and if there is no breach of fiduciary duty.

Some studies have been performed that examine the ethics of bribery from various religious perspectives (McGee et al., 2023c), including *atheism* (McGee et al., 2023d), *Buddhism* (McGee et al., 2023e), *Christianity* (McGee et al., 2023f), *Hinduism* (McGee et al., 2023g), *Judaism* (McGee et al., 2023h), and *Islam* (McGee et al., 2023a). Demographic research includes the results of some studies on various demographic variables (McGee & Benk, 2023e), such as *confidence in government* (McGee & Benk, 2023a), *confidence in the police* (McGee & Benk, 2023b), *confidence in the justice system* (McGee & Benk, 2023c), *political viewpoint* (McGee & Benk, 2023d), *gender* (McGee & Benk, 2023g, v), *age* (McGee & Benk, 2023h, w), *education level* (McGee & Benk, 2023i, x), *income level* (McGee & Benk, 2023j, y), *social class* (McGee & Benk, 2023k, z), *ethnicity* (McGee & Benk, 2023l), *marital status* (McGee & Benk, 2023m), *employment status* (McGee & Benk, 2023n), *sector of employment* (McGee & Benk, 2023p), *religious denomination* (McGee & Benk, 2023q), *religiosity* (McGee & Benk, 2023r), *happiness* (McGee &

Benk, 2023s), *health* (McGee & Benk, 2023t), *size of town* (McGee & Benk, 2023u), and whether *urban dwellers* view bribery differently than *rural dwellers* (McGee & Guadron, 2023).

The second volume in the series presents the results of several country studies on the ethics of bribery (McGee & Benk, 2023f). McGee and Zhou (2023) ranked 52 countries based on the prevalence of bribery. Romania ranked No. 40, slightly better than Pakistan and Nigeria and slightly worse than Vietnam and Lebanon.

A recent study investigated ways to uncover bribery by applying mathematical techniques, using Romania as a case study (Batrancea et al., 2023a). Another recent Romanian study focused on bribery in the healthcare industry, and found that it had increased as a result of the Covid-19 pandemic (Bîzoi & Bîzoi, 2023). A Turkish study of public procurement during Covid-19 also found that the incidence of bribery had greatly increased during this period (Dikmen & Cicek, 2023). Another Turkish study examined primary documents and reported on the corruption, tax evasion, and bribery that took place during the last days of the Ottoman Empire (Akdemir & Yeşilyurt, 2023).

A recent longitudinal study on attitudes toward bribery in 75 countries found that accepting a bribe had become significantly more acceptable over time in 45.3% of the surveyed countries, and significantly less acceptable in only 30.7% of the countries, with no significant difference of opinion in 24.0% of the surveyed countries. In Romania, taking a bribe has become significantly less acceptable between 1998 and 2017. Other countries in the region where bribery has become significantly less acceptable over time include Bulgaria, the Czech Republic, Estonia, Poland, and Slovenia. Some of the countries where bribery has become significantly more acceptable over time include Russia, Serbia, and Slovenia. Attitudes toward bribery have not changed significantly over time in Belarus, Bosnia and Herzegovina, Hungary, Moldova, Montenegro, North Macedonia, and Ukraine (McGee et al., 2023b).

There is a widespread belief that bribery is always unethical. But is it? Philosophers seldom use the word *always* in their philosophical treatises. There always seems to be an exception. Such is the case with bribery, as we shall see below.

How about tax evasion? Is it *always* unethical? By now you might expect that the answer to that question is *no*, and you would be right. Well, maybe you would be right. Smith and Kimball (1998) examined the literature of the Church of Jesus Christ of Latter-Day Saints and could not find a single passage that would justify tax evasion, although they did find a few passages that condemned evasion. Block (1998), on the other hand, examined the economic literature and could not find a single convincing argument to justify taxation.

What if you were a Jew living in Nazi Germany? Would you have a moral obligation to pay taxes to Hitler? Almost everyone would say *no*. However, a survey of Orthodox Jewish students found that there was some support for the idea that even Jews living in Nazi Germany had some obligation to pay taxes to Hitler (McGee & Cohn, 2006, 2008), a conclusion that seems outrageous on its surface. However, there is some support in the Jewish literature in favor of this view. Cohn (2012) gave the following four reasons:

1. Jews must follow the laws of the country in which they live.
2. Jewish law prohibits lying.
3. A Jew must not do anything that would discredit the religion.
4. Jews must perform a maximum number of mitzvot (commandments and good deeds). They must stay out of jail in order to do that. Evading taxes may result in a jail sentence, which would prevent them from following the commandment to perform good deeds (McGee, 2022).

None of these arguments would hold up to philosophical analysis, but we will save these points of discussion for a later date. Tamari (1998), another Jewish scholar, surveyed the Jewish literature and concluded that tax evasion is almost always unethical.

The literature of the Baha'i faith takes the position that tax evasion is always unethical, and that there is a moral obligation to pay taxes even to Hitler. The only exception to this position is in cases where some government persecutes members of the Baha'i faith (DeMoville, 1998).

The Christian literature is mixed. Martin Crowe (1944), a Catholic priest, surveyed 500 years of religious and philosophical literature, much of which was in the Latin language. What he found was that the vast majority of scholars were usually against tax evasion, but with exceptions. The usual exceptions were in cases where people cannot afford to pay, or where the government is corrupt, or where the people do not receive much in benefits in return for their tax payments or where the taxes are too high. He found a few scholars who believed there is never any moral duty to pay taxes because all governments are illegitimate. He also found a few scholars who think that tax evasion is always unethical. All three of these views are discussed by McGee (1994, 1998b, 2006a). He expanded the categories to four views a few years later (McGee, 2012j).

Pennock (1998) justified tax evasion as a means of war tax resistance. Schansberg (1998) took a Biblical position and asked whether there are limits to rendering unto Caesar. Gronbacher (1998) addressed Catholic social thought on the issue, from the perspective of classical liberalism. A few scholars have written on the Muslim perspective. Murtuza and Ghazanfar (1998) discussed Zakat, the voluntary offering Muslims give to charity as a form of voluntary taxation. McGee (1998) wrote a book chapter on tax evasion in Islam that was based on the work of two Muslim scholars who believed tax evasion is justified in a number of cases, such as when taxes cause prices to increase, or when a tax is imposed on income. Jalili (2012) wrote a book chapter that disagreed with the McGee chapter. McGee (2012g) responded to the Jalili chapter. According to Jalili's interpretation of the Muslim view, tax evasion is always unethical because Allah owns everything, and evading taxes is akin to stealing from Allah. However, he prefaces that position by stating that this view only applies to cases where the government has adopted Sharia law. Thus, in a secular society, evasion might be ethically possible, although Jalili carefully avoided saying that.

A number of surveys based on the Crowe (1944) findings were distributed to various groups over the years. The findings of 49 of them were summarized by

McGee (2012k). Those surveys consisted of 18 statements that begin with the phrase "Tax evasion is ethical if …" The statements are based on 15 of the reasons Crowe found in the literature that had been used over the centuries to justify tax evasion, and were supplemented by three more recent arguments to justify tax evasion. One of these surveys was distributed to 134 Romanian graduate and upper division undergraduate business students (McGee 2006b, c). The survey found that some reasons to justify tax evasion were significantly stronger than other arguments, and that males were more opposed to tax evasion in 12 of 18 cases. The six strongest arguments to justify tax evasion were as follows:

1. Tax evasion is ethical if the tax system is unfair.
2. Tax evasion is ethical if the government discriminates against me because of my religion, race, or ethnic background.
3. Tax evasion is ethical if I can't afford to pay.
4. Tax evasion is ethical if tax rates are too high.
5. Tax evasion is ethical if a significant portion of the money collected winds up in the pockets of corrupt politicians or their families and friends.
6. Tax evasion is ethical if the government imprisons people for their political opinions (McGee, 2012k, pp. 570).

Some studies have been written from a practitioner's perspective. Armstrong and Robison (1998), Oliva (1998), and Englebrecht et al. (1998) all addressed certain aspects of evasion from a practitioner's perspective. Batrancea et al. (2023b) addressed some issues relating to gender inequities in the tax system.

The present research has tried to draw a profile of fraudster based on several individual or social patterns. In this view, the most recent research conducted by the Association of Certified Fraud Examiners (2022) was based on 2000 real cases of fraud affecting organizations in 133 countries and 23 industries, which provided interesting results. Regarding the fraudster's profile by gender, the mentioned research shows that men are much more inclined to take risks than women, and thus the number of frauds in which they are involved is significantly higher than that of women. More exactly, according to this study, 73% of the perpetrators are male, while only 27% are women. However, median losses caused by men were only 25% higher than median losses caused by women. The mentioned study also revealed high gender disparities from one region of the world to another. For example, the highest percentages in which women were involved in occupational frauds were found in the United States of America and Canada (38%) followed by Asia and the Pacific (28%) and the regions of Latin America and the Caribbean and sub-Saharan Africa (each of them with 25%). The smallest percentage of women fraudsters (5%) is found in southern Asia.

Regarding the profile of the fraudster by age, a study conducted by the Association of Certified Fraud Examiners (2022) found that the highest number of frauds (54%) had been committed by people between the ages of 31 and 45. However, the amount of fraud losses increased as the fraudster's age increased, so that the losses caused by people over the age of 60 were the largest.

When we talk about the educational profile of the fraudster, the results are somewhat interesting, because, perhaps, we would expect a better education to give better compliance with the rules. We found that the maximum number of frauds (about 47%) was caused by people who have a university degree.

In addition, the amount of fraud losses increased for fraudsters who held more degrees and were better educated (Association of Certified Fraud Examiners 2020, 2022).These results could be explained by the fact that a better education ensures a better understanding of the functioning mechanisms of the economic, financial, and information flows, and in this way, they may easily find an opportunity to obtain illicit benefits.

Similarly, the studies carried out in the specialized literature (Queloz, 2002; Leția, 2014, p. 14; Aniței & Lazăr, 2016, p. 16; Șcheau, 2018) identified another feature of economic crime, mainly that it requires high professional knowledge and skills, namely a specialized knowledge on the part of those who commit it. In this context, economic and financial crime is closely linked to economic change and development (Merton, 1968). In the age of the internet and artificial intelligence, such innovations are closely linked to cybercrime, which requires financial transfers: "special skills, work and a lot of perseverance" (Șcheau, 2018, p.17). In a constantly changing society, adaptation to new socioeconomic conditions can be performed differently by individuals in society. Thus, business people can invent different forms of white-collar crime in the form of tax evasion or money laundering, while the poor can engage in illegal activities such as prostitution, gambling, or drug sales (Aniței & Lazăr, 2016, p.17–18).

According to Klapper et al. (2015) Romania has the lowest level of financial education in the European Union. The countries with the highest level of financial education are the countries in the northwest of the EU (Denmark, Sweden, the Netherlands, and Germany) and those with the lowest levels are found in southeastern Europe (Greece, Italy, Portugal, and Romania).

However, interesting results regarding the different impact of intelligence on the two subgroups of high-income and low-income were found by Achim et al. (2020) in their study conducted on 182 countries for the time span 2012–2017. Thus, they found a positive coefficient for the impact of intelligence on economic and financial crimes, meaning that increased intellectual capacities of people from these countries, including high professional knowledge and skills, were used to break the traditional technology in order to obtain illegal benefits. On the other hand, for the low-income countries, the level of intelligence was not a significant factor affecting the impact of financial crime.

Regarding the profile of the fraudster by level of authority, the same Association of Certified Fraud Examiners studies (2020, 2022) found that the frauds committed by owners and executives were much more harmful, even if the percentage of cases was higher for employee and managers.

Regarding the tenure or experience in the same company, the same research found that fraudsters having worked for the same company for 6–10 years or more had the highest losses for the companies they worked for.

When a person commits fraud, that person will often display certain behavioral patterns that tend to be associated with fraudulent conduct. The most common red flag in every study since 2008 was the fraudster living beyond his or her means (to have luxury cars, helicopters, to spend money on exotic holidays or other similar expenses).

References

Achim, M. V., & Borlea, N. S. (2020). *Economic and financial crime. Corruption, shadow economy, and money laundering*. Springer Nature. https://doi.org/10.1007/978-3-030-51780-9

Achim, M. V., Borlea, S. N., Găban, L. V., & Cuceu, I. C. (2018a). Rethinking the shadow economy in terms of happiness. Evidence for the European Union member states. *Technological and Economic Development of Economy, 24*(1), 199–228. https://doi.org/10.3846/20294913.2016.1209250

Achim, M. V., Borlea, S. N., & Anghelina, A. M. (2018b). The impact of fiscal policies on corruption: A panel analysis. *South African Journal of Economic and Management Sciences, 21*(1), a1970. https://doi.org/10.4102/sajems.v21i1.1970

Achim, M. V., Borlea, N. S., Gaban, L. V., & Mihaila, A. A. (2019). The shadow economy and culture: Evidence in European countries. *Eastern European Economics*. https://doi.org/10.1080/00128775.2019.1614461

Achim, M. V., Borlea, N. S., Văidean, V. L., Rus, A. I. D., & Dobre, F. (2020). The impact of intelligence on economic and financial crime: A cross-country study. *Singapore Economic Review*. https://doi.org/10.1142/S0217590820500782

Achim, M. V., Văidean, V. L., & Borlea, N. S. (2021). Does technology matter for combating economic and financial crime? A panel data study. *Technological and economic development of economy., 27*(1), 223–261. https://doi.org/10.3846/tede.2021.13977

Achim, M. V., Mirza, N., & Văidean, V. L. (2022). The asymmetric impact of tax burden structures on the shadow economy: A panel analysis of old and new European Union countries. *Applied Economics Letters*. https://doi.org/10.1080/13504851.2022.2094876

Akdemir, T., & Yeşilyurt, S. (2023). Corruption and bribery in ottoman tax management: An evaluation of the period 1876–1909. In R. W. McGee & S. Benk (Eds.), *The ethics of bribery: Theoretical and empirical studies*. Springer, forthcoming.

Alm, J., & Torgler, B. (2006). Culture differences and tax morale in the United States and Europe. *Journal of Economic Psychology, 27*(2), 224–246.

Aniţei, N. C., & Lazăr, R. E. (2016). *Evaziunea fiscală între legalitate şi infracţiune (Fiscal evasion between legality and crime)*. Universul Juridic Publishing House.

Armstrong, M. B., & Robison, J. (1998). Ethics in taxation. In R. W. McGee (Ed.), *The ethics of tax evasion* (pp. 330–348). The Dumont Institute for Public Policy Research. Summarized in McGee, Robert W., The Ethics of Tax Evasion: Summaries of 21 Studies (March 12, 2022). https://doi.org/10.2139/ssrn.4056290

Association of Certified Fraud Examiners. (2020). *Report to the nations. Global study on occupational fraud and abuse*.

Association of Certified Fraud Examiners. (2022). *Occupational Fraud 2022: A report to the nations*.

Batrancea, L., Gómez, F. J. B., Nichita, A., & Dragolea, L.-L. (2023a). Crunching numbers in the quest for spotting bribery acts: A cross-cultural rundown. In R. W. McGee & S. Benk (Eds.), *The ethics of bribery: Theoretical and empirical studies*. Springer, forthcoming.

Batrancea, L., Nichita, A., Batrancea, I., & Dragolea, L. (2023b). Are we taxed in the same manner while making a purchase? A brief inquiry into taxation, gender equity and evasion. In

R. W. McGee & S. Benk (Eds.), *The ethics of bribery, volume 2: Country studies*. Springer, forthcoming.
Bîzoi, A.-C., & Bîzoi, C.-G. (2023). Primum non-nocere: How to fight the 'pandemic' of health-care corruption. In R. W. McGee & S. Benk (Eds.), *The ethics of bribery: Theoretical and empirical studies*. Springer, forthcoming.
Block, W. (1998). The justification for taxation in the economics literature. In R. W. McGee (Ed.), *The ethics of tax evasion* (pp. 36–88). The Dumont Institute for Public Policy Research. Summarized in McGee, Robert W., The Ethics of Tax Evasion: Summaries of 21 Studies (March 12, 2022). https://doi.org/10.2139/ssrn.4056290
Borlea, S. N., Achim, M. V., & Rus, A. I. D. (2019). Behavioral determinants of corruption. A cross-country survey. *Studia Universitatis Vasile Goldiş Arad, Seria Ştiinţe Economice, 29*(1), 21–39.
Bose, S. (2012). Hindu ethical considerations in relation to tax evasion. In R. W. McGee (Ed.), *The ethics of tax evasion: Perspectives in theory and practice* (pp. 135–147). Springer. Summarized in McGee (2023d).
Brosio, G., Cassone, A., & Ricciuti, R. (2002). Tax evasion across Italy: Rational noncompliance or inadequate civic concern? *Public Choice, 112*(3-4), 259–273.
Chelliah, R. J. (1971). Trends in taxation in developing countries. *Staff Papers, International Monetary Fund, 18*, 254–0331.
Cohn, G. (2012). The traditional Jewish view of paying taxes. In R. W. McGee (Ed.), *The ethics of tax evasion: Perspectives in theory and practice* (pp. 149–158). Springer. Summarized in McGee (2023d).
Crowe, M.T. (1944). *The moral obligation of paying just taxes*. The Catholic University of America Studies in Sacred Theology No. 84.
Cubillas, E., & Suárez, N. (2018). Bank market power and lending during the global financial crisis. *Journal of International Money and Finance, 89*, 1–22.
Çule, M., & Fulton, M. (2009). Business culture and tax evasion: Why corruption and the unofficial economy can persist. *Journal of Economic Behavior & Organization, 72*(3), 811–822.
DeMoville, W. (1998). The ethics of tax evasion: A Baha'i perspective. In R. W. McGee (Ed.), *The ethics of tax evasion* (pp. 230–240). The Dumont Institute for Public Policy Research. Summarized in McGee, Robert W., The Ethics of Tax Evasion: Summaries of 21 Studies (March 12, 2022). https://doi.org/10.2139/ssrn.4056290
Devereux, M. P., & De Mooij, R. A. (2009). *Alternative systems of business tax in Europe: An applied analysis of ACE and CBIT reforms*. Study for the European Commission, DG Taxation and Customs Union.
Dikmen, S., & Cicek, H. G. (2023). Fighting against corruption and bribery in public procurements during the Covid-19 pandemic. In R. W. McGee & S. Benk (Eds.), *The ethics of bribery: Theoretical and empirical studies*. Springer, forthcoming.
Dreher, A., & Schneider, F. (2010). Corruption and the shadow economy. An empirical analysis. *Public Choice, 144*, 215–238.
Dreher, A., & Siemers, L. H. R. (2009). The nexus between corruption and capital account restrictions. *Public Choice, 140*, 245–265.
Englebrecht, T. D., Folami, B., Lee, C., & Masselli, J. J. (1998). The impact of ethics on tax compliance behavior: A multidimensional analysis. In R. W. McGee (Ed.), *The ethics of tax evasion* (pp. 372–402). The Dumont Institute for Public Policy Research. Summarized in McGee (2022).
Enste, D. H. (2010). Regulation and shadow economy: Empirical evidence for 25 OECD-countries. *Constitutional Political Economy, 21*(3), 231–248.
European Commission. (2012).
European Commission. (2013). Project 'ECOLEF' The economic and legal effectiveness of anti money laundering and combating terrorist financing policy, Project funded by the European Commission DG Home Affairs JLS/2009/ISEC/AG/087 February 2013.
European Payment Index. (2012).

Frey, B. S., & Stutzer, A. (2012). The use of happiness research for public policy. *Social Choice and Welfare, 38*(4), 659–674.

Gaspareniene, L., Remeikiene, R. R., & Navickas, V. (2016). The concept of digital shadow economy: Consumer's attitude. *Procedia Economics and Finance, 39*, 502–509.

Gronbacher, G. M. A. (1998). Taxation: Catholic social thought and classical liberalism. In R. W. McGee (Ed.), *The ethics of tax evasion* (pp. 158–167). The Dumont Institute for Public Policy Research. Summarized in McGee, Robert W., The Ethics of Tax Evasion: Summaries of 21 Studies (March 12, 2022). https://doi.org/10.2139/ssrn.4056290

Halla, M. (2010). *The link between the intrinsic motivation to comply and compliance behavior: A critical appraisal of existing evidence*. IZA Discussion Paper.

Hassan, M., & Schneider, F. (2016). *Size and development of the shadow economies of 157 countries worldwide: Updated and new measures from 1999 to 2013*. Available at SSRN 2861026.

Head, K. (2003). *Gravity for beginner*. Mimeo, University of British Columbia.

Helliwell, J. F. (2000). *Language and trade, gravity modelling of trade flows and the role of language*. The Department of Canadian Heritage.

Jalili, A. R. (2012). The ethics of tax evasion: An Islamic perspective. In R. W. McGee (Ed.), *The ethics of tax evasion: Perspectives in theory and practice* (pp. 167–199). Springer. Summarized in McGee (2023d).

Johnson, S., Kaufmann, D., & Sleifer, A. (1997). The unofficial economy in transition. *Brooking Papers on Economic Activity, 1997*, 159–221.

Kelmson, B., Kirabaeva, K., Medina, L. Mircheva, B. and Weiss, J. (2019). *Explaining the shadow economy in Europe: Size, causes and policy options*. IMF Working Paper European Department, WP/19/278, page 1–29.

Kirchler, E. (2007). *The economic psychology of tax behavior*. Cambridge, UK.

Klapper, L., Lusardi, A., & Van Oudheusden, P. (2015). *Financial literacy around the world. World Bank*. World Bank.

Kogler, C., Bătrancea, L., Nichita, A., Pantya, J., & Belianin, A. (2013). Trust and power as determinants of tax compliance: Testing the assumptions of the slippery slope framework in Austria, Hungary, Romania and Russia. *Journal of Economic Psychology, 34*, 169–180.

Leţia, A. A. (2014). *Investigation of business crime: Money laundering, corruption and tax fraud, theoretical and practical aspects*. Universal Juridic Publishing House.

Mara, S. (2021). Drivers of the shadow economy in European Union welfare states: A panel data analysis. *Economic Analysis and Policy, 72*, 309–325.

Masca, S. G., & Pitea, C. (2021). *Tax Evasion within European Union – Trends and Determinants (June 23, 2021)*. https://ssrn.com/abstract=4153727

McGee, R. W. (1994). Is tax evasion unethical? *University of Kansas Law Review, 42*(2), 411–435.

McGee, R. W. (1997). *The ethics of tax evasion and trade protectionism from an Islamic perspective*. Available at SSRN 461397.

McGee, R. W. (1998a). The ethics of tax evasion in Islam. In R. W. McGee (Ed.), *The ethics of tax evasion* (pp. 214–219). The Dumont Institute for Public Policy Research. Summarized in McGee, Robert W., The Ethics of Tax Evasion: Summaries of 21 Studies (March 12, 2022). https://doi.org/10.2139/ssrn.4056290

McGee, R. W. (1998b). When is tax evasion unethical? In R. W. McGee (Ed.), *The ethics of tax evasion* (pp. 5–35). The Dumont Institute for Public Policy Research. Summarized in McGee, Robert W., The Ethics of Tax Evasion: Summaries of 21 Studies (March 12, 2022). https://doi.org/10.2139/ssrn.4056290

McGee, R. W. (1999). *Why people evade taxes in Armenia: A look at an ethical issue based on a summary of interviews*. https://ssrn.com/abstract=242568.

McGee, R. W. (2006a). Three views on the ethics of tax evasion. *Journal of Business Ethics, 67*(1), 15–35.

McGee, R.W. (2006b). The Ethics of Tax Evasion; A Survey of Romanian Business Students and Faculty. *The ICFAI Journal of Public Finance* 4(2): 38-68. Summarized in McGee (2012k) at pp. 569-571.

McGee, R. W. (2006c). The ethics of tax evasion; A Survey of Romanian Business Students and Faculty. Reprinted in R.W. McGee & G.G. Preobragenskaya, *Accounting and Financial System Reform in Eastern Europe and Asia* (pp. 299–334). Springer, 2006. Summarized in McGee (2012k) at pp. 569-571.

McGee, R. W. (Ed.). (2012). *The ethics of tax evasion: Perspectives in theory and practice*. Springer. Summarized in McGee (2023d).

McGee, R. W. (2012a). Gender and the ethics of tax evasion; an empirical study of 82 countries. In R. W. McGee (Ed.), *The ethics of tax evasion: Perspectives in theory and practice* (pp. 415–439). Springer. Summarized in McGee (2023d).

McGee, R. W. (2012b). Age and the ethics of tax evasion. In R. W. McGee (Ed.), *The ethics of tax evasion: Perspectives in theory and practice* (pp. 441–449). Springer. Summarized in McGee (2023d).

McGee, R. W. (2012c). Education level and the ethics of tax evasion. In R. W. McGee (Ed.), *The ethics of tax evasion: Perspectives in theory and practice* (pp. 451–457). Springer. Summarized in McGee (2023d).

McGee, R. W. (2012d). Religious practice and the ethics of tax evasion. In R. W. McGee (Ed.), *The ethics of tax evasion: Perspectives in theory and practice* (pp. 459–469). Springer. Summarized in McGee (2023d).

McGee, R. W. (2012e). Religion and the ethics of tax evasion. In R. W. McGee (Ed.), *The ethics of tax evasion: Perspectives in theory and practice* (pp. 471–473). Springer. Summarized in McGee (2023d).

McGee, R. W. (2012f). Marital status and the ethics of tax evasion. In R. W. McGee (Ed.), *The ethics of tax evasion: Perspectives in theory and practice* (pp. 475–484). Springer. Summarized in McGee (2023d).

McGee, R. W. (2012g). The ethics of tax evasion in Islam: A comment. In R. W. McGee (Ed.), *The ethics of tax evasion: Perspectives in theory and practice* (pp. 159–165). Springer. Summarized in McGee (2023d).

McGee, R. W. (2012h). Christina views on the ethics of tax evasion. In R. W. McGee (Ed.), *The ethics of tax evasion: Perspectives in theory and practice* (pp. 201–210). Springer. Summarized in McGee (2023d).

McGee, R. W. (2012i). Income level and the ethics of tax evasion. In R. W. McGee (Ed.), *The ethics of tax evasion: Perspectives in theory and practice* (pp. 485–495). Springer. Summarized in McGee (2023d).

McGee, R. W. (2012j). Four views on the ethics of tax evasion. In R. W. McGee (Ed.), *The ethics of tax evasion: Perspectives in theory and practice* (pp. 3–33). Springer. Summarized in McGee (2023d).

McGee, R. W. (2012k). Annotated bibliography: 18 statement surveys. In R. W. McGee (Ed.), *The ethics of tax evasion: Perspectives in theory and practice* (pp. 499–598). Springer. An updated summary will appear in McGee & Shopovski (2023a).

McGee, R. W. (2012l). Christian views on the ethics of tax evasion. In R. W. McGee (Ed.), *The ethics of tax evasion: Perspectives in theory and practice* (pp. 201–210). Springer. Summarized in McGee (2023d).

McGee, R.W. (2022). *The ethics of tax evasion: Summaries of 21 studies*. Working Paper. https://doi.org/10.13140/RG.2.2.12914.79049 Note: A slightly different version of this paper will appear in R. W. McGee & J. Shopovski (Eds.), The Ethics of Tax Evasion, Volume 2: New Perspectives in Theory and Practice. Switzerland: Springer, 2023, forthcoming.

McGee, R. W. (2023a). The ethics of bribery: Summaries of 24 studies. In R. W. McGee & S. Benk (Eds.), *The ethics of bribery: Theoretical and empirical studies*. Springer, forthcoming.

McGee, R. W. (2023b). The ethics of bribery: Summaries of 28 studies. In R. W. McGee & S. Benk (Eds.), *The ethics of bribery: Theoretical and empirical studies*. Springer, forthcoming.

McGee, R. W. (2023c). The Rothbard-Block theory of bribery. In R. W. McGee & S. Benk (Eds.), *The ethics of bribery: Theoretical and empirical studies*. Springer, forthcoming.

McGee, R. W. (2023d). *The ethics of tax evasion: Summaries of 35 studies* (Working Paper).

McGee, R. W., & Benk, S. (2023a). Confidence in government and attitudes toward bribery: Summaries of 15 studies. In R. W. McGee & S. Benk (Eds.), *The ethics of bribery: Theoretical and empirical studies*. Springer, forthcoming.
McGee, R. W., & Benk, S. (2023b). Confidence in the police and attitudes toward bribery: Summaries of 6 studies. In R. W. McGee & S. Benk (Eds.), *The ethics of bribery: Theoretical and empirical studies*. Springer, forthcoming.
McGee, R. W., & Benk, S. (2023c). Confidence in the justice system and attitudes toward bribery: Summaries of 15 studies. In R. W. McGee & S. Benk (Eds.), *The ethics of bribery: Theoretical and empirical studies*. Springer, forthcoming.
McGee, R. W., & Benk, S. (2023d). Political viewpoint and attitudes toward bribery: Summaries of 16 studies. In R. W. McGee & S. Benk (Eds.), *The ethics of bribery: Theoretical and empirical studies*. Springer, forthcoming.
McGee, R. W., & Benk, S. (Eds.). (2023e). *The ethics of bribery: Theoretical and empirical studies*. Springer.
McGee, R. W., & Benk, S. (Eds.). (2023f). *The ethics of bribery, Vol. 2: Country studies*. Springer.
McGee, R. W., & Benk, S. (2023g). Gender and attitudes toward bribery: Summaries of 31 studies. In R. W. McGee & S. Benk (Eds.), *The ethics of bribery: Theoretical and empirical studies*. Springer, forthcoming.
McGee, R. W., & Benk, S. (2023h). Age and attitudes toward bribery: Summaries of 26 studies. In R. W. McGee & S. Benk (Eds.), *The ethics of bribery: Theoretical and empirical studies*. Springer, forthcoming.
McGee, R. W., & Benk, S. (2023i). Education level and attitudes toward bribery: Summaries of 23 studies. In R. W. McGee & S. Benk (Eds.), *The ethics of bribery: Theoretical and empirical studies*. Springer, forthcoming.
McGee, R. W., & Benk, S. (2023j). Income level and attitudes toward bribery: Summaries of 18 studies. In R. W. McGee & S. Benk (Eds.), *The ethics of bribery: Theoretical and empirical studies*. Springer, forthcoming.
McGee, R. W., & Benk, S. (2023k). Social class and attitudes toward bribery: Summaries of 20 studies. In R. W. McGee & S. Benk (Eds.), *The ethics of bribery: Theoretical and empirical studies*. Springer, forthcoming.
McGee, R. W., & Benk, S. (2023l). Ethnicity and attitudes toward bribery: Summaries of 8 studies. In R. W. McGee & S. Benk (Eds.), *The ethics of bribery: Theoretical and empirical studies*. Springer, forthcoming.
McGee, R. W., & Benk, S. (2023m). Marital status and attitudes toward bribery: Summaries of 20 studies. In R. W. McGee & S. Benk (Eds.), *The ethics of bribery: Theoretical and empirical studies*. Springer, forthcoming.
McGee, R. W., & Benk, S. (2023n). Employment status and attitudes toward bribery: Summaries of 17 studies. In R. W. McGee & S. Benk (Eds.), *The ethics of bribery: Theoretical and empirical studies*. Springer, forthcoming.
McGee, R. W., & Benk, S. (2023p). Sector of employment and attitudes toward bribery: Summaries of 14 studies. In R. W. McGee & S. Benk (Eds.), *The ethics of bribery: Theoretical and empirical studies*. Springer, forthcoming.
McGee, R. W., & Benk, S. (2023q). Religious denomination and attitudes toward bribery: Summaries of 19 studies. In R. W. McGee & S. Benk (Eds.), *The ethics of bribery: Theoretical and empirical studies*. Springer, forthcoming.
McGee, R. W., & Benk, S. (2023r). Religiosity and attitudes toward bribery: Summaries of 12 studies. In R. W. McGee & S. Benk (Eds.), *The ethics of bribery: Theoretical and empirical studies*. Springer, forthcoming.
McGee, R. W., & Benk, S. (2023s). Happiness and attitudes toward bribery: Summaries of 19 studies. In R. W. McGee & S. Benk (Eds.), *The ethics of bribery: Theoretical and empirical studies*. Springer, forthcoming.

McGee, R. W., & Benk, S. (2023t). Health and attitudes toward bribery: Summaries of 11 studies. In R. W. McGee & S. Benk (Eds.), *The ethics of bribery: Theoretical and empirical studies*. Springer, forthcoming.
McGee, R. W., & Benk, S. (2023u). Size of town and attitudes toward bribery: Summaries of 10 studies. In R. W. McGee & S. Benk (Eds.), *The ethics of bribery: Theoretical and empirical studies*. Springer, forthcoming.
McGee, R. W., & Benk, S. (2023v). Gender and attitudes toward bribery. In R. W. McGee & S. Benk (Eds.), *The ethics of bribery: Theoretical and empirical studies*. Springer, forthcoming.
McGee, R. W., & Benk, S. (2023w). Age and attitudes toward bribery. In R. W. McGee & S. Benk (Eds.), *The ethics of bribery: Theoretical and empirical studies*. Springer, forthcoming.
McGee, R. W., & Benk, S. (2023x). Education level and attitudes toward bribery. In R. W. McGee & S. Benk (Eds.), *The ethics of bribery: Theoretical and empirical studies*. Springer, forthcoming.
McGee, R. W., & Benk, S. (2023y). Income level and attitudes toward bribery. In R. W. McGee & S. Benk (Eds.), *The ethics of bribery: Theoretical and empirical studies*. Springer, forthcoming.
McGee, R. W., & Benk, S. (2023z). Social class and attitudes toward bribery. In R. W. McGee & S. Benk (Eds.), *The ethics of bribery: Theoretical and empirical studies*. Springer, forthcoming.
McGee, R. W., & Block, W. E. (2023). Helping hand v. greedy hand bribery. In R. W. McGee & S. Benk (Eds.), *The ethics of bribery: Theoretical and empirical studies*. Springer, forthcoming.
McGee, R. W. & Cohn, G. M. (2006). Jewish Perspectives on the Ethics of Tax Evasion. *Andreas School of Business Working Paper*, Barry University, Miami Shores, FL 33161 USA, September. https://doi.org/10.2139/ssrn.929027.
McGee, R. W., & Cohn, G. M. (2008). Jewish perspectives on the ethics of tax evasion. *Journal of Legal, Ethical and Regulatory Issues, 11*(2), 1–32.
McGee, R. W., & Guadron, M. (2023). Do urban dwellers view bribery differently than rural dwellers? An empirical study of views in 76 countries. In R. W. McGee & S. Benk (Eds.), *The ethics of bribery: Theoretical and empirical studies*. Springer, forthcoming.
McGee, R. W., & Petrides, Y. (2023a). How risky is it to give or receive a bribe? A ranking of 56 countries. In R. W. McGee & S. Benk (Eds.), *The ethics of bribery: Theoretical and empirical studies*. Springer, forthcoming.
McGee, R. W., & Petrides, Y. (2023b). Are some forms of bribery more serious than others? In R. W. McGee & S. Benk (Eds.), *The ethics of bribery: Theoretical and empirical studies*. Springer, forthcoming.
McGee, R. W., & Ross, A. (2014). *Education level and ethical attitude toward tax evasion: A six-country study*. https://doi.org/10.2139/ssrn.2410582.
McGee, R. W., & Rossi, M. J. (2006). *The ethics of tax evasion: A survey of law and business students in Argentina*. https://doi.org/10.2139/ssrn.875892.
McGee, R. W., & Shopovski, J. (Eds.). (2023a). *The ethics of tax evasion, volume 2: New perspectives in theory and practice*. Springer, forthcoming.
McGee, R. W., & Shopovski, J. (Eds.). (2023b). *The ethics of tax evasion: Country studies*. Springer. forthcoming.
McGee, R. W., & Smith, S. R. (2012). Ethics, tax evasion, and religion: A survey of opinion of members of the Church of Jesus Christ of latter-day saints. In R. W. McGee (Ed.), *The ethics of tax evasion: Perspectives in theory and practice* (pp. 211–226). Springer. Summarized in McGee (2023d).
McGee, R. W., & Tyler, M. (2006). *Tax evasion and ethics: A demographic study of 33 countries*. https://doi.org/10.2139/ssrn.940505.
McGee, R. W., & Zhou, E. (2023). How prevalent is bribery? A ranking of 52 countries. In R. W. McGee & S. Benk (Eds.), *The ethics of bribery: Theoretical and empirical studies*. Springer, forthcoming.
McGee, R. W., Nickerson, I., & Fees, W. (2006, July). German and American opinion on the ethics of tax evasion. In *Allied academies international conference. academy of legal, ethical and regulatory issues. Proceedings* (Vol. 10, No. 2, p. 31). https://doi.org/10.2139/ssrn.936743

McGee, R. W., Benk, S., & Budak, T. (2023a). Muslim attitudes toward bribery. In R. W. McGee & S. Benk (Eds.), *The ethics of bribery: Theoretical and empirical studies*. Springer, forthcoming.
McGee, R. W., Benk, S., & Pardisi, A. (2023b). Has the attitude toward bribery changed over time? A longitudinal study of 75 countries. In R. W. McGee & S. Benk (Eds.), *The ethics of bribery, volume 2: Country studies*. Springer, forthcoming.
McGee, R. W., Benk, S., & Yüzbaşı, B. (2023c). Religious attitudes toward bribery: A comparative study. In R. W. McGee & S. Benk (Eds.), *The ethics of bribery: Theoretical and empirical studies*. Springer, forthcoming.
McGee, R. W., Benk, S., & Yüzbaşı, B. (2023d). Atheist attitudes toward bribery. In R. W. McGee & S. Benk (Eds.), *The ethics of bribery: Theoretical and empirical studies*. Springer, forthcoming.
McGee, R. W., Benk, S., & Yüzbaşı, B. (2023e). Buddhist attitudes toward bribery. In R. W. McGee & S. Benk (Eds.), *The ethics of bribery: Theoretical and empirical studies*. Springer, forthcoming.
McGee, R. W., Benk, S., & Yüzbaşı, B. (2023f). Christian attitudes toward bribery. In R. W. McGee & S. Benk (Eds.), *The ethics of bribery: Theoretical and empirical studies*. Springer, forthcoming.
McGee, R. W., Benk, S., & Yüzbaşı, B. (2023g). Hindu attitudes toward bribery. In R. W. McGee & S. Benk (Eds.), *The ethics of bribery: Theoretical and empirical studies*. Springer, forthcoming.
McGee, R. W., Benk, S., & Yüzbaşı, B. (2023h). Jewish attitudes toward bribery. In R. W. McGee & S. Benk (Eds.), *The ethics of bribery: Theoretical and empirical studies*. Springer, forthcoming.
Medina, L., & Schneider, F. (2018). *Shadow economies around the world: What did we learn over the last 20 years?* International Monetary Fund Working Paper, WP/18/17.
Merton, R. K. (1968). *Social theory and social structure* (Enlarged Ed ed.). Free Press.
Murtuza, A., & Ghazanfar, S. M. (1998). Taxation as a form of worship: Exploring the nature of zakat. In R. W. McGee (Ed.), *The ethics of tax evasion* (pp. 190–212). The Dumont Institute for Public Policy Research. Summarized in McGee, Robert W., The Ethics of Tax Evasion: Summaries of 21 Studies (March 12, 2022). https://doi.org/10.2139/ssrn.4056290
Oliva, R. R. (1998). The schism between tax practitioners' ethical and legal obligations: Recommendations for the fusion of law and ethics. In R. W. McGee (Ed.), *The ethics of tax evasion* (pp. 350–371). The Dumont Institute for Public Policy Research. Summarized in McGee, Robert W., The Ethics of Tax Evasion: Summaries of 21 Studies (March 12, 2022). https://doi.org/10.2139/ssrn.4056290
Pennock, R. T. (1998). Death and taxes: On the justice of conscientious war tax resistance. In R. W. McGee (Ed.), *The ethics of tax evasion* (pp. 124–142). The Dumont Institute for Public Policy Research. Summarized in McGee, Robert W., The Ethics of Tax Evasion: Summaries of 21 Studies (March 12, 2022). https://doi.org/10.2139/ssrn.4056290
Preobragenskaya, G. G., & McGee, R. W. (2016). A demographic study of Russian attitudes toward tax evasion. *Journal of Accounting, Ethics & Public Policy, 17*(1), 137–207. http://ssrn.com/abstract=2745666
Queloz, N. (2002). Criminalité économique et criminalité organisée. *L'Économie politique, 3*(15), 58–67.
Remeikiene, R., Gaspareniene, L., & Schneider, F. (2017). The definition of digital shadow economy. *Technological and Economic Development of Economy, 24*(2), 1–22.
Satalkina, L., & Steiner, G. (2020). Digital entrepreneurship and its role in innovation systems: A systematic literature review as a basis for future research avenues for sustainable transitions. *Sustainability, 12*(7), 2764.
Schansberg, D. E. (1998). The ethics of tax evasion within biblical Christianity: Are there limits to "rendering unto Caesar?". In R. W. McGee (Ed.), *The ethics of tax evasion* (pp. 144–157). The Dumont Institute for Public Policy Research. Summarized in McGee, Robert W., The Ethics of Tax Evasion: Summaries of 21 Studies (March 12, 2022). https://doi.org/10.2139/ssrn.4056290
Scheau, M. C. (2018). *Criminalitatea informatica privind transferurile financiare*. Editura Economica Bucuresti.

Schneider, F., & Buehn, A. (2016). *Estimating the size of the shadow economy: Methods, problems and open questions.* IZA Discussion Paper No. 9820.

Schneider, F. H., & Klinglmair, R. (2004). *Shadow economies around the world: what do we know?* Universität Linz, Working Paper No. 0403.

Smith, S. R., & Kimball, K. C. (1998). Tax evasion and ethics: A perspective from members of the Church of Jesus Christ of latter-day saints. In R. W. McGee (Ed.), *The ethics of tax evasion* (pp. 220–229). The Dumont Institute for Public Policy Research. Summarized in McGee, Robert W., The Ethics of Tax Evasion: Summaries of 21 Studies (March 12, 2022). https://doi.org/10.2139/ssrn.4056290

Tamari, M. (1998). Ethical issues in tax evasion: A Jewish perspective. In R. W. McGee (Ed.), *The ethics of tax evasion* (pp. 168–178). The Dumont Institute for Public Policy Research. Summarized in McGee, Robert W., The Ethics of Tax Evasion: Summaries of 21 Studies (March 12, 2022). https://doi.org/10.2139/ssrn.4056290

Torgler, B. (2002). *The economic analysis of 'creative' compliance.* WWZ-Discussion Paper.

Torgler, B. (2004). Tax Morale in Asian countries. *Journal of Asian Economics, 15*, 237–266.

Torgler, B., & Schneider, F. (2009). The impact of tax morale and institutional quality on the shadow economy. *Journal of Economic Psychology, 30*(3), 228–245.

Williams, C. C. (2020). Tackling informal entrepreneurship in east-Central Europe: From a deterrence to preventative approach. *Journal of Developmental Entrepreneurship, 25*(4), 1–20.

Williams, C. C., & Shahid, M. S. (2016). Informal entrepreneurship and institutional theory: Explaining the varying degrees of (in)formalization of entrepreneurs in Pakistan. *Entrepreneurship & Regional Development, 28*(1-2), 1–25.

Yew, B. K., Milanov, V. B., & McGee, R. W. (2015). An analysis of individual tax morale for Russia: Before and after flat tax reform. *International Business Research, 8*(1), 60–80. http://ssrn.com/abstract=2544702

Monica Violeta Achim is full professor and doctoral supervisor in the field of finance at the Faculty of Economics and Business Administration, Babeş-Bolyai University, Cluj-Napoca, Romania. With over 24 years of experience in academia, she has authored and coauthored over 150 scientific articles and 25 books. Her most recent reference work is the book *Economic and Financial Crime: Corruption, Shadow Economy and Money Laundering*, published by Springer. In 2020 she received an Award for Excellence in Scientific Research at Babeş-Bolyai University, Faculty of Economics and Business Administration, Cluj-Napoca, Romania, in recognition of the results obtained in her research activity. She heads a big grant titled "Intelligent analysis and prediction of the economic and financial crime in a cyber-dominated and interconnected business world," conducted over the period 2021–2023, financed by the Romanian Ministry of Education and Research, CNCS – UEFISCDI, project number PN-III-P4-ID-PCE-2020-2174 (www.fincrime.net).

Sorin Nicolae Borlea is a professor and doctoral supervisor in the field of finance at the University of Oradea and Vasile Goldiş University, and an associate scientific researcher at the European Research Institute of Babeş-Bolyai University, Cluj-Napoca. He has over 16 years of experience in the academic field and 30 years in the business environment. He has authored over 90 scientific articles and 20 books. His most recent reference work is the coauthored book *Economic and Financial Crime: Corruption, Shadow Economy and Money Laundering*, published by Springer. In parallel with the academic field, he works in the business environment as financial auditor, accounting expert, tax consultant, and financial analyst, being strongly anchored in economic and financial crime issues in the files managed by the Court of Cluj-Napoca. He is well known in the business environment as a perfectionist, being ranked in the top10 accounting experts in Cluj County (2017). He is a member of the project titled "Intelligent analysis and prediction of the economic and financial crime in a cyber-dominated and interconnected business world," conducted over the period 2021–2023, financed by the Romanian Ministry of Education and Research, CNCS – UEFISCDI, project number PN-III-P4-ID-PCE-2020-2174 (www.fincrime.net).

Robert W. McGee is a business professor at Fayetteville State University, USA. He holds 23 academic degrees, including 13 doctorates from universities in the USA and 4 European countries. He has authored more than 60 books, including several novels, and more than 1000 articles, book chapters, conference papers, and working papers. Various studies have ranked him No. 1 in the world for both accounting ethics and business ethics scholarship. He is an attorney and Certified Public Accountant (CPA) (retired) and has worked or lectured in more than 30 countries. He drafted the accounting law for Armenia and Bosnia and reviewed the accounting law for Mozambique. He was in charge of assisting the Finance Ministries of Armenia and Bosnia convert their countries to International Financial Reporting Standards. He is also a world champion in taekwondo, karate, kung fu, and tai chi (both Yang and Sun styles) and has won more than 900 gold medals.

Gabriela-Mihaela Mureşan holds a PhD in Finance and works as lecturer at the Department of Finance, Faculty of Economics and Business Administration, Babeş-Bolyai University. She has authored more than 20 research papers, 2 international books, and 2 national books, and attended several international conferences. Her research interests are broadly focused in the field of insurance, financial analysis, and economic psychology. She is especially interested in human behavior, manipulation, money addiction, culture, happiness, ethics, corruption, fraud, corporate performance, bankruptcy, and creative accounting. She is a member of the project titled "Intelligent analysis and prediction of the economic and financial crime in a cyber-dominated and interconnected business world," conducted over the period 2021–2023, financed by the Romanian Ministry of Education and Research, CNCS – UEFISCDI, project number PN-III-P4-ID-PCE-2020-2174 (www.fincrime.net).

Ioana Lavinia Safta (Plesa) has a degree in Economics, with a master's degree in Audit and Control Accounting Management. She is a second-year PhD student in Finance, with an interest in economics, "The relationship between creative accounting and fraud, models for detecting the risk of fraud at the level of economic entities." She worked as an assistant professor at the Department of Finance, Faculty of Economics and Business Administration, Babeş-Bolyai University in Cluj-Napoca. She gained over 3 years of experience in accounting, working as an accountant in a financial expertise and audit firm. She is the author/coauthor of scientific articles in her studies area. Her research interests are focused on finance and accounting. Lately, she has given special attention on issues related to economic and financial crime. She is a member of the project titled "Intelligent analysis and prediction of the economic and financial crime in a cyber-dominated and interconnected business world," conducted over the period 2021–2023, financed by the Romanian Ministry of Education and Research, CNCS – UEFISCDI, project number PN-III-P4-ID-PCE-2020-2174 (www.fincrime.net).

Viorela-Ligia Văidean is an associate professor in the field of finance at the Faculty of Economics and Business Administration, Babeş-Bolyai University, Cluj-Napoca. She holds a bachelor's degree in Finance and Banking from Babeş-Bolyai University (BBU), Cluj-Napoca, Romania in 2006, further graduating from a master's program in Corporate Finance and Insurances and another degree in Project Management and Evaluation. She successfully followed a full-time PhD program, obtaining her PhD in Finance, in 2010. In 2015 she graduated from a postdoctoral study program. She has worked as a teaching assistant and then a lecturer at the Finance Department within BBU, Cluj-Napoca. She has also worked as an expert for different EU-financed projects and grants. She has written more than 40 research papers and attended several international conferences. She has been the author or coauthor of ten books and international book chapters. Her research interests cover the areas of health economics, corporate finance, financial management, organized crime, and fiscal policies. She is a member of the project titled "Intelligent analysis and prediction of the economic and financial crime in a cyber-dominated and interconnected business world," conducted over the period 2021–2023, financed by the Romanian Ministry of Education and Research, CNCS – UEFISCDI, project number PN-III-P4-ID-PCE-2020-2174 (www.fincrime.net).

Chapter 3
Bibliometric Analysis of Financial Crime Links Using Visual Maps

Monica Violeta Achim, Robert W. McGee, and Ioana Lavinia Safta (Pleşa)

Abstract This chapter provides a bibliometric analysis of financial crime, and includes visual maps to assist in the understanding of the issues involved. Bibliometrics deals with the collection, processing, and quantitative analysis of bibliographic data from scientific publications and, using statistical methods, assesses the academic quality of the publications analyzed. Depending on the methods used, bibliometric analyses of citations, co-citation, coauthorship, use of certain terms, bibliographic sources, etc. can be carried out through various factor analyses as well as content analyses. The main objective of this subsection is to quantify the state of the art in terms of research identified as having been carried out according to scientific articles queried via the Web of Science (WoS) platform.

Keywords Financial crime · Bibliometric analysis · Tax compliance · Tax morale · Corruption · Money laundering

In this section we conducted an investigation of financial crime links using visual maps. More exactly, through bibliometric analysis, we quantified the current state of knowledge regarding the correlation between various patterns associated with financial crime such as tax compliance, tax attitude, tax morale, corruption, or money laundering and even possible determining factors such as age, gender, education, region, or professional status, using a set of scientific materials

M. V. Achim (✉)
Faculty of Economics and Business Administration, Babeş-Bolyai University, Cluj-Napoca, Romania
e-mail: monica.achim@econ.ubbcluj.ro

R. W. McGee
Fayetteville State University, Fayetteville, NC, USA

I. L. Safta (Pleşa)
Faculty of Economic Sciences and Business Administration, Babeş-Bolyai University, Cluj-Napoca, Romania

M. V. Achim, R. W. McGee (eds.), *Financial Crime in Romania*, SpringerBriefs in Finance, https://doi.org/10.1007/978-3-031-27883-9_3

collected from the Web of Science platform and their analysis through the VOSviewer software. The main objective of this analysis was to study the research trend in the field of interest.

Bibliometrics is a field of research that uses mathematical computing and statistical techniques to study publications and communication patterns in the distribution of information (Diodato & Gellatly, 2013).

Bibliometrics deals with the collection, processing, and quantitative analysis of bibliographic data from scientific publications and, using statistical methods, assesses the academic quality of the publications analyzed. Depending on the methods used, bibliometric analyses of citations, co-citation, coauthorship, use of certain terms, bibliographic sources, etc. can be carried out through various factor analyses as well as content analyses.

The main objective of this subsection is to quantify the state of the art in terms of research identified as having been carried out according to scientific articles queried via the Web of Science (WoS) platform.

Looking at the graphs of keyword maps and the most relevant terms as a starting point, through deductive reasoning, we identified the most addressed research. Searches were conducted on the Web of Science platform including keywords for the 1996–2022 period.

For this purpose, we produced five maps in which we analyzed the keyword group associations according to which the Web of Science search was carried out, using the total count method (Van Eck & Waltman, 2011). The data were extracted from the WoS platform for the period 1996 to 2022.

A number of initial terms were identified for each group, but then 10% of them were eliminated based on the relevance score criteria calculated by the software. Furthermore, in the term-checking stage, some terms were deselected, i.e., common terms such as author, study, research, article, year, data, paper, etc., as these terms distorted the maps because they were not directly related to the initial searches.

VOSviewer revealed the field of research studies to be correlated with terms such as age, gender, education, region, and professional status. The maps contain a number of different clusters, but we individually analyzed only the clusters with the highest relevance to our searches, as follows.

Figure 3.1 shows the terms with which the attitude toward taxes correlates. Out of the 3160 initial terms, the software retained 2188 terms with at least 10 uses. Subsequently, from the list of 2188 terms, 15% of them are eliminated according to the relevance score criteria calculated by the software. In the next step, common terms such as author, study, research, article, year, date, paper, etc. are also deselected, so in the very end 300 terms remain, presented in Fig. 3.2. As such, the network of the most relevant and frequently used terms in our research being the association between tax attitudes and searched keywords, generated in the VOSviewer software according to bibliometric data extracted from the WoS platform in the 1996–2022 period, reveals that the *attitude toward taxes* is correlated with terms such as age, gender, gender-different, taxes, culture, education, region, corruption. The generated map shows six clusters, but for our research the most

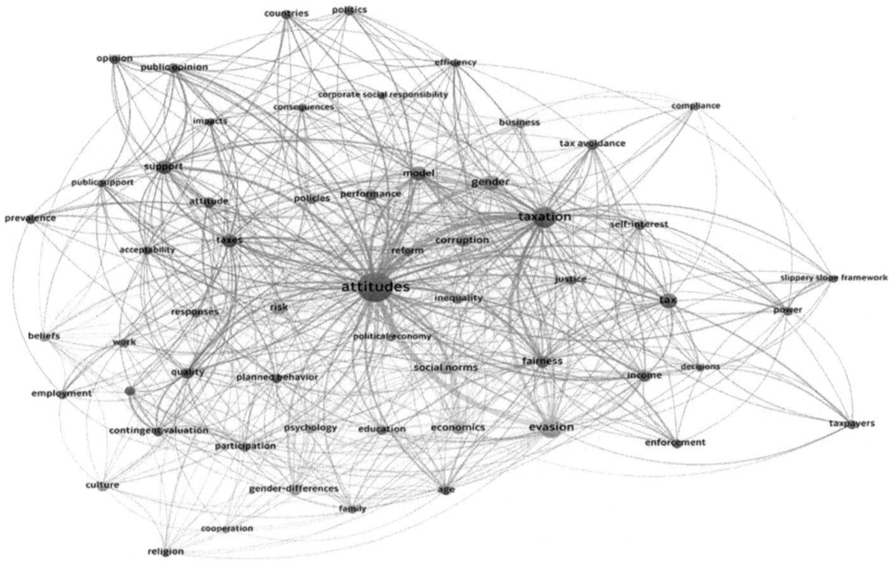

Fig. 3.1 Map showing the relationship between attitude toward taxes and groups of keywords. (Source: own processing, VOSviewer software)

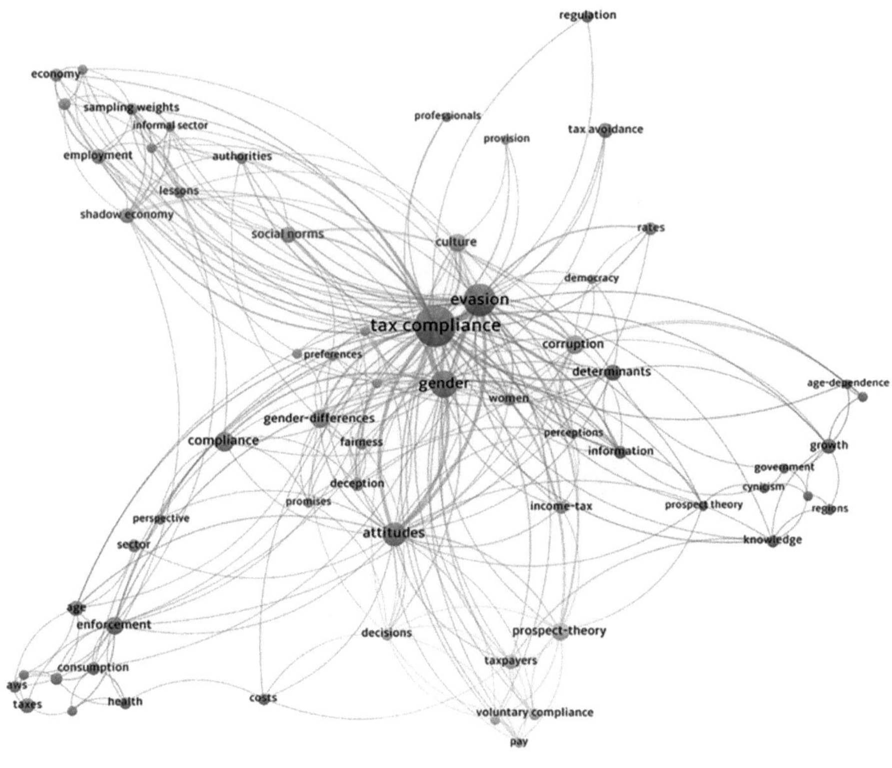

Fig. 3.2 Map showing the link between tax compliance and groups of keywords. (Source: own processing, VOSviewer software)

relevant cluster is the third cluster, since the frequency with which words are linked in the initial search have a link strength of 411.

Figure 3.2 investigates tax compliance links. Out of the 1020 initial terms, the software retained 500 terms with at least 10 uses. After removing irrelevant terms, we kept 202 terms in the analysis. For this analysis the map consists of 9 clusters; the cluster we analyzed is cluster number 8, which captures a linkage strength of 160 between keywords; besides keywords we may also observe a linkage to other words such as culture, gender, attitude, income tax, corruption, shadow economy, sector, perspectives.

Figure 3.3 shows the map of corruption links. The map identifies both the keywords in our search and other words with a high relevance for corruption, which indicates that researchers are paying more and more attention to this concept, in order to better understand it and to identify ways to stop it or rather to reduce it. In this figure we find a number of 8 clusters, which is a small number in terms of this concept, but this small number of clusters is due to the fact that there are extremely strong links between this concept and the keywords in our search; the software includes them in the same cluster, we find a strength of the link even of 1145.

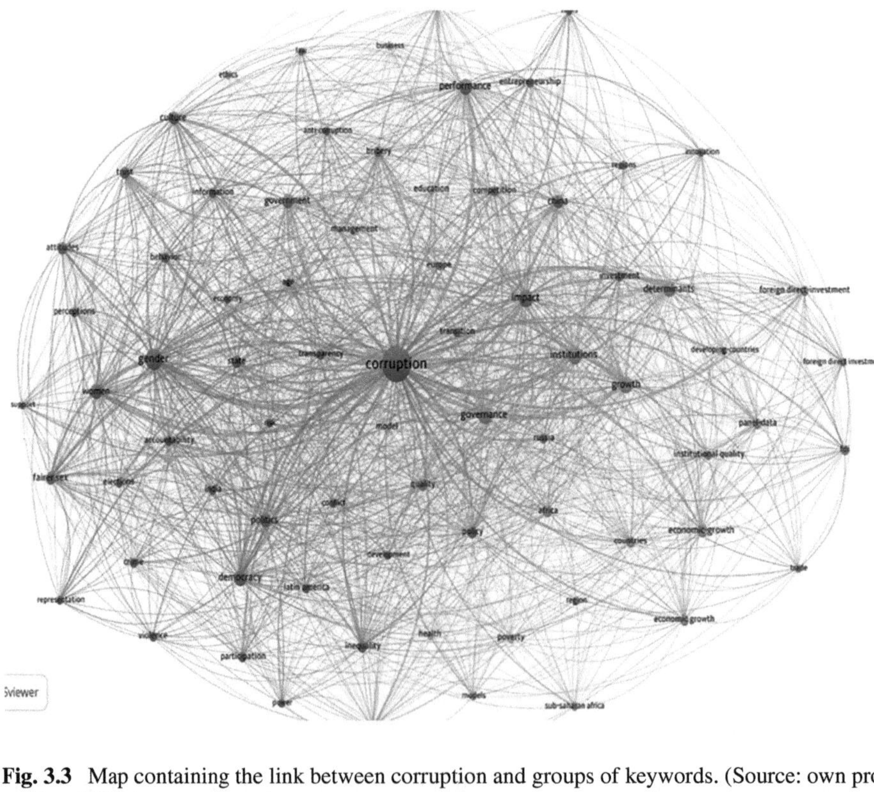

Fig. 3.3 Map containing the link between corruption and groups of keywords. (Source: own processing, VOSviewer software)

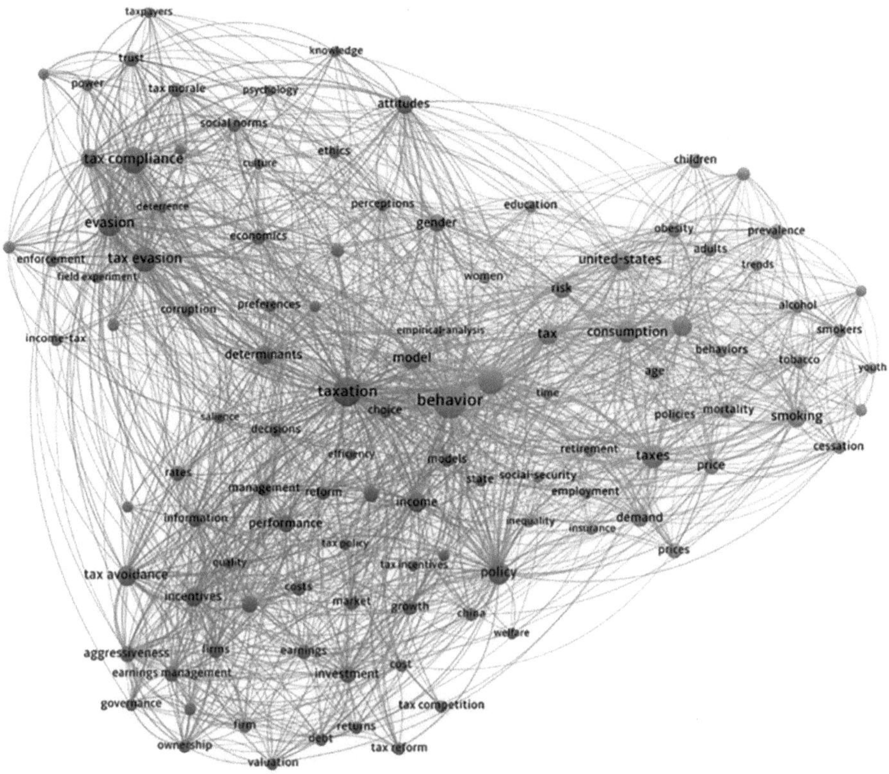

Fig. 3.4 Map containing the link between tax behavior and groups of keywords. (Source: own processing, VOSviewer software)

Cluster number 1 is the largest cluster, where we find corruption correlated with gender, age, education, region, risk, culture, anti-corruption.

Figure 3.4 shows the link between tax behavior and keywords. Out of the 5643 initial terms, the software retained 376 terms with at least 10 uses. Subsequently, from the list of 376 terms, 15% of them are eliminated according to the relevance score criteria calculated by the software. This leaves 280 for analysis. The map shows 6 clusters. We may observe from the map that terms such as behavior, taxes, gender, culture, perception, tax morale, social norms, and psychology highly correlate with tax behavior along with other economic and political determinants.

Figure 3.5 shows that tax morale correlates with terms such as trust, attitude, tax behavior, education, gender, or culture along with other economic and political determinants.

In order to more clearly highlight the keywords that are found in the searches of interest in our research, we have selected the words with the highest frequency in the published articles and we have also made a representation of them in the form of a WordCloud (Fig. 3.6).

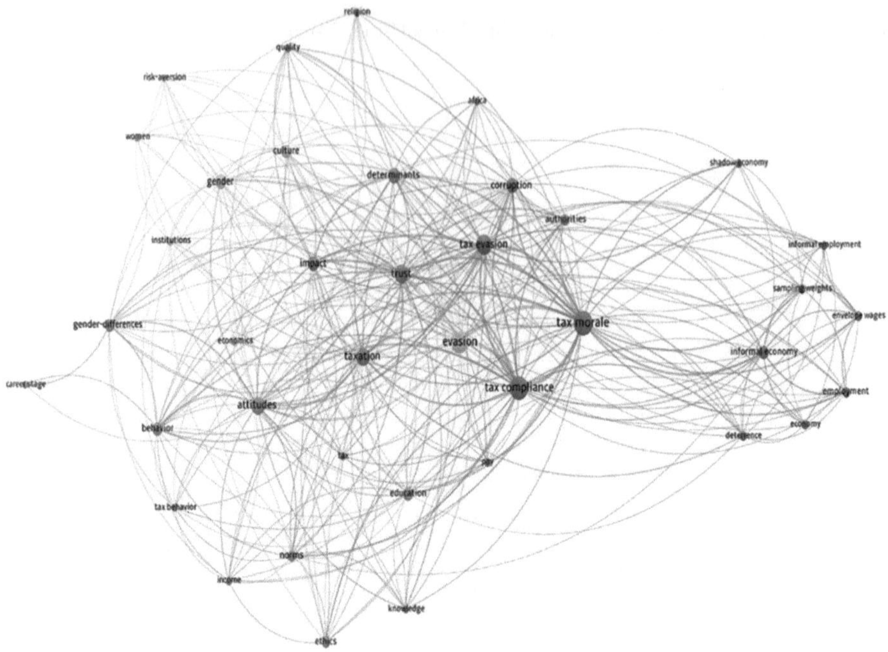

Fig. 3.5 Map containing the link between tax morale and groups of keywords. (Source: own processing, VOSviewer software)

Fig. 3.6 WordCloud of most frequent keywords in this research. (Source: own processing, WordCloud software)

It can be seen that the higher the font of the keywords is, the higher their frequency in searches is, more precisely meaning that they are found more often, for example corruption is found in 99% of searches, behavior is found in over 80%, education in 82%, gender-difference is found in about 70% of searches, and so on.

References

Diodato, V. P., & Gellatly, P. (2013). *Dictionary of Bibliometrics*. 1st ed. Taylor and Francis, New York.

Van Eck, N. J., & Waltman, L. (2011). Text mining and visualization using VOSviewer. *ISSI Newsletter, 7*(3), 50–54.

Monica Violeta Achim is full professor and doctoral supervisor in the field of Finance at the Faculty of Economics and Business Administration, Babeş-Bolyai University, Cluj-Napoca, Romania. With over 24 years of experience in academia, she has published, as author and co-author, over 150 scientific articles and 25 books. Her most recent reference work is the book *Economic and Financial Crime. Corruption, Shadow Economy and Money Laundering*, published by Springer. In 2020 she earned an Award for Excellence in Scientific Research at Babeş-Bolyai University, Faculty of Economics and Business Administration, Cluj-Napoca, Romania, in recognition of the results obtained in her research activity. She heads a big grant titled "Intelligent analysis and prediction of economic and financial crime in a cyber-dominated and interconnected business world," conducted over the period 2021-2023, financed from the Romanian Ministry of Education and Research, CNCS-UEFISCDI, project number PN-III-P4-ID-PCE-2020-2174 (www.fincrime.net).

Robert W. McGee is business professor at Fayetteville State University, USA. He has earned 23 academic degrees, including 13 doctorates from universities in the United States and 4 European countries. He has published more than 60 books, including several novels, and more than 1000 articles, book chapters, conference papers, and working papers. Various studies have ranked him #1 in the world for both accounting ethics and business ethics scholarship. He is an attorney and CPA (retired) and has worked or lectured in more than 30 countries. He drafted the accounting law for Armenia and Bosnia and reviewed the accounting law for Mozambique. He was in charge of assisting the Finance Ministries of Armenia and Bosnia convert their countries to International Financial Reporting Standards. He is also a world champion in taekwondo, karate, kung fu, and tai chi (both Yang and Sun styles) and has won more than 900 gold medals.

Ioana Lavinia Safta (Pleşa) has a degree in Economics, with a Master's degree in Audit and Control Accounting Management. She is currently a second-year PhD student in Finance, with an interest in economics, "The relationship between creative accounting and fraud, models for detecting the risk of fraud at the level of economic entities." She worked as assistant professor at the Department of Finance, Faculty of Economics and Business Administration, Babeş-Bolyai University in Cluj-Napoca. She gained over 3 years of experience in accounting, working as an accountant in a financial expertise and audit firm. She is the author/co-author of scientific articles in her studies area. Her research interests are focused on finance and accounting. Lately, she has given special attention on issues related to economic and financial crime. She is a member of the project titled "Intelligent analysis and prediction of economic and financial crime in a cyber-dominated and interconnected business world," conducted over the period 2021-2023, financed from the Romanian Ministry of Education and Research, CNCS-UEFISCDI, project number PN-III-P4-ID-PCE-2020-2174 (www.fincrime.net).

Chapter 4
Hypotheses Development

Monica Violeta Achim and Robert W. McGee

Abstract This chapter discusses the hypotheses development that was used in the study. There were five sets of research hypotheses, referring to: tax compliance; attitude toward accepting cheating on taxes; how the perception of corruption might be related to certain demographic variables, such as gender, age, level of education, professional status, and geographic region; how skills detect the risk of money laundering, taking certain demographic variables into account; and responding to information requests from bank officers.

Keywords Tax compliance · Tax evasion · Corruption · Demographic variables · Money laundering · Disclosure

In the line of the aforementioned literature, we propose to respond to the following five sets of research hypotheses, each of them containing five research questions (RQ). Therefore, we sum up to 25 research questions, as follows:

I. **The first set of research questions: referring to tax compliance**

RQ1.1: *How does tax compliance depend on age?*
RQ1.2: *How does tax compliance depend on gender?*
RQ1.3: *How does tax compliance depend on Romanian regions (Banat, Bucovina, Crisana, Dobrogea, Maramureş, Moldova, Muntenia, Oltenia, Transylvania)?*
RQ1.4: *How does tax compliance depend on professional status?*
RQ1.5: *How does tax compliance depend on education?*

M. V. Achim
Faculty of Economics and Business Administration, Babeş-Bolyai University, Cluj-Napoca, Romania

R. W. McGee (✉)
Fayetteville State University, Fayetteville, NC, USA

M. V. Achim, R. W. McGee (eds.), *Financial Crime in Romania*, SpringerBriefs in Finance, https://doi.org/10.1007/978-3-031-27883-9_4

II. **The second set of research questions: referring to the attitude toward accepting cheating on taxes (is there an active, proactive, or passive attitude of people toward the taxation of goods and services?)**

RQ2.1: *How does tax morale depend on age?*
RQ2.2: *How does tax morale depend on gender?*
RQ2.3: *How does tax morale depend on Romanian regions (Banat, Bucovina, Crisana, Dobrogea, Maramureş, Moldova, Muntenia, Oltenia, Transylvania)?*
RQ2.4: *How does tax morale depend on professional status?*
RQ2.5: *How does tax morale depend on education?*

III. **The third set of research questions: referring to how the perception of corruption levels depends on age, gender, regions, etc.**

RQ3.1: *How does the perception of corruption depend on age?*
RQ3.2: *How does the perception of corruption depend on gender?*
RQ3.3: *How does the perception of corruption depend on the Romanian regions (Banat, Bucovina, Crisana, Dobrogea, Maramureş, Moldova, Muntenia, Oltenia, Transylvania)?*
RQ3.4: *How does the perception of corruption depend on professional status?*
RQ3.5: *How does the perception of corruption depend on education?*

IV. **The fourth set of research questions: referring to how the possessed skills detect the risk of money laundering depending on gender, age, region, etc.**

RQ4.1: *How does the level of skills in anti money laundering (AML) depend on age?*
RQ4.2: *How does the level of skills in AML depend on gender?*
RQ4.3: *How does the level of skills in AML depend on Romanian regions (Banat, Bucovina, Crisana, Dobrogea, Maramureş, Moldova, Muntenia, Oltenia, Transylvania)?*
RQ4.4: *How does the level of skills in AML depend on professional status?*
RQ4.5: *How does the level of skills in AML depend on education?*

V. **The fifth set of research questions: covering the attitude toward responding to information requests from the bank officers (we actually want to determine how aware the population is of the fact that banks have their own needs with respect to getting to know their customers)**

RQ5.1: *How does the attitude toward the job of bank officers depend on age?*
RQ5.2: *How does the attitude toward the job of bank officers depend on gender?*
RQ5.3: *How does the attitude toward the job of bank officers depend on Romanian regions (Banat, Bucovina, Crisana, Dobrogea, Maramureş, Moldova, Muntenia, Oltenia, Transylvania)?*
RQ5.4: *How does the attitude toward the job of bank officers depend on professional status?*
RQ5.5: *How does the attitude toward the job of bank officers depend on education?*

Monica Violeta Achim is full professor and doctoral supervisor in the field of Finance at the Faculty of Economic Sciences and Business Administration, Babeş-Bolyai University, Cluj-Napoca, Romania. With over 24 years of experience in academia, she has published, as author and co-author, over 150 scientific articles and 25 books. Her most recent reference work is the book *Economic and Financial Crime. Corruption, Shadow Economy and Money Laundering*, published by Springer. In 2020 she earned an Award for Excellence in Scientific Research at Babeş-Bolyai University, Faculty of Economics and Business Administration, Cluj-Napoca, Romania, in recognition of the results obtained in her research activity. She heads a big grant titled "Intelligent analysis and prediction of economic and financial crime in a cyber-dominated and interconnected business world," conducted over the period 2021-2023, financed from the Romanian Ministry of Education and Research, CNCS-UEFISCDI, project number PN-III-P4-ID-PCE-2020-2174 (www.fincrime.net).

Robert W. McGee is business professor at Fayetteville State University, USA. He has earned 23 academic degrees, including 13 doctorates from universities in the United States and 4 European countries. He has published more than 60 books, including several novels, and more than 1000 articles, book chapters, conference papers, and working papers. Various studies have ranked him #1 in the world for both accounting ethics and business ethics scholarship. He is an attorney and CPA (retired) and has worked or lectured in more than 30 countries. He drafted the accounting law for Armenia and Bosnia and reviewed the accounting law for Mozambique. He was in charge of assisting the Finance Ministries of Armenia and Bosnia convert their countries to International Financial Reporting Standards. He is also a world champion in taekwondo, karate, kung fu, and tai chi (both Yang and Sun styles) and has won more than 900 gold medals.

Chapter 5
Methodology and Data

Monica Violeta Achim, Sorin Nicolae Borlea, Mihai Gaicu, Codruța Mare, Robert W. McGee, Gabriela-Mihaela Mureşan, Ioana Lavinia Safta (Pleşa), Mircea Constantin Şcheau, and Viorela-Ligia Văidean

Abstract This chapter discusses the methodology used in the study and how the data were gathered. A questionnaire was distributed to 1856 Romanians comprising a wide range of demographic variables, including gender, age, education level, professional status, and geographic region of the country.

Keywords Survey · Romania · Demographic variables · Tax compliance · Corruption · Money laundering

M. V. Achim (✉) · G.-M. Mureşan · I. L. Safta (Pleşa) · V.-L. Văidean
Faculty of Economics and Business Administration, Babeş-Bolyai University, Cluj-Napoca, Romania
e-mail: monica.achim@econ.ubbcluj.ro

S. N. Borlea
Faculty of Economics, University of Oradea, Oradea, Romania

Faculty of Economics, Computer Science and Engineering, "Vasile Goldiş" Western University of Arad, Arad, Romania

European Research Institute, Babeş-Bolyai University, Cluj-Napoca, Romania

M. Gaicu
SAS Institute, Brussels, Belgium

C. Mare
Faculty of Economics and Business Administration, Babeş-Bolyai University, Cluj-Napoca, Romania

Interdisciplinary Centre for Data Science, Babeş-Bolyai, Cluj-Napoca, Romania

R. W. McGee
Fayetteville State University, Fayetteville, NC, USA

M. C. Şcheau
European Research Institute, Babeş-Bolyai University, Cluj-Napoca, Romania

M. V. Achim, R. W. McGee (eds.), *Financial Crime in Romania*, SpringerBriefs in Finance, https://doi.org/10.1007/978-3-031-27883-9_5

5.1 Description of the Sample

For our purpose a survey based on a questionnaire was conducted among 1856 respondents for the period May 27 to June 6, 2022. In order for the result of the study to be eloquent and to reflect the actual situation, with the lowest possible degree of subjectivism, we addressed the most heterogeneous segments of respondents.

Figure 5.1 shows the results by age. About 30% of the respondents belonged to the 16–25 year-old age group, 20% were between 36 and 45 years, and another 20% were 46–55 years old; 16% were between 26 and 35 years and the remaining 13% were above 56 years old.

Figure 5.2 reflects the content of our sample by gender. Among the 1856 respondents, the great majority of about three quarters of the respondents were female while only one quarter was represented by males.

Figure 5.3 reflects the sample population by region. About 34% of the respondents belong to the Transylvanian region, following by about 20% from Muntenia. About 12% and 11% of the respondents came from Moldova and Oltenia, respectively, and the remaining 23% were divided among the remaining regions (about 9% came from Banat, about 5% from Bucovina, and Crisana, Dobrogea and Maramureş, each of them with about 3–4%).

The level of their professional status was another observed variable. Thus, according to Fig. 5.4, about half of the respondents were employees, followed by students (25%); 19% of the respondents held management positions, 6% represent retired people while only less than 1% of respondents were unemployed.

Finally, the level of education was another important pattern that we wanted to examine, as one potential determinant of citizens' understanding and compliance with the law. Figure 5.5 shows that about 45% of the respondents had bachelor degrees, 30% of the respondents had master studies, about 19% were high school graduates or less, 4% had doctoral studies, while less than 2% had postdoctoral studies.

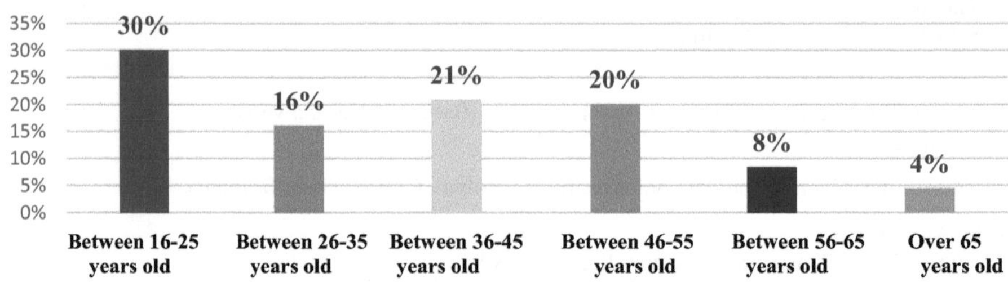

Fig. 5.1 Sample percentage by age. (Note: Data survey, with a sample of 1856 individuals)

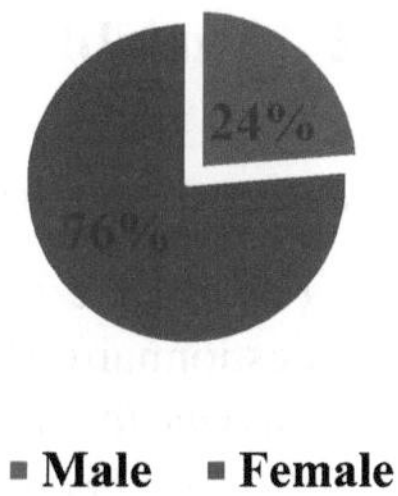

Fig. 5.2 Sample percentage by gender. (Note: Data survey, with a sample of 1856 individuals)

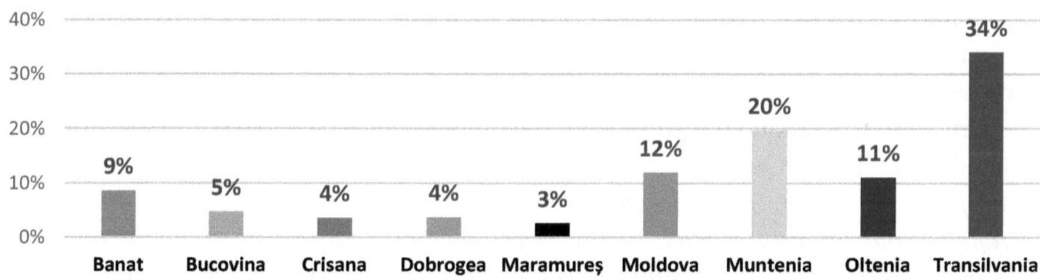

Fig. 5.3 Sample percentage by region of Romania. (Note: Data survey, with a sample of 1856 individuals)

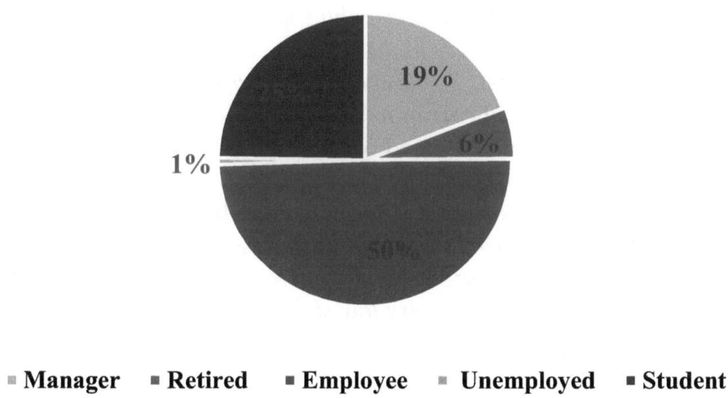

Fig. 5.4 Sample percentage by professional status. (Note: Data survey, with a sample of 1856 individuals)

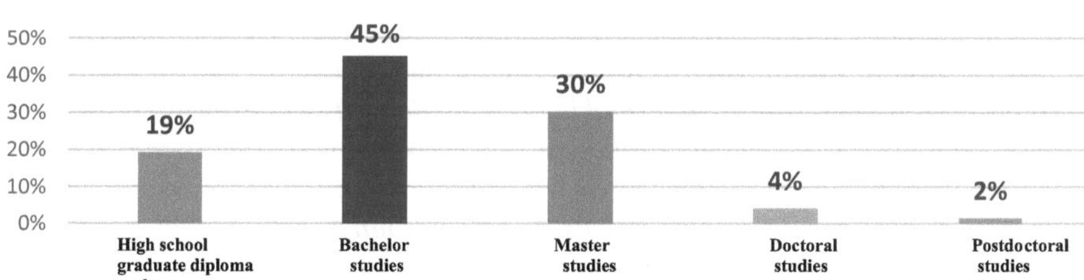

Fig. 5.5 Sample percentage by level of education. (Note: Data survey, with a sample of 1856 individuals)

5.2 Variables and Data

The dependent variables that we analyzed are represented by:

Tax compliance (Q1) was captured by the answers to the first question from the questionnaire (Q1) that was formulated as follows: Question 1:*Let's start with how you feel about taxes. Regarding paying your tax duties, which one of the following behaviors is common for you and people around you: Taxes are paid long before the deadline, to get the benefit of some discounts from the whole amount; Taxes are paid long before the deadline, regardless of any discounts; Taxes are paid very close to the deadline; Taxes are paid over the deadline.*

Tax morale (Q2) was estimated by the *attitude toward accepting cheating on taxes*, taken from the second question from the questionnaire. The question was formulated as follows: Question 2: *When you receive goods and services from the shops, restaurants, hotels, salons, etc., please choose the situation that best reflects your opinion: Always receiving the receipt; Usually receiving the receipt; Always asking for the receipt; Receiving the receipt but leaving it there; Not bothered by not receiving the receipt.*

Perception of corruption (Q3) of the Romanian citizens was taken from question three. This question was formulated as follows: Question 3: *How do you perceive the level of corruption of Romanian public institutions, on a scale between 1 point (very low) to 5 points (very high)? Please choose one of the following: 1 – very low level of corruption; 2 – low level of corruption; 3 – average level of corruption; 4 – high level of corruption; 5 – very high level of corruption.*

AML skills (Q4) were determined based on the fourth question (Q4), which evaluates the level of *skills possessed by the citizens in order to detect the risk of money laundering*. The question was formulated as follows: Question 4: *Related to the risk of money laundering, do you think that people have suitable knowledge in order to be able to recognize a suspicious transaction in a business? Please choose one of the following: 1 – very low skills to detect the risk of money laundering in a business; 2 – low skills to detect the risk of money laundering in a business; 3 – average skills to detect the risk of money laundering in a business; 4 – high skills to detect the risk of money laundering in a business; 5 – very high skills to detect the risk of money laundering in a business.*

Attitude toward KYC (Know Your Clients) procedures (Q5) was measured based on the fifth question (Q5), which deals with the *attitude toward providing information to the bank officers to apply the "Know Your Clients (KYC)" procedures.* The question was formulated as follows: Question 5: *When you or people around you ask for a bank transaction (making a bank deposit, withdrawing cash from the account, etc.), and the bank officer asks you to complete some details regarding the provenience of the money, or where that amount goes, generally you or people around have different reactions. To help us analyze your responses, please indicate which of the following categories best represents you: Refuse to offer any of the required details, banks have to satisfy the people's needs and that's all; Bothered of these required details but finally providing the asked information;*

Offer any asked details, banks must apply their "know your clients" principle to do their job.

The independent variables were represented by age, gender, professional status, education, and region. The data referring to them were collected from the questions Q6 to Q10 from the survey questionnaire.

5.3 Methods

The first step of the analysis was data curation. Finally, a sample of 1856 Romanian respondents remained in the analysis.

The dataset consisted of qualitative and ordinal variables dealing with financial crime perceptions such as tax, corruption, and money laundering behavioral aspects along with demographic characteristics. The first step was the descriptive assessment of data. For this, we computed frequencies and percentages, and we constructed pie and bar charts. In the second step of the analysis, we conducted relationship assessments. Given the nature of our data, we used the Chi-square test, along with the contingency coefficient. Clustered bar charts were constructed for visualization purposes. Statistical significance was considered at a critical level of 10%. Analyses were conducted in Excel (MS Office 365), Tableau 2022.1, and IBM SPSS 24.

In order to make proper analyses and comparisons we also calculated scores for each variable of financial crime behavior (Q1 – Tax compliance, Q2 – Tax morale, Q3 – Perception of corruption, Q4 – AML skills, and Q5 – attitude toward KYC), as an average frequency of occurrence of each option within an analyzed category of determinants (age, gender, region, professional status or education), as follows:

Tax compliance score (Q1) = $(1*N1\% + 2*N2\% + 3*N3\% + 4*N4\%)i$, where the numbers 1, 2, 3, and 4 represent the numbers assigned to the following responses regarding the time of paying taxes:

1-Long before the deadline, regardless of the discounts
2-Long before the deadline to benefit from discounts
3-Very close to the deadline
4-Past the deadline

and N1%, N2%, N3%, and N4% represent the relative frequencies of occurrence for each option 1, 2, 3, or 4 within an analyzed "i" category of determinants (age, gender, region, professional status, or education).

Tax compliance score ranged from 1 – the best attitude to 4 – the worst attitude toward paying tax duties.

Tax morale score (Q2) = $(1*N1\% + 2*N2\% + 3*N3\% + 4*N4\% + 5*N5\%)i$, where the numbers 1, 2, 3, 4, and 5 represent the numbers assigned to the following responses regarding the adopted behavior when people receive goods and services from the shops, restaurants, hotels, salons, etc.:

1-Always receiving the receipt
2-Usually receiving the receipt
3-Always asking for the receipt
4-Receiving receipt but leaving it there
5-Not bothered by not receiving the receipt

and N1%, N2%, N3%, N4%, and N5% represent the relative frequencies of occurrence for each option 1,2, 3, 4, or 5 within an analyzed "i" category of determinants (age, gender, region, professional status, or education).

Tax morale score ranged from 1 – the most active (ethical) attitude to 5 – the most passive (unethical) attitude toward cheating on taxes.

Perception of corruption score (Q3) = (1*N1% + 2*N2% + 3*N3% + 4*N4% + 5*N5%)i, where the numbers 1,2, 3, 4, and 5 represent the number assigned to the following responses regarding the level of perceived corruption:

1-very low level of corruption
2-low level of corruption
3-average level of corruption
4-high level of corruption
5-very high level of corruption

and N1%, N2%, N3%, N4%, and N5% represent the relative frequency of occurrence for each option 1,2, 3, 4, or 5 within an analyzed "i" category of determinants (age, gender, region, professional status, or education).

Perception of corruption score ranged from 1 – the lowest level of corruption to 5 – the highest level of corruption.

AML skills score (Q4) = (1*N1% + 2*N2% + 3*N3% + 4*N4% + 5*N5%)i, where the numbers 1,2, 3, 4, and 5 represent the numbers assigned to the following responses regarding the level of AML skills possessed:

1-very low skills to detect the risk of money laundering in business
2-low skills to detect the risk of money laundering in business
3-average skills to detect the risk of money laundering in business
4-high skills to detect the risk of money laundering in business
5-very high skills to detect the risk of money laundering in business

and N1%, N2%, N3%, N4%, and N5% represent the relative frequencies of occurrence for each option 1,2, 3, 4, or 5 within an analyzed "i" category of determinants (age, gender, region, professional status, or education).

AML skills score ranged from 1 – very low skills to 5 – very high skills.

KYC attitude score (Q5) = (1*N1% + 2*N2% + 3*N3%)i, where the numbers 1, 2, and 3 represent the number assigned to the following responses regarding the adopted behavior when bank officers ask for details:

1-Offer any asked details, banks must apply their "know your clients" principle to do their job
2-Bothered of these required details but finally providing the asked information
3- Refuse to offer any required details, banks have to satisfy the people's needs and that's all

and N1%, N2%, and N3% represent the relative frequency of occurrence for each option 1, 2, or 3 within an analyzed "i" category of determinants (age, gender, region, professional status, or education). KYC attitude score ranges from 1 – the best attitude to 3 – the worst attitude.

Monica Violeta Achim is full professor and doctoral supervisor in the field of Finance at the Faculty of Economics and Business Administration, Babeş-Bolyai University, Cluj-Napoca, Romania. With over 24 years of experience in academia, she has published as author and co-author, over 150 scientific articles and 25 books. Her most recent reference work is the book Economic and Financial Crime. Corruption, Shadow Economy and Money Laundering, published by Springer. In 2020 she earned an Award for Excellence in Scientific Research at Babeş-Bolyai University, Faculty of Economics and Business Administration, Cluj-Napoca, Romania, in recognition of the results obtained in her research activity. She heads a big grant titled "Intelligent analysis and prediction of economic and financial crime in a cyber-dominated and interconnected business world," conducted over the period 2021–2023, financed from the Romanian Ministry of Education and Research, CNCS – UEFISCDI, project number PN-III-P4-ID-PCE-2020-2174 (www.fincrime.net).

Sorin Nicolae Borlea is professor and doctoral supervisor in the field of Finance at the University of Oradea and Vasile Goldiş University, and associate scientific researcher at the European Research Institute of Babeş-Bolyai University Cluj-Napoca. He has over 16 years of experience in the academic field and 30 years in the business environment. He has published over 90 scientific articles and 20 books. His most recent reference work is the co-authored book *Economic and Financial Crime: Corruption, shadow economy and money laundering,* published by Springer. In parallel with the academic field, he works in the business environment as financial auditor, accounting expert, tax consultant, and financial analyst, being strongly anchored in economic and financial crime issues in the files managed by the Court of Cluj-Napoca. He is well known in the business environment as a perfectionist, being ranked in the top10 accounting experts in Cluj County (2017). He is a member of the project titled "Intelligent analysis and prediction of the economic and financial crime in a cyber-dominated and interconnected business world," conducted over the period 2021–2023, financed from the Romanian Ministry of Education and Research, CNCS – UEFISCDI, project number PN-III-P4-ID-PCE-2020-2174 (www.fincrime.net).

Mihai Gaicu holds a BSc and an MSc in Business Engineering from Solvay Brussels School and a specialized master's in Data Science, Big Data from the Free University of Brussels. He acquired experience over two years in the banking sector and the IT industry, focusing on financial crime and artificial intelligence. He is a subject-matter expert in anti-money laundering (AML) and is working as Global Solution Advisor at SAS Institute. His role consists of collaborating with R&D and delivery teams to deploy industry best practices for AML solutions and helping financial institutions around the world to fight fraud and to meet regulatory compliance.

Codruţa Mare is a professor at the Department of Statistics-Forecasts-Mathematics and PhD coordinator in the field of cybernetics and statistics, Faculty of Economics and Business Administration, and the Scientific Director of the Interdisciplinary Centre for Data Science, Babeş-Bolyai University, Cluj-Napoca, Romania. She teaches several types of statistics and econometrics methods, from descriptive statistics to economic forecasting and spatial econometrics. She has expertise in consultancy and research projects conducted both for public institutions (The World Bank, European Commission, Romanian Ministry of Structural Funds, Cluj-Napoca City Hall, etc.) and for private companies, along with delivering training both in data analysis and in visualization, in Romania and abroad. Results of her research were published in books and articles in prestigious international journals. She is a member of the project titled "Intelligent analysis and prediction of the economic and financial crime in a cyber-dominated and interconnected business world," conducted over the period 2021–2023, financed by the Romanian Ministry of Education and Research, CNCS – UEFISCDI, project number PN-III-P4-ID-PCE-2020-2174 (www.fincrime.net).

Robert W. McGee is a business professor at Fayetteville State University, USA. He has earned 23 academic degrees, including 13 doctorates from universities in the USA and four European Countries. He has published more than 60 books, including several novels, and more than 1000 articles, book chapters, conference papers and working papers. Various studies have ranked him #1 in the world for both accounting ethics and business ethics scholarship. He is an attorney and CPA (retired) and has worked or lectured in more than 30 countries. He drafted the accounting law for Armenia and Bosnia and reviewed the accounting law for Mozambique. He was in charge of assisting the Finance Ministries of Armenia and Bosnia convert their countries to International Financial Reporting Standards. He is also a world champion in taekwondo, karate, kung fu and tai chi (both Yang and Sun styles) and has won more than 900 gold medals.

Gabriela-Mihaela Mureşan holds a PhD in Finance and currently works as lecturer at the Department of Finance, Faculty of Economics and Business Administration Babeş-Bolyai University. She has published more than 20 research papers, 2 international books, 2 national books, and attended several international conferences. Her research interests are broadly focused in the field of insurance, financial analysis and economic psychology. She is especially interested in human behavior, manipulation, money addiction, culture, happiness, ethics, corruption, fraud, corporate performance, bankruptcy and creative accounting. She is member of the project titled "Intelligent analysis and prediction of the economic and financial crime in a cyber-dominated and interconnected business world", conducted over the period 2021–2023, financed from the Romanian Ministry of Education and Research, CNCS – UEFISCDI, project number PN-III-P4-ID-PCE-2020-2174 (www.fincrime.net).

Ioana Lavinia Safta (Pleşa) has a degree in economics, with a master's degree in Audit and Control Accounting Management. She is currently a second-year PhD student in Finance, with an interest in economics, "The relationship between creative accounting and fraud, models for detecting the risk of fraud at the level of economic entities." She worked as an assistant professor at the Department of Finance, Faculty of Economics and Business Administration, Babeş Bolyai University in Cluj-Napoca. She gained over 3 years of experience in accounting, working as an accountant in a financial expertise and audit firm. She is the author / co-author of scientific articles in her studies area. Her research interests are focused on finance and accounting. Lately, she has given special attention on issues related to economic and financial crime. She is a member of the project titled "Intelligent analysis and prediction of economic and financial crime in a cyber-dominated and interconnected business world," conducted over the period 2021–2023, financed from the Romanian Ministry of Education and Research, CNCS – UEFISCDI, project number PN-III-P4-ID-PCE-2020-2174 (www.fincrime.net).

Mircea Constantin Şcheau is a PhD in Public Order and National Security with a topic of interest for economic and security fields, "Cybercrime on financial transfers," who received the "Victor Slavescu Prize" awarded by the Romanian Academy. Author / co-author of three volumes, more than forty scientific articles on management, law enforcement, critical infrastructure, information technology, defense, lecturer at numerous international conferences and member, inter alia, of the "Policies and strategies in the European Union's single market" research group of the European Research Institute of Babeş-Boyai University, Cluj-Napoca. He is a member of the project titled "Intelligent analysis and prediction of the economic and financial crime in a cyber-dominated and interconnected business world," conducted over the period 2021–2023, financed from the Romanian Ministry of Education and Research, CNCS – UEFISCDI, project number PN-III-P4-ID-PCE-2020-2174 (www.fincrime.net).

Viorela-Ligia Văidean is Associate professor in the field of Finance at the Faculty of Economic Sciences and Business Administration, Babeş-Bolyai University, Cluj-Napoca. She obtained a Bachelor Degree in Finance and Banking from 'Babeş – Bolyai' University (BBU) Cluj-Napoca, Romania in 2006, further graduating from a Master program in Corporate Finance and Insurances and another degree in Project Management and Evaluation. She successfully followed a full time PhD program, obtaining her PhD in the Finance field, in 2010. In 2015 she graduated from a post-doctoral study program. She has worked as a Teaching Assistant and then a Lecturer for the Finance Department within BBU Cluj-Napoca. She has also worked as an Expert for different EU financed projects and grants. She has published more than 40 research papers and attended several international conferences. She has been the author or co-author of ten books and international book chapters. Her research interests cover the areas of Health Economics, Corporate Finance, Financial Management, Organized Crime and Fiscal Policies. She is member of the project titled "Intelligent analysis and prediction of the economic and financial crime in a cyber-dominated and interconnected business world," conducted over the period 2021–2023, financed from the Romanian Ministry of Education and Research, CNCS – UEFISCDI, project number PN-III-P4-ID-PCE-2020-2174 (www.fincrime.net).

Chapter 6
Results

Monica Violeta Achim, Sorin Nicolae Borlea, Mihai Gaicu, Codruța Mare, Robert W. McGee, Gabriela-Mihaela Mureşan, Mircea Constantin Șcheau, and Viorela-Ligia Văidean

Abstract This chapter discloses and discusses the results of the study. The first objective of the study consisted of finding the main patterns that characterize the Romanian community, related to the level of tax compliance, attitude of citizens toward accepting cheating on taxes, the perception of corruption level in the Romanian public institutions, the level of skills possessed by citizens to detect the risk of money laundering, and the attitude toward providing information to bank officers. A series of color charts are included to make it easier for the reader to visualize the results.

Keywords Survey · Romania · Demographic variables · Tax compliance · Corruption · Money laundering

6.1 Descriptive Statistics

The first objective of our study consisted in finding the main patterns that characterize the Romanian community, related to the level of tax compliance, attitude of citizens toward accepting cheating on taxes, the perception of corruption level in the Romanian public institutions, the level of skills possessed by citizens to detect the risk of money laundering, the attitude toward providing information to bank officers.

In order to address this objective, a series of descriptive statistics were used. We started with the answers to the first question from the questionnaire (Q1) that dealt with *tax compliance*. According to our results presented in Fig. 6.1, a plurality of respondents (36%) declared that they pay taxes long before the deadline in order to

M. V. Achim · S. N. Borlea · C. Mare · G.-M. Mureşan · M. C. Șcheau · V.-L. Văidean
Babeş-Bolyai University, Cluj-Napoca, Romania

M. Gaicu
SAS Institute, Brussels, Belgium

R. W. McGee (✉)
Fayetteville State University, Fayetteville, NC, USA

M. V. Achim, R. W. McGee (eds.), *Financial Crime in Romania*, SpringerBriefs in Finance, https://doi.org/10.1007/978-3-031-27883-9_6

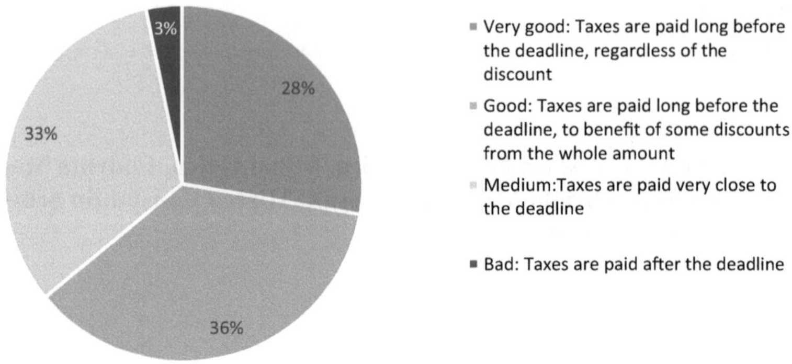

Fig. 6.1 Tax compliance. (Note: Data survey, with a sample of 1856 individuals)

benefit from some discounts from the whole due amount, while 28% declare that they pay taxes long before the deadline, regardless of the discounts. About 64% of the interviewed citizens had a good or very good level of tax compliance: they declared that they pay taxes long before the deadline (for discount benefits or not). Thirty-three percent (33%) had a medium level of tax compliance, declaring that they pay taxes very close to the deadline. A small percentage of 3% declared that they paid the taxes after the deadline; therefore they face a low level of compliance.

The second question (Q2) dealt with the *attitude toward accepting cheating on taxes*. Regarding the proactive attitude of citizens toward accepting cheating on taxes, Fig. 6.2 shows that more than half of the interviewed citizens declared that they usually receive their receipt (55% of the whole sample) while 20% of the respondents declared that they always receive the receipt. However, about 13% declared that they always ask for their receipt. Eight percent (8%) declared that they receive a receipt but left it there without picking it up, while 5% of the respondents were not bothered by not receiving the receipt.

In Fig. 6.3 we reorganized the concluding results. Thus, 74% of the respondents had an active attitude (they usually/always receive the receipt and take it). About 13% of the respondents had a proactive attitude (they do not receive but ask for the receipt). Finally, a similar percentage of about 13% of respondents had a passive attitude (if they receive or don't receive a receipt, it doesn't matter).

Question 3 investigated the *perception of the corruption level* among Romanian citizens. Figure 6.4 reflects the answers for Question 3 regarding the perception of citizens about corruption levels in Romania. About two-thirds (66.33%) of the sample declared that they perceive the level of corruption in Romania as being high or very high, while about 25% considered that there was a medium level of corruption in Romania, comparable with other countries. However, 8.14% of the citizens perceived a low or very low level of corruption in Romania.

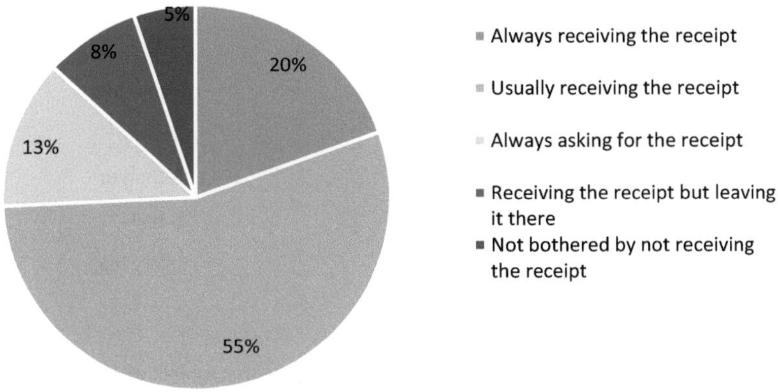

Fig. 6.2 Tax morale (attitude toward accepting cheating on taxes – general view). (Note: Data survey, with a sample of 1856 individuals)

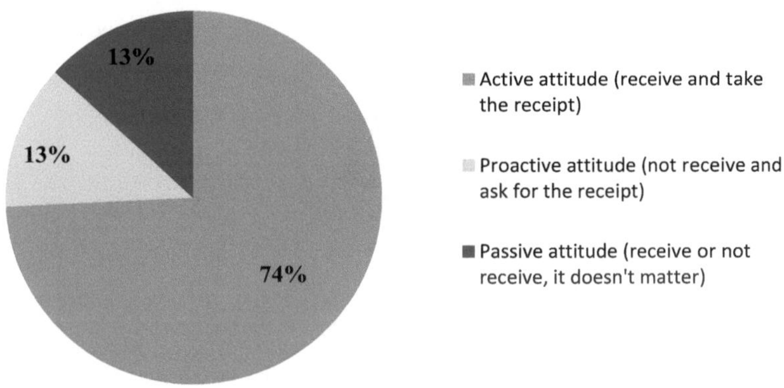

Fig. 6.3 Tax morale (attitude toward accepting cheating on taxes – active, proactive, or passive attitude). (Note: Data survey, with a sample of 1856 individuals)

The fourth question (Q4) dealt with *skills possessed to detect the risk of money laundering*. Figure 6.5 reflects the answers to question 4 and investigates the level of skills possessed by citizens in order to detect suspicious transactions and the risk of money laundering. The results show that a majority of 70% of the citizens had low or very low skills to detect the risk of money laundering in business. About 25% of those interviewed considered that they possessed medium skills, while only about 5% of our sample considered having high or very high skills to detect suspicious transactions.

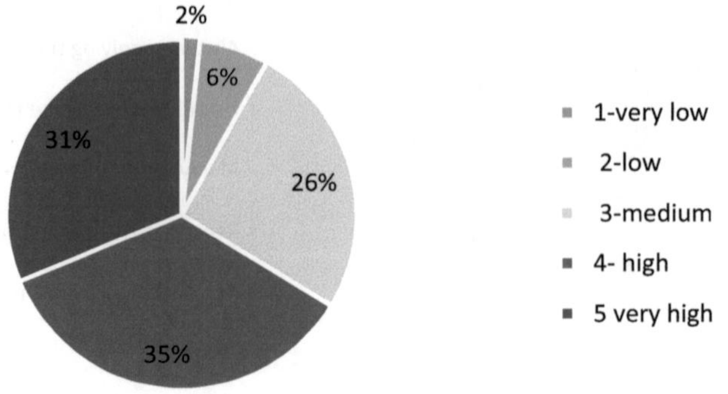

Fig. 6.4 Perception of corruption level. (Note: Data survey, with a sample of 1856 individuals)

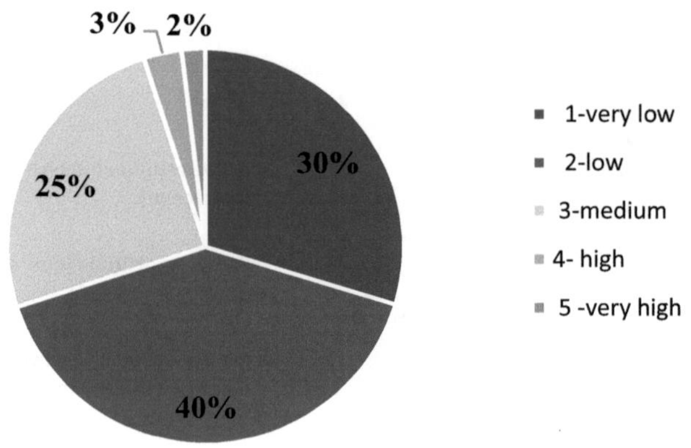

Fig. 6.5 AML skills (skills possessed to detect the risk of money laundering). (Note: Data survey, with a sample of 1856 individuals)

The fifth question (Q5) dealt with the *attitude toward providing information to bank officers*. Figure 6.6 shows the results of question 5 investigating the attitude toward providing information to bank officers. We may depict from Fig. 6.49 that a majority of about 68% of those interviewed had a good attitude toward being asked for information from bank officers (they offer any required details because they know the banks must apply their "know your clients" principle to do their job and they comply), while 32% had a medium or bad attitude. More exactly, 23% of those surveyed had a medium attitude, meaning that they were bothered by these required details but finally provided the requested information. Only 9% of respondents had a bad attitude, meaning that they refused to provide any requested details to the banks; they considered that banks had to satisfy the people's needs and that's all.

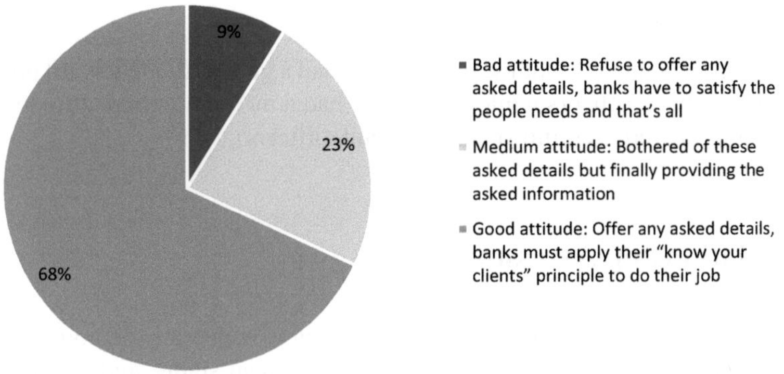

Fig. 6.6 Attitude toward KYC procedures (attitude toward providing information to bank officers). (Note: Data survey, with a sample of 1856 individuals)

Preliminary Conclusions

- *Tax compliance* (Q1)

A majority (64%) of those interviewed had a good or very good level of tax compliance; they declared that they pay taxes long before the deadline (for discount benefits or not). About 33% had a medium level of tax compliance while they declare that they pay taxes very close to the deadline. A small percentage (about 3%) declares that they pay the taxes after the deadline, thus having a bad level of compliance.

- *Tax morale* (Q2)

A majority (74%) of the respondents had an active attitude *toward accepting cheating on taxes* (they usually/always receive the receipt and take it). About 13% of the respondents had a proactive attitude (they do not receive but ask for receipt). Finally, a similar percentage of about 13% of the respondents had a passive attitude (if they receive the receipt or not, it doesn't matter).

- *Perception of corruption level* (Q3)

A majority of about 66% of those interviewed declared that they perceive the level of corruption in Romania as being high or very high, while about 25% considered the level of corruption as being medium; however, about 8% of the sample perceived a low or very low level of corruption in Romania.

- *AML Skills* (Q4)

A majority of about 70% of the sample had low or very low skills to detect the risk of money laundering in businesses; about 25% had medium skills, while only about 5% had high or very high skills to detect suspicious transactions.

- *Attitude toward KYC procedures* (Q5)

A majority of about 68% of the respondents had a good attitude toward providing information to bank officers while about 32% had a medium or bad attitude (refuse or hardly provide required information to bank officers).

6.2 Relationship Assessment

The second objective of the study was to investigate whether any demographic variables were significant (age, gender, region, professional status, and education) for the level of tax compliance, tax morale expressed by the attitude of citizens toward accepting cheating on taxes, perception of corruption level in the Romanian public institutions, the level of skills possessed by citizens to detect the risk of money laundering, and attitude toward providing information to bank officers. For this purpose, as stated in the methodological section, we employed the Chi-square test, with the contingency coefficient attached.

6.2.1 Relationship Characteristics

Table 6.1 presents the results of the relationship assessment based on the Chi-square test, while in Table 6.2 we present the estimated contingency coefficients meant to evaluate the intensity of the relationship between the demographic variables and the fiscal perceptions and behavior of the respondents.

With respect to *age*, we can see that in all cases, all types of financial crime perception variables are significantly dependent on the age group. Consequently, we can conclude that there are significant differences of financial crime perception among the age groups. Table 6.2 shows that the relationship intensity is low, with all

Table 6.1 Relationship existence – Chi-square test results

Variables	Age	Gender	Education	Professional status	Region
Q1 – Tax compliance	48.2 (0.000)	9.14 (0.028)	28.98 (0.004)	34.99 (0.000)	40.8 (0.018)
Q2 – Tax morale	59.47 (0.000)	2.94 (0.568)	21.8 (0.150)	51.23 (0.000)	60.75 (0.002)
Q3 – Perception of corruption	37.64 (0.010)	9.3 (0.054)	46.84 (0.000)	15.99 (0.453)	34.49 (0.350)
Q4 – AML skills	121.05 (0.000)	7.66 (0.105)	49.4 (0.000)	72.22 (0.000)	45.99 (0.052)
Q5 – Attitude toward KYC procedures	59.91 (0.000)	8.00 (0.018)	27.62 (0.001)	38.16 (0.000)	30.21 (0.017)

Note: Chi-square (*p*-value)

Table 6.2 Intensity assessment – contingency coefficient results

Variable	Age	Gender	Education	Professional status	Region
Q1 – Tax compliance	0.159	0.07	0.124	0.136	0.147
Q2 – Tax morale	0.176	0.04	0.108	0.164	0.178
Q3 – Perception of corruption	0.141	0.071	0.157	0.092	0.135
Q4 – AML skills	0.247	0.064	0.161	0.194	0.155
Q5 – Attitude toward KYC procedures	0.172	0.066	0.121	0.142	0.127

contingency coefficients being below 0.3. But, in the case of tax compliance (Q1), the level of skills possessed by citizens to detect the risk of money laundering (AML skills – Q4), and the attitude toward banks asking for information (Q5 – attitude toward KYC procedure), the association intensity is the highest with age. This shows that different age groups have different levels of compliance or of understanding financial crime issues. These will be developed in more depth in the following part.

Gender is significantly associated with tax compliance (Q1), corruption perception regarding public institutions in Romania (Q3), and the attitude toward banks asking personal information (Q5). However, the contingency coefficients have very small values (0.07, 0.071, and 0.066, respectively). This shows that attitudinal and behavioral differences are much smaller between genders than between age groups. Males and females had similar characteristics for tax morale (attitude toward cheating on taxes) and capacity/skills to detect money laundering risk.

Tax morale (Q2) is also similar for different educational levels. But all of the other four financial crime behavioral variables (Q1, Q3, Q4, and Q5) were significantly impacted by the level of education. The most important differences given by the level of education are to be found for the skills that allow citizens to detect the risk of money laundering (contingency coefficient of 0.161). Next comes corruption perception, followed by tax compliance, and, in the end, the attitude of citizens related to personal information asked by banks. *Professional status* also had significant differences, except for corruption perception (Q3). This is quite an interesting result. While age, gender, and education all had significant differences in the way different groups of respondents perceived the level of corruption in Romania, professional status did not. This means that all professional status groups had similar characteristics when corruption perception was assessed. Indeed, when going deeper into analysis and evaluating RQ 3.4, Figs. 6.108, 6.109, 6.110, and 6.111 it clearly showed that different types of groups have similar features for the different corruption levels. Always, employees come first, followed by managers and students. Once again, the highest impact was upon the issue of detecting money laundering situations, followed by tax morale.

The last considered demographic aspect was the part of Romania where the respondent lives, proxied by its *historical regions*. We do not opt for the classical county-level assessment, as there is evidence for historical differences in perceptions and behaviors, due to interactions with different types of people and cultures. Once again, there is no difference with respect to corruption perception. The distribution of different corruption perception levels in the Romanian historical regions is similar. What may be noticed when dealing with RQ3.3 is that the general perception is that of high corruption in Romania. Tax morale (Q2) registered the highest differences among Romanian regions – just as expected (contingency coefficient of 0.178).

6.2.2 *Analytical Results*

6.2.2.1 How Does Tax Compliance Depend on Age, Gender, Romanian Regions, Professional Status, and Education?

The first set of research questions refers to checking how tax compliance depends on age, gender, Romanian regions, professional status, and education.

6.2.2.1.1 Tax Compliance and Age

This section is dedicated to respond to our first research question, RQ1.1: *How does tax compliance depend on age?*

In Tables 6.1 and 6.2 from the Sect. 6.2.1, we find that the level of tax compliance differs significantly by age groups, at the 1% level. The following Figs. 6.7, 6.8, 6.9, and 6.10 provide us with additional useful information. We may see from Fig. 6.9 that a majority of 70%, 72%, and 71%, respectively, from people aged 16–25, 26–35, and over 65 pay their tax duties long before the deadline (with or without relying on any discount) while these percentages are significantly lower, of 55% and 57%, for people aged 46–55 and 56–65, respectively. The most people paying taxes after the deadline (5%) belong to the 36–45 age group, while older people, especially people over 65, are more inclined to pay their taxes on time.

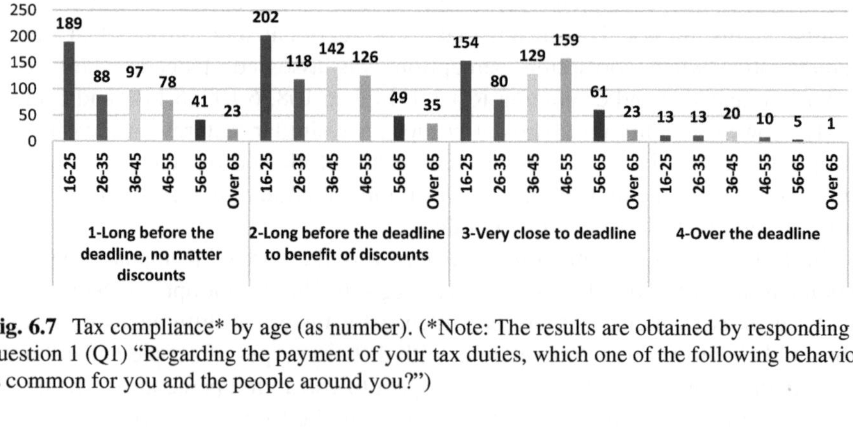

Fig. 6.7 Tax compliance* by age (as number). (*Note: The results are obtained by responding to question 1 (Q1) "Regarding the payment of your tax duties, which one of the following behaviors is common for you and the people around you?")

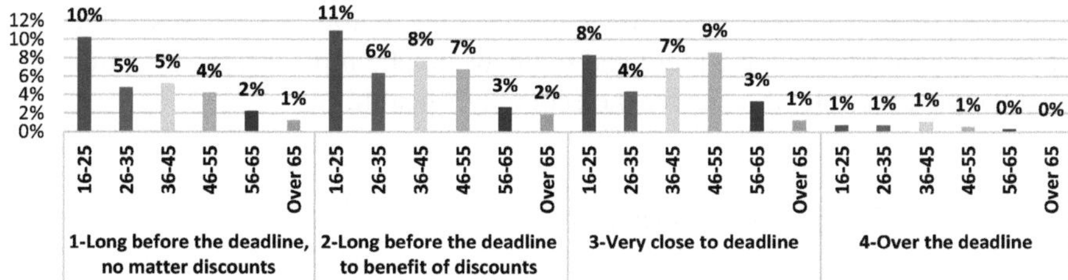

Fig. 6.8 Tax compliance by age* (as % in the grand total). (*Note: The results are obtained by responding to question 1 (Q1) "Regarding the payment of your tax duties, which one of the following behaviors is common for you and the people around you?")

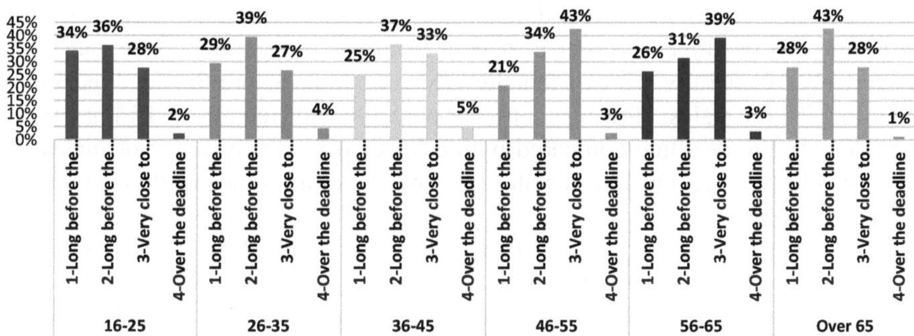

Fig. 6.9 Tax compliance by age* (as % of the total). (*Note: The results are obtained by responding to question 1 (Q1) "Regarding the payment of your tax duties, which one of the following behaviors is common for you and the people around you?")

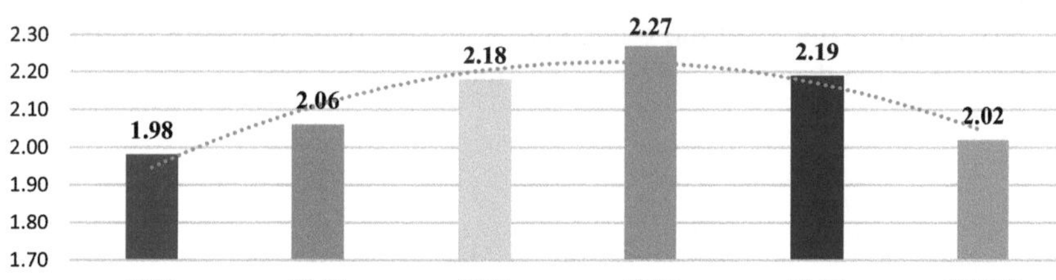

Fig. 6.10 Tax compliance score by age. (Note: The tax compliance scores range from 1 – the best attitude to 4 – the worst attitude toward paying tax duties)

All in all, the level of tax compliance score calculated and presented in Fig. 6.10 shows that people between 46 and 55 have the worst attitude toward paying their tax duties followed by the people aged 36–45 and 36–45 (with tied scores of 2.19 and 2.18, respectively). The best attitude toward paying taxes is found at the extreme limits of age – the group aged 16–25 (1.98) and at the age group above 65 (2.02).

An inverted U shape between age and tax compliance is found: As age increases until the age 46–55, taxpayers tend to have a bad attitude toward their tax obligations (they pay taxes very close to the deadline or after the deadline). After the age of 55, taxpayers become more and more aware about paying taxes on time and about the positive role of taxes for the economy's health.

6.2.2.1.2 Tax Compliance and Gender

This section responds to our second research question RQ1.2: *How does tax compliance depend on gender?*

In Tables 6.1 and 6.2 from the Sect. 6.2.1, we find that the level of tax compliance differs significantly by gender, at the 5% level of significance. The following Figs. 6.11, 6.12, 6.13, and 6.14 provide us with useful additional information. We may see from these figures that both majorities of females and males pay taxes long before the last deadline, in order to benefit from some discounts (36% and 37%, respectively). Generally, 63% of females pay taxes long before the deadline, compared to 67% for males. However, a higher percentage of females (34%) pay taxes very close to the deadline compared with a lower percentage (28%) of males. In addition, a lower percentage of females (3%) pay taxes after the deadline compared to 5% for males.

The tax compliance score calculated and presented in Fig. 6.14 shows that generally females have a weaker attitude toward paying tax liabilities than males (the score for females is 2.12, which is higher than the score of 2.07 found for males). Indeed, the percentage of males paying taxes long before the deadline is 67% and the remaining 33% stands for very close to the deadline or even after the deadline. For females the percentage of those paying taxes long before the deadline is 63% and the remaining percentage reflecting payments very close to the deadline or even after the deadline is 37%. However, females, although they are more inclined to pay taxes very close to the deadline compared to males, they are more inclined than males to respect the deadline, not to go past the deadline.

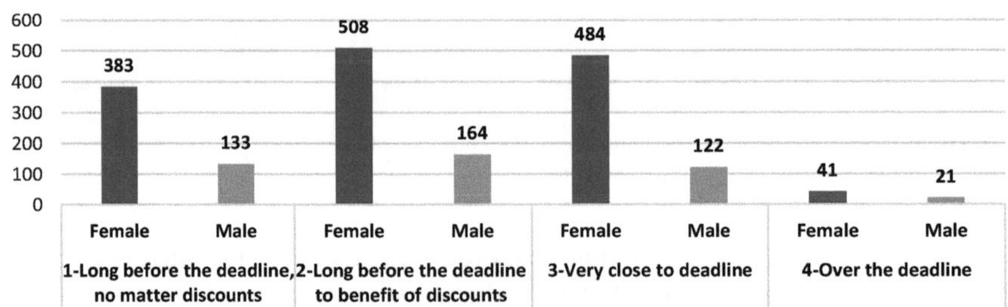

Fig. 6.11 Tax compliance by gender* (as number). (*Note: The results are obtained by responding to question 1 (Q1) "Regarding the payment of your tax duties, which one of the following behaviors is common for you and the people around you?")

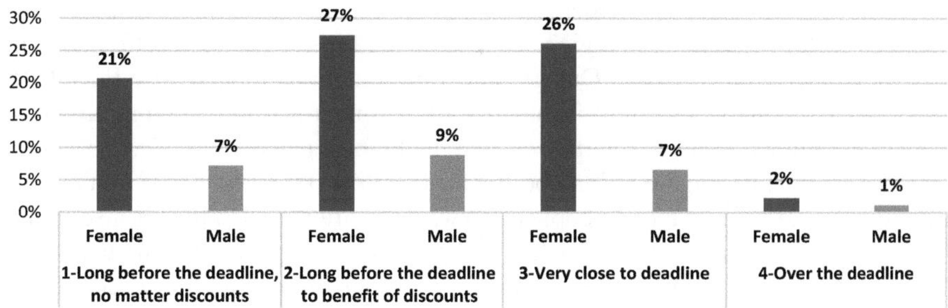

Fig. 6.12 Tax compliance by gender* (as % in the grand total). (*Note: The results are obtained by responding to question 1 (Q1) "Regarding the payment of your tax duties, which one of the following behaviors is common for you and the people around you?")

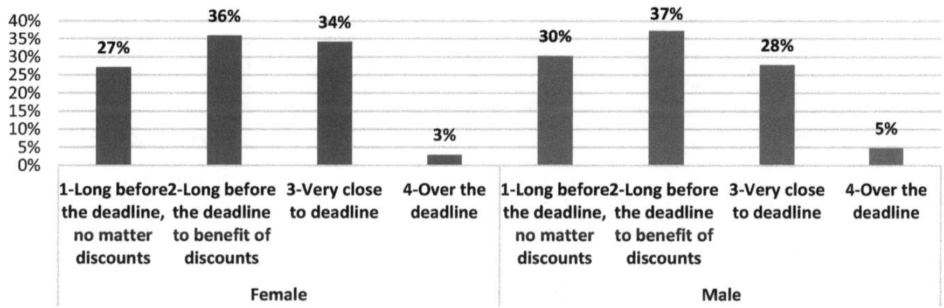

Fig. 6.13 Tax compliance by gender* (as % of the total). (*Note: The results are obtained by responding to the question 1 (Q1) "Regarding the payment of your tax duties, which one of the following behaviors is common for you and the people around you?")

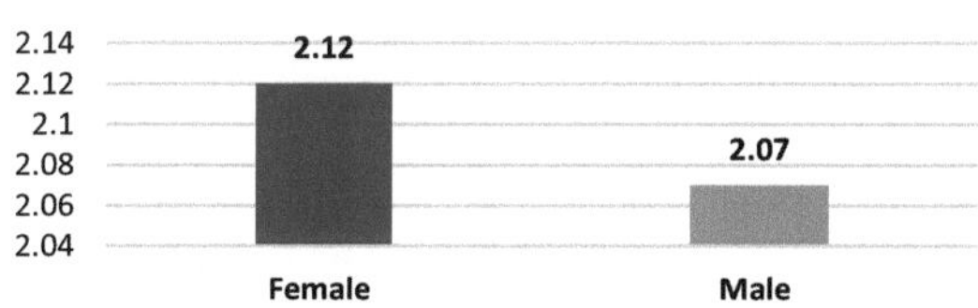

Fig. 6.14 Tax compliance score by gender. (Note: Tax compliance scores range from 1 – the best attitude to 4 – the worst attitude toward paying tax duties)

6.2.2.1.3 Tax Compliance and the Romanian Regions

This section reveals the response to our third research question RQ1.3: *How does tax compliance depend on Romanian regions (Banat, Bucovina, Crisana, Dobrogea, Maramureş, Moldova, Muntenia, Oltenia, Transylvania)?*

In Tables 6.1 and 6.2 from Sect. 6.2.1, we find that tax compliance does not significantly differ by Romanian region. The following Figs. 6.15, 6.16, 6.17, 6.18, and 6.19 show useful information. Our graphical presentations reflected by Figs. 6.15, 6.16, and 6.17 show different behaviors of people regarding paying taxes by Romanian regions. Thus, in Oltenia we find the highest percentage (77%) of all the regions of people paying taxes long before the deadline (targeting a discount or not), while the lowest percentage of people (1%) who pay after the deadline is also found. Moldova lies at the opposite side, where the percentage of people paying taxes very close to the deadline is the highest among all regions (44%) and the percentage of people paying taxes after the deadline is the highest among all regions (5%) (Fig. 6.17).

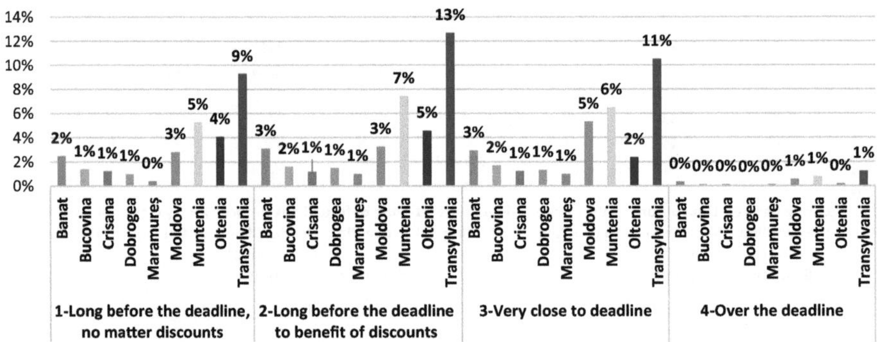

Fig. 6.15 Tax compliance by Romanian region * (as number). (*Note: The results are obtained by responding to question 1 (Q1) "Regarding the payment of your tax duties, which one of the following behaviors is common for you and the people around you?")

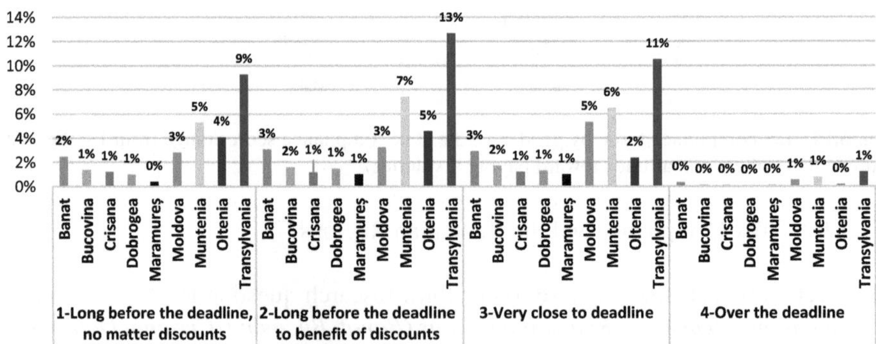

Fig. 6.16 Tax compliance by Romanian regions * (as % in the grand total). (*Note: The results are obtained by responding to question 1 (Q1) "Regarding the payment of your tax duties, which one of the following behaviors is common for you and the people around you?")

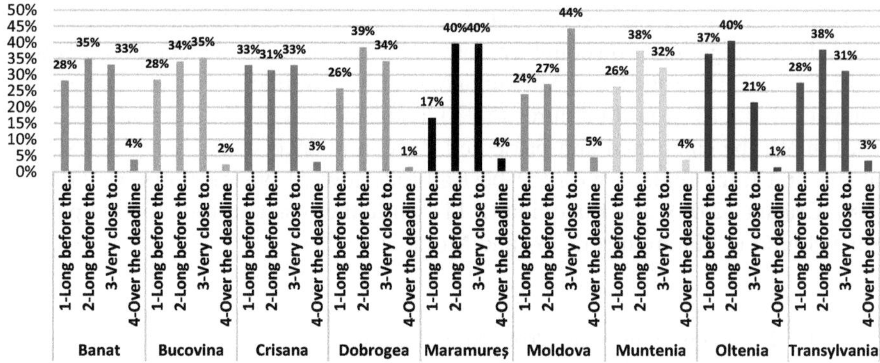

Fig. 6.17 Tax compliance by Romanian regions * (as % of the total). (*Note: The results are obtained by responding to question 1 (Q1) "Regarding the payment of your tax duties, which one of the following behaviors is common for you and the people around you?")

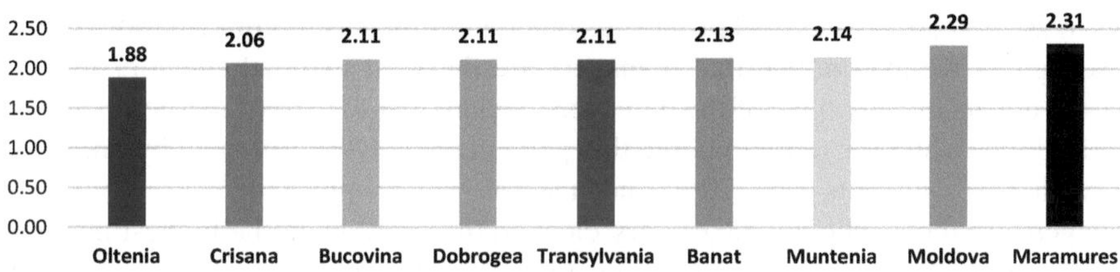

Fig. 6.18 Tax compliance score by Romanian regions (bars). (Note: Tax compliance scores range from 1 – the best attitude to 4 – the worst attitude toward paying tax duties)

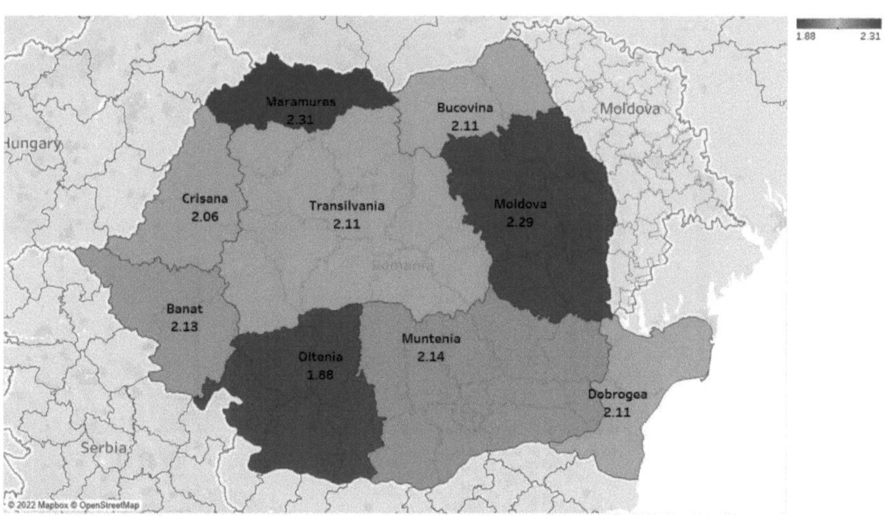

Fig. 6.19 Tax compliance scores by Romanian region (map). (Note: Tax compliance scores range between minimum 1 – the best attitude (colored in green) to maximum 4 – the worst attitude toward paying tax duties (colored in red))

Oltenia registers the highest percentage of people (77%) paying taxes long before the deadline (targeting a discount or not), followed by a far distant Transylvania (65%), Crisana, Dobrogea, and Muntenia (each 63%). While at the very end are the regions of Banat (61%), Maramures (56%), and Moldova (51%) (Fig. 6.64).

All in all, the calculated and presented tax compliance score by regions shows that the first three regions with the best attitude toward paying taxes are Oltenia (1.88), Crisana (2.06), and Bucovina (2.11) while the worst attitude toward paying taxes is found in Maramures (2.31) and Moldova (2.29).

6.2.2.1.4 Tax Compliance and Professional Status

This section discloses the results of our fourth research question RQ1.4: *How does tax compliance depend on professional status?*

In Tables 6.1 and 6.2 from Sect. 6.2.1, we find that the level of tax compliance differs significantly by professional status, at a 5% significance level. The following Figs. 6.20, 6.21, 6.22, and 6.23 provide us other additional useful information. From these figures we may notice that managers are the least inclined category to pay taxes in advance. Only 55% of the managers declare that they pay taxes long before the deadline, while for retired people this percentage is 64%, followed by employees with 65%, students with 70%, and unemployed people with 71%. However, managers are those who pay taxes very close to the deadline in the highest percent (42%) among all professional categories. Only 4% of managers pay taxes after the deadline. At the opposite side, with the highest percentage of people paying taxes in advance are the unemployed (71%) and students (70%), these categories being the tax payers who pass the deadline for paying taxes with the lowest percentage.

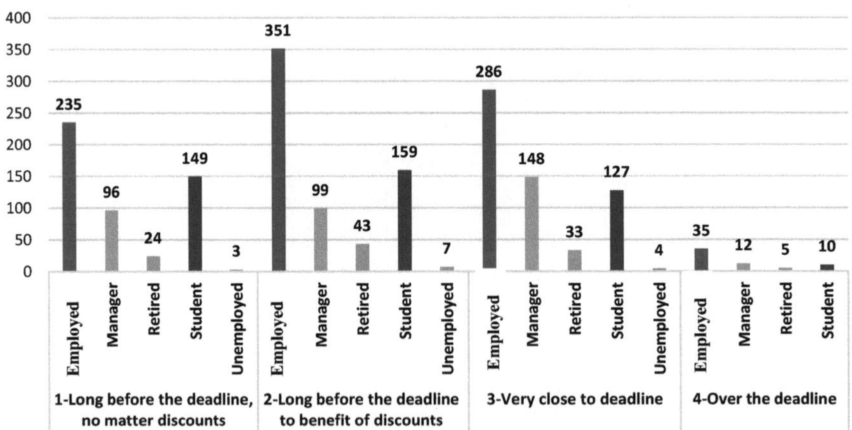

Fig. 6.20 Tax compliance by professional status* (as number). (*Note: The results are obtained by responding to question 1 (Q1) "Regarding the payment of your tax duties, which one of the following behaviors is common for you and the people around you?")

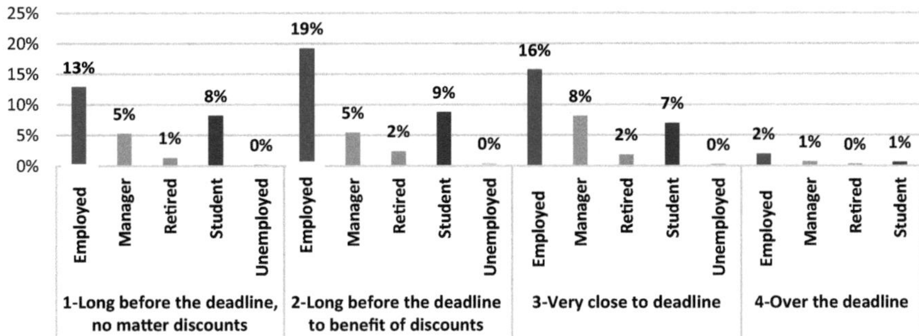

Fig. 6.21 Tax compliance by professional status*(as % in the grand total). (*Note: The results are obtained by responding to question 1 (Q1) "Regarding the payment of your tax duties, which one of the following behaviors is common for you and the people around you?")

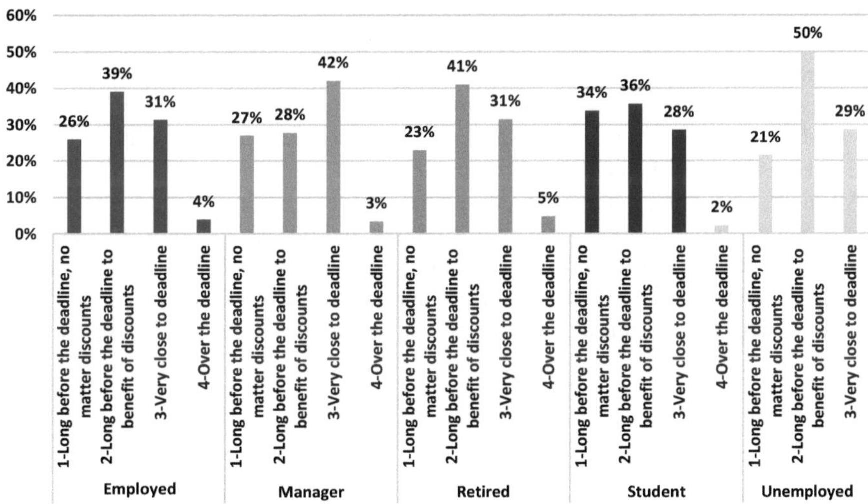

Fig. 6.22 Tax compliance by professional status*(as % of the total). (*Note: The results are obtained by responding to question 1 (Q1) "Regarding the payment of your tax duties, which one of the following behaviors is common for you and the people around you?")

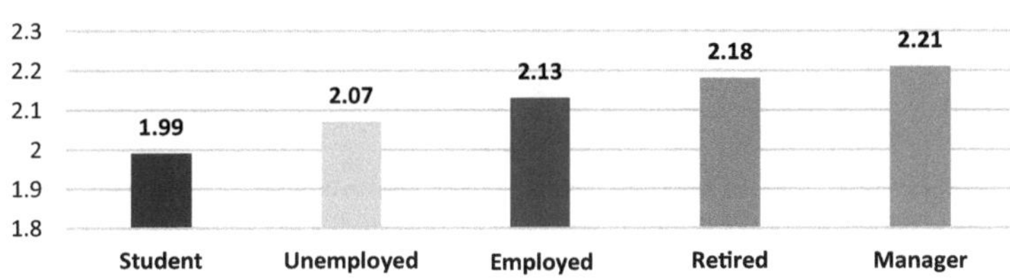

Fig. 6.23 Tax compliance score by professional status. (Note: Tax compliance scores range from 1 – the best attitude to 4 – the worst attitude toward paying tax duties)

All in all, the calculated and presented tax compliance scores by professional status show that managers and retired people have the worst attitude toward paying taxes (with the highest scores of 2.21 and 2.18) while the best attitude toward paying taxes are students (1.99), followed by the unemployed (2.07) (Fig. 6.69).

6.2.2.1.5 Tax Compliance and Education

This section discusses the answer to our fifth research question RQ1.5: *How does tax compliance depend on education?*

In Tables 6.1 and 6.2 from the Sect. 6.2.1, we find that the level of tax compliance significantly differs by education, at the 1% significance. The following Figs. 6.24, 6.25, 6.26, and 6.27 may help us extract other additional results. From these figures we may see that the more educated people are, the more they become aware of paying their taxes on time, trying to maximize some benefits in the form of discounts. Thus, the percentage of taxpayers that pay taxes far in advance in order to get benefits in the form of discounts increases from 31% (high school graduates or less), to 32% (bachelor's studies), 35% (master's studies) 42% (doctoral studies), and even 50% (postdoctoral studies). Therefore, in order to understand the role of discounts provided by the government, to attract people to pay their taxes on time, citizens have to be as highly educated as possible.

All in all, after calculating a tax compliance score, we may conclude that as the level of education increases at bachelor's degree and master's studies, the level of compliance decreases. Furthermore, getting a doctoral degree means getting more complex knowledge that results in understanding the role of regulations and to better comply with them. Thus at this level of education, the degree of passive attitude

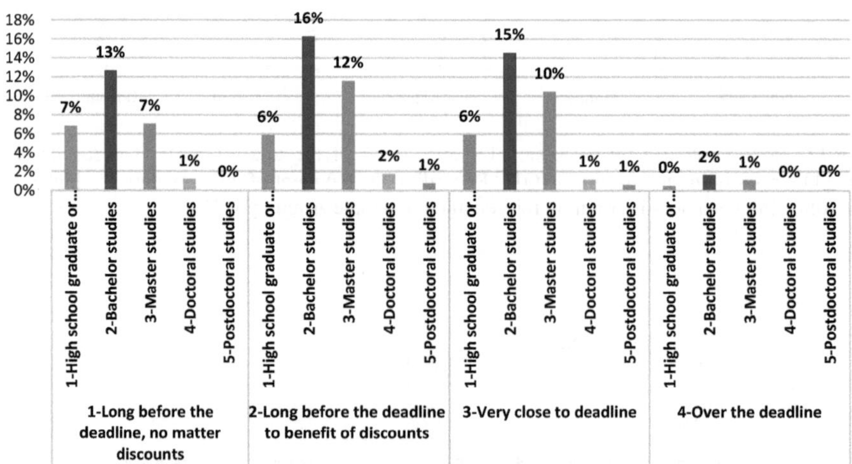

Fig. 6.24 Tax compliance by education* (as number). (*Note: The results are obtained by responding to question 1 (Q1) "Regarding the payment of your tax duties, which one of the following behaviors is common for you and the people around you?")

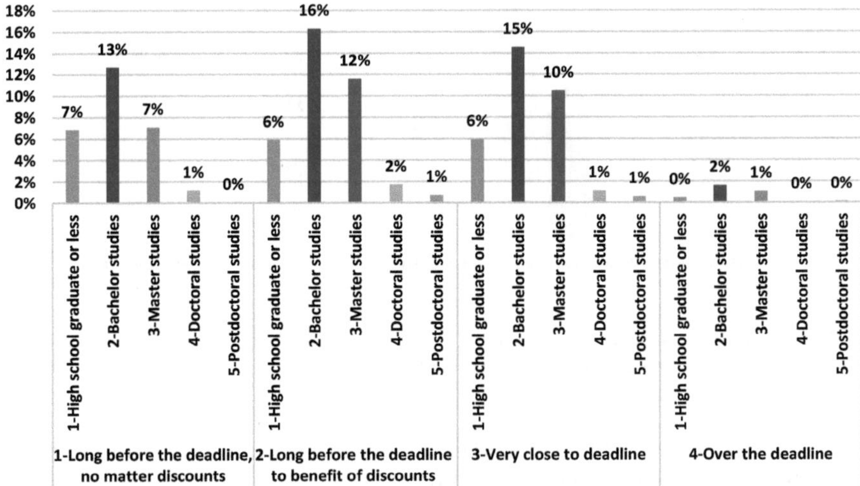

Fig. 6.25 Tax compliance by education* (as % in the grand total). (*Note: The results are obtained by responding to question 1 (Q1) "Regarding the payment of your tax duties, which one of the following behaviors is common for you and the people around you?")

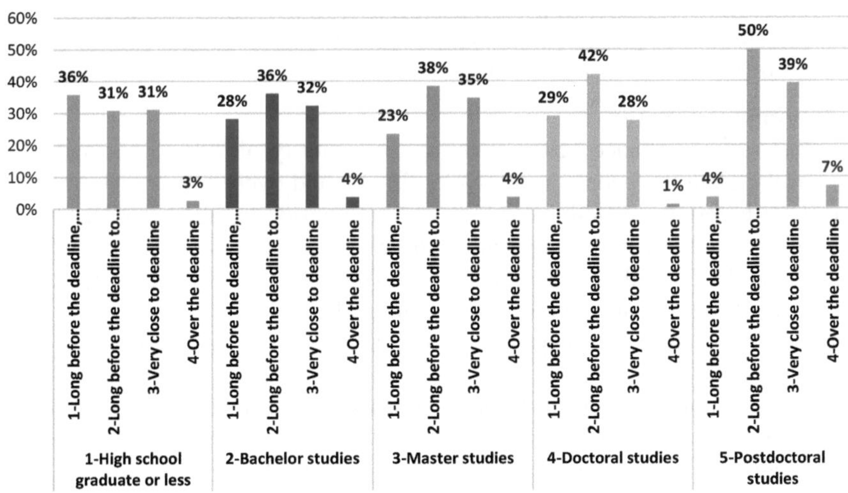

Fig. 6.26 Tax compliance by education* (as % of the total). (*Note: The results are obtained by responding to question 1 (Q1) "Regarding the payment of your tax duties, which one of the following behaviors is common for you and the people around you?")

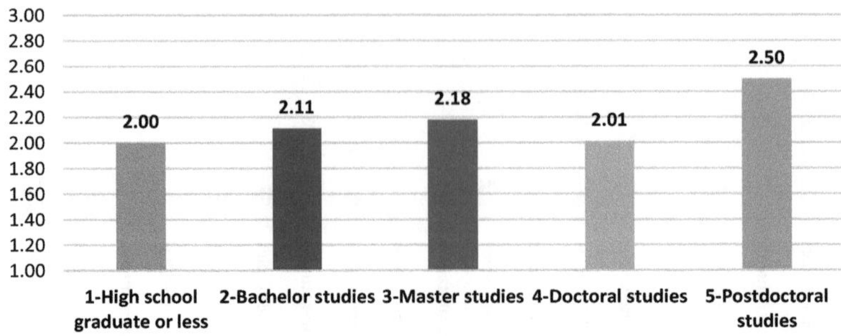

Fig. 6.27 Tax compliance score by education. (Note: Tax compliance scores range from 1 – the best attitude to 4 – the worst attitude toward paying tax duties)

is reduced. However, postdoctoral studies are correlated with the highest level of noncompliance (the score is maximum) (Fig. 6.27).

6.2.2.1.6 Concluding Remarks

According to our results the levels of tax compliance are significantly impacted by the demographic variables of age, gender, professional status, and education at the 1% and 5% levels of significance. Even if there is an impact of region on tax compliance, this difference is not significant.

Tax Compliance by Age

Regarding tax compliance behavior by age, a majority of 70%, 72%, and 71%, respectively, from the people aged 16–25, 26–35, and over 65 years pay their tax duties long before the deadline (with or without considering the advantage of any discounts) while these percentages are significantly lower, only 55% and 57%, for people aged 46–55 and 56–65, respectively. The highest percentage (5%) of age category paying taxes after the deadline belongs to the people aged 36–45, while elderly people, especially people aged over 65, are more inclined to pay taxes on time.

All in all, people between 46–55 have the worst attitude toward paying tax duties followed by the people aged 56–65 and 36–45 (with tied scores of 2.19 and 2.18). The best attitude toward paying taxes is found at the extreme limits of age, at the 16–25 age group and people aged above 65.

An inverted U shape between age and tax compliance is found: As the age increases until the age 46–55, taxpayers tend to have a bad attitude toward tax duties (they pay taxes very close to the deadline or after the deadline). After 55, taxpayers become more and more aware about paying taxes on time and about the positive role of taxes for the economy's health while the best attitude toward paying taxes is found in the age group over 65, who are the most conscientious taxpayers among all age groups.

Tax Compliance by Gender
In relation to gender, a smaller majority of 63% of females pay taxes long before the deadline, compared to 67% for males. However, a higher percentage of females (34%) pay taxes very close to the deadline compared with a lower percentage (28%) for males. Despite this, females are more inclined to respect the deadlines, not to surpass them, than males are. In addition, a lower percentage of females (3%) pay taxes past the deadline compared to 5% for males. Accounting for all aspects, females have a quite better attitude toward paying tax duties than males.

Tax Compliance by Region
The first three regions with the best attitude toward paying taxes are Oltenia, Crisana, and Bucovina while the regions with the worst attitude toward paying taxes are in the northern part of the country, in Maramures and Moldova.

Tax Compliance by Professional Status
Managers and retired people have the worst attitude toward paying taxes while the best attitude toward paying taxes is found in students followed by unemployed people. Managers are the least inclined category to pay taxes in advance; actually, they only pay taxes very close to the deadline, in the highest percentage of 42% among all the professional categories.

Tax Compliance by Education
As people become more educated, they seem to become more aware of paying their taxes in time, trying to maximize some benefits in the form of discounts. However, the percentage of those who pay after the deadlines increases as the level of education increases, reaching the maximum level of 7% for postdoctoral studies.

All in all, after calculating a tax compliance score, we may conclude that as the level of education increases at bachelor's degree and master's studies, the level of compliance decreases. Further, getting a doctoral degree means getting more complex knowledge that permits the understanding of the role of regulations and the need to better comply with them. Thus, at this level of education, the degree of passive attitude is reduced. However, postdoctoral studies are correlated with the highest level of noncompliance (the score is maximum).

6.2.2.2 How Does Tax Morale Depend on Age, Gender, Romanian Region, Professional Status, and Education?

The second set of research questions we launch refers to checking how tax morale depends on age, gender, Romanian region, professional status, and education.

6.2.2.2.1 Tax Morale and Age

This section reports on the answers to our research question RQ2.1: *How does tax morale depend on age?*

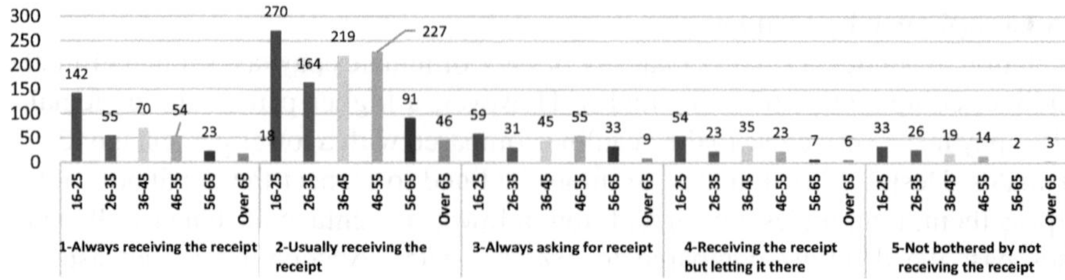

Fig. 6.28 Tax morale by age* (as number). (*Note: The results are obtained by responding to question 2 (Q2): "Upon receiving goods and services from the shops, restaurants, hotels, salons, etc., please choose one or more of the following, that fit you better…")

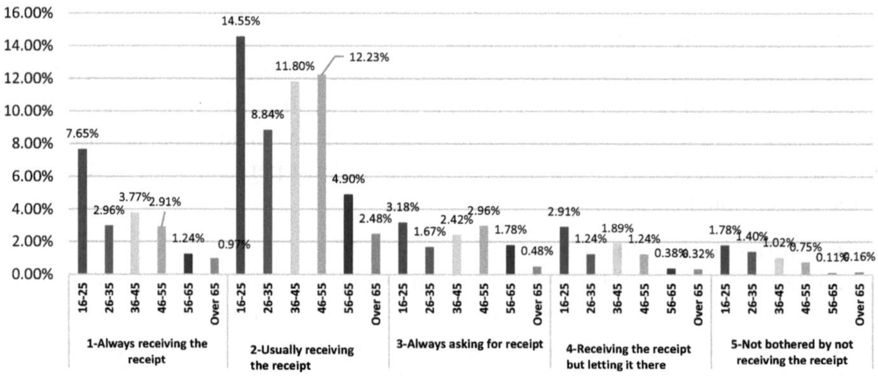

Fig. 6.29 Tax morale by age * (as % in the grand total). (*Note: The results are obtained by responding to question 2 (Q2): "Upon receiving goods and services from the shops, restaurants, hotels, salons, etc., please choose one or more of the following, that fit you better..")

In Tables 6.1 and 6.2 from Sect. 6.2.1, we find that the level of tax morale significantly differs by age, at the 1% level of significance. The following Figs. 6.28, 6.29, and 6.30 provide us with additional useful information. The largest majority of respondents in each of the age groups declare that they usually receive receipts when they buy goods and services from the shops, restaurants, hotels, salons, etc. However, when we analyze the age groups, we find that the highest level of this percentage is found in the 46–55 age group. More exactly, 66% of the people belonging to the 46–55 age group declare that they usually receive receipts when they buy goods and services, followed by people belonging to the 56–65 age group (with 58%) and then people over 65 and people aged between 36–45 (with the same percentage of 56%). The lowest level of people declaring they usually receive receipts belongs to the 16–25 age group (48%). The groups of respondents aged 46–55 and 56–65 are also those who are the most interested in asking for receipts (the percentages in which they ask for receipts are 15% and 21%, respectively); therefore they have the highest level of proactive attitudes in all the groups and the lowest level of passive attitudes (the percentages of those who respond they are not

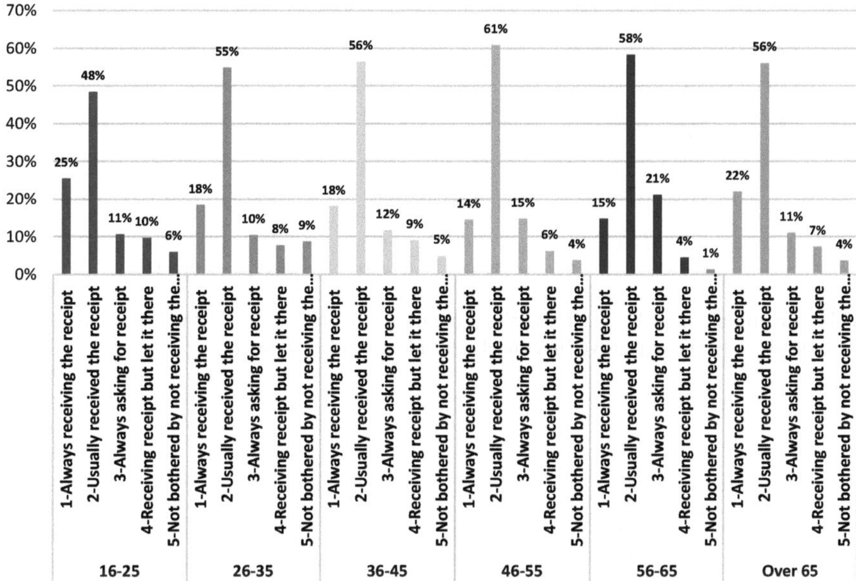

Fig. 6.30 Tax morale by age * (as % of the total). (*Note: The results are obtained by responding to question 2 (Q2): "Upon receiving goods and services from the shops, restaurants, hotels, salons, etc., please choose one or more of the following, that fit you better..")

interested in receiving receipts are 10% and 5%, respectively, among the total of these groups).

All in all, the tax morale score calculated and presented in Fig. 6.31 shows that a higher age level is associated with an increasingly active (ethical) attitude toward cheating on taxes. Indeed, starting with the age group 26–35, the tax morale score systematically decreases from one age group to another. The most ethical attitude toward cheating on taxes is found in the eldest group of respondents.

6.2.2.2.2 Tax Morale and Gender

This section discusses the results of our research question RQ2.2: *How does tax morale depend on gender?*

In Tables 6.1 and 6.2 from Sect. 6.2.1, we find that the level of tax morale does not differ significantly by gender. However, several analyses are made based on Figs. 6.32, 6.33, and 6.34. The largest majority of male or female respondents state that they usually receive receipts when they buy goods and services from the shops, restaurants, hotels, salons, etc. they visit. However, our results show that 75% of the female respondents have an active attitude (usually or always receiving the receipt) while this percentage is 73% for male respondents. The same percentage (13%) of each of the groups shows they have a proactive attitude asking for the receipt. Going further, the percentage of females having a passive attitude (they are not interested

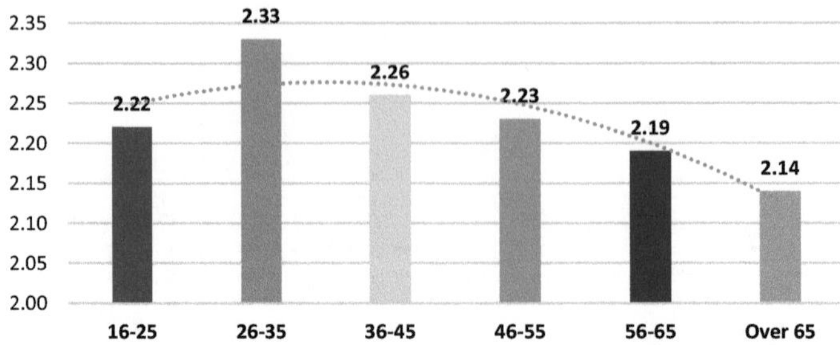

Fig. 6.31 Tax morale score by age. (Note: Tax morale score ranges from 1 – the most active (ethical) attitude to 5 – the most passive (unethical) attitude toward cheating taxes)

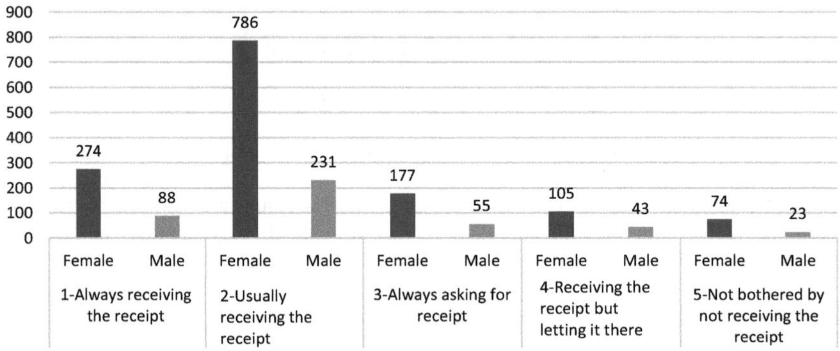

Fig. 6.32 Tax morale by gender* (as number). (*Note: The results are obtained by responding to question 2 (Q2): "Upon receiving goods and services from the shops, restaurants, hotels, salons, etc., please choose one or more of the following, that fit you better…")

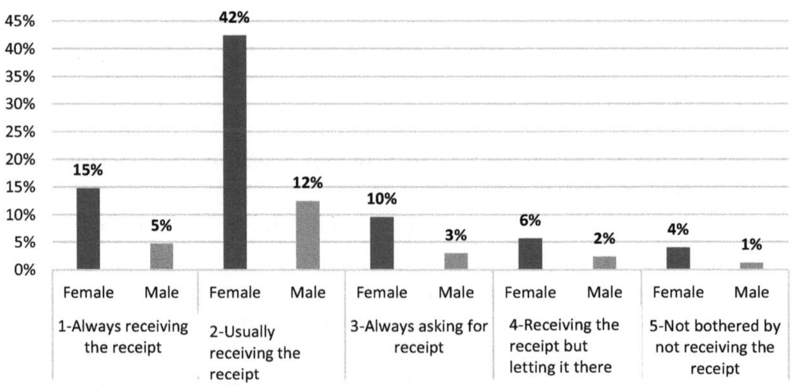

Fig. 6.33 Tax morale by gender *(as % in the grand total). (*Note: The results are obtained by responding to question 2 (Q2): "Upon receiving goods and services from the shops, restaurants, hotels, salons, etc., please choose one or more of the following, that fit you better…")

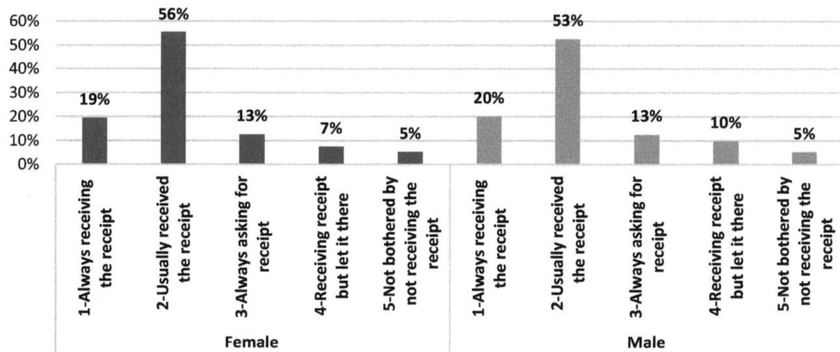

Fig. 6.34 Tax morale by gender *(as % of the total). (*Note: The results are obtained by responding to question 2 (Q2): "Upon receiving goods and services from the shops, restaurants, hotels, salons, etc., please choose one or more of the following, that fit you better…")

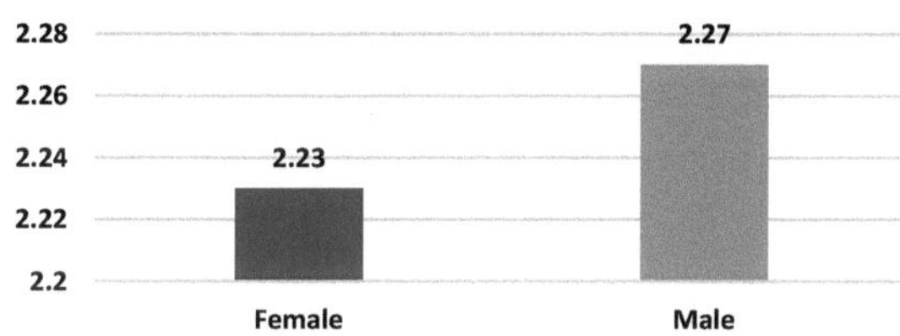

Fig. 6.35 Tax morale score by gender. (Note: Tax morale scores range from 1 – the most active (ethical) attitude to 5 – the most passive (unethical) attitude toward cheating taxes)

in receiving a receipt) is 12% compared to a higher percentage of 15% for the males. We may conclude that females are more active and less passive in relation to accepting cheating taxes compared to males.

Indeed, tax morale scores calculated and presented in Fig. 6.35 show that males have a quite higher unethical attitude toward cheating on taxes than females, being also more inclined to accept cheating than females.

6.2.2.2.3 Tax Morale and Romanian Region

This section discusses the answers to our research question RQ2.3: *How does tax morale depend on Romanian regions (Banat, Bucovina, Crisana, Dobrogea, Maramureş, Moldova, Muntenia, Oltenia, Transylvania)?*

In Tables 6.1 and 6.2 from Sect. 6.2.1, we find that the level of tax morale significantly differs by Romanian region at the 1% level. The following Figs. 6.36, 6.37, 6.38, 6.39, and 6.40 provide other insightful details. The majority of respondents in each region declare that they usually receive their receipts from the shops, restaurants, etc. they visit. However, when we check for the highest active attitude (usually and always receiving a receipt), the highest percentage of 80% is found in

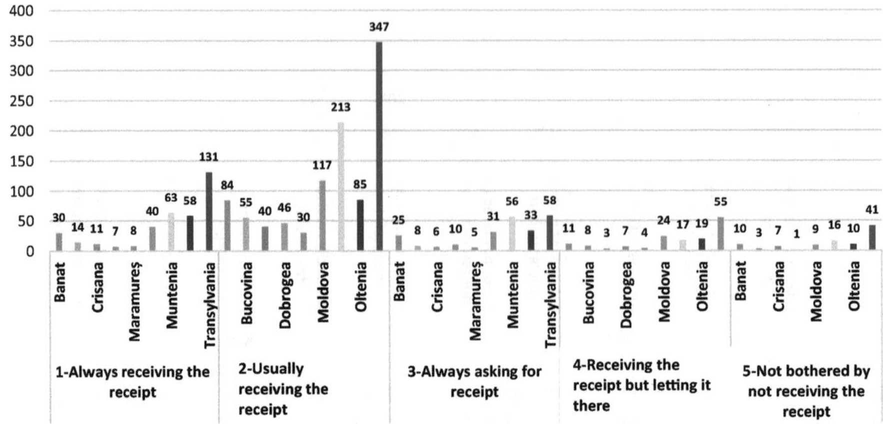

Fig. 6.36 Tax morale by Romanian region* (as number). (*Note: The results are obtained by responding to question 2 (Q2): "Upon receiving goods and services from the shops, restaurants, hotels, salons, etc., please choose one or more of the following, that fit you better…")

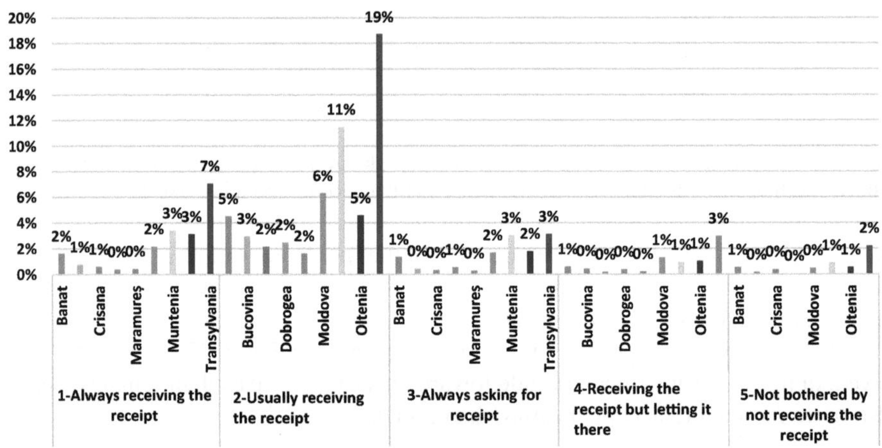

Fig. 6.37 Tax morale by region* (as % in the grand total). (*Note: The results are obtained by responding to question 2 (Q2): "Upon receiving goods and services from the shops, restaurants, hotels, salons, etc., please choose one or more of the following, that fit you better)

Maramures, followed by Bucovina (79%) and Muntenia (75%).The highest percentage of proactive attitudes (asking for receipts) is held by people from Banat and Oltenia (each of them with 16%) while the lowest level of proactive attitude is found in Bucovina, Crisana, and Transylvania (each of them with 9%). The highest passive attitude of people is found in Moldova and Transylvania (each of them with 15%) followed by Oltenia (14%) and Banat (13%).

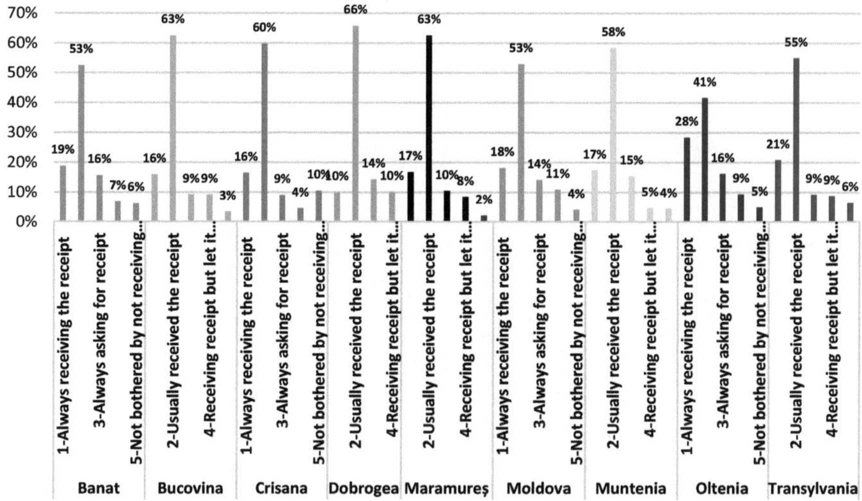

Fig. 6.38 Tax morale by region* (as % of the total). (*Note: The results are obtained by responding to question 2 (Q2): "Upon receiving goods and services from the shops, restaurants, hotels, salons, etc., please choose one or more of the following, that fit you better…")

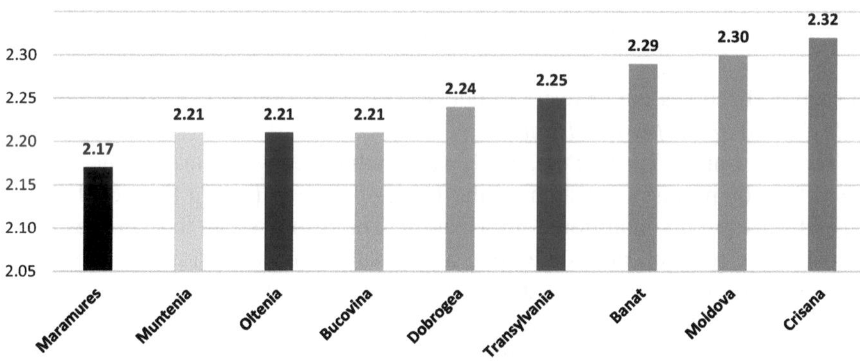

Fig. 6.39 Tax morale score by region (bars). (Note: Tax morale scores range from 1 – the most active (ethical) attitude to 5 – the most passive (unethical) attitude toward cheating taxes)

All in all, the level of the tax morale score calculated and presented in Fig. 6.86 shows that the most ethical respondents in terms of the attitude toward cheating taxes are found in Maramures (2.17), followed by Muntenia, Oltenia, and Bucovina (with the same score of 2.21). At the opposite pole, the most unethical regions in terms of accepting cheating on taxes are Crisana (2.32), followed by Moldova (2.3) and Banat (2.29).

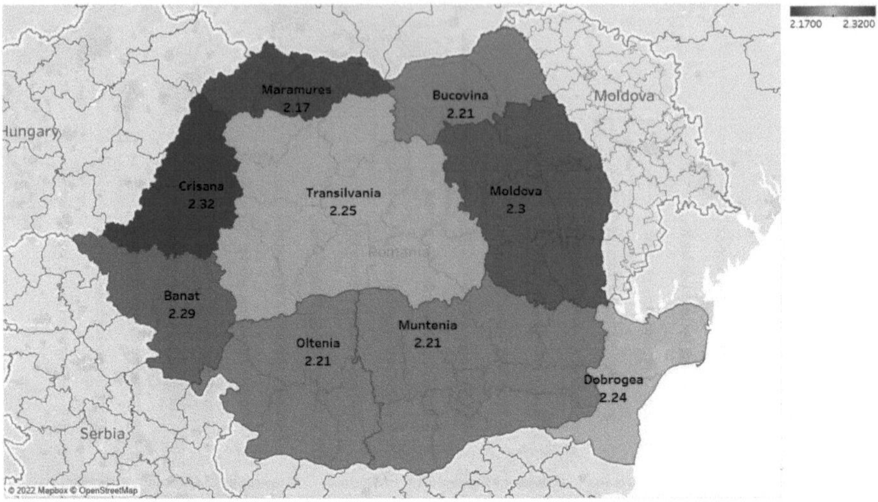

Fig. 6.40 Tax morale score by regions (map). (Note: Tax morale score ranges from 1 – the most active (ethical) attitude (colored in green) to 5 – the most passive (unethical) attitude toward cheating taxes (colored in red))

6.2.2.2.4 Tax Morale and Professional Status

This section discusses the answers to our research question RQ2.4: *How does tax morale depend on professional status?*

In Tables 6.1 and 6.2 from Sect. 6.2.1, we find that the level of tax morale significantly differs by professional status at the 1% level. The following Figs. 6.41, 6.42, 6.43, and 6.44 provide additional information. The results show that retirees have the most active (ethical) attitude among all the surveyed professional groups. The largest majority in the retirees' category (79%) declares that they receive receipts from the shops, restaurants, etc. they go to (always or usually). This majority is followed by students and unemployed people (78%), managers (75%), and employees (with only 72%). The highest proactive attitude (always asking for receipt) is found for managers (16%), followed by employees (13%) while the lowest proactive attitude is found in students (9%) and unemployed people (7%). The highest passive attitude (unethical attitude) is found for employees (15%), followed by students and unemployed (14%). The two categories consisting of managers and retirees have the least passive attitudes (9%).

All in all, after calculating a tax morale score by professional status, it is found that employees have the lowest level of ethical attitude in relation to accepting cheating on taxes, followed by unemployed. At the opposed pole, with the highest ethical attitude in relation to accepting cheating on taxes are retirees and students.

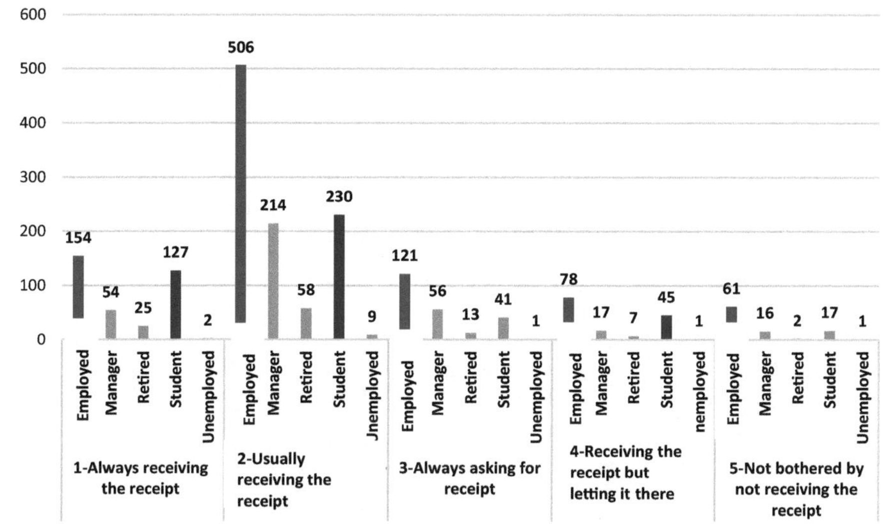

Fig. 6.41 Tax morale by professional status* (as number). (*Note: The results are obtained by responding to question 2 (Q2): "Upon receiving goods and services from the shops, restaurants, hotels, salons, etc., please choose one or more of the following, that fit you better…")

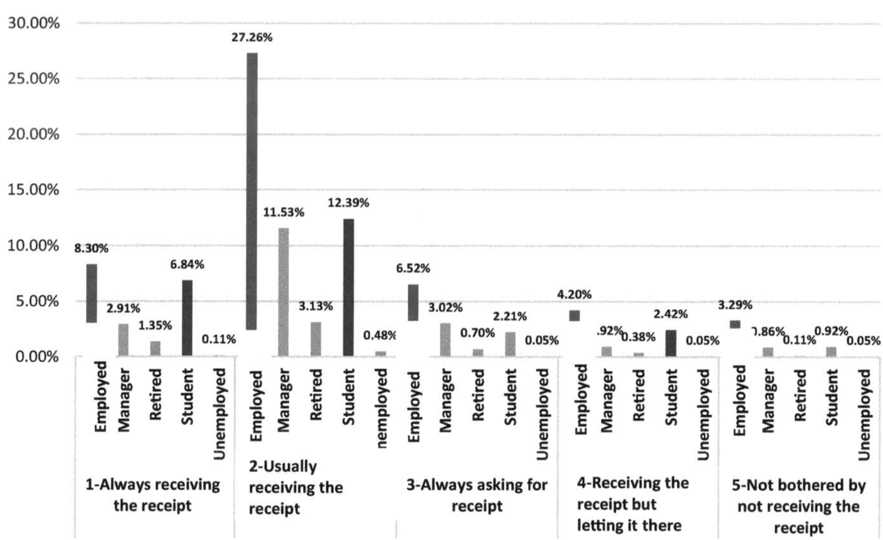

Fig. 6.42 Tax morale by professional status* (as % in the grand total). (*Note: The results are obtained by responding to question 2 (Q2): "Upon receiving goods and services from the shops, restaurants, hotels, salons, etc., please choose one or more of the following, that fit you better…")

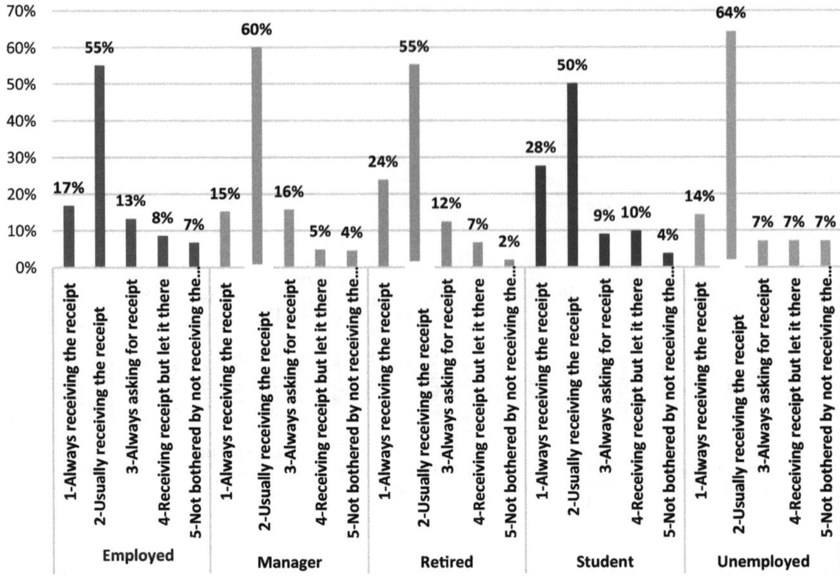

Fig. 6.43 Tax morale by professional status* (as % of the total). (*Note: The results are obtained by responding to question 2 (Q2): "Upon receiving goods and services from the shops, restaurants, hotels, salons, etc., please choose one or more of the following, that fit you better…")

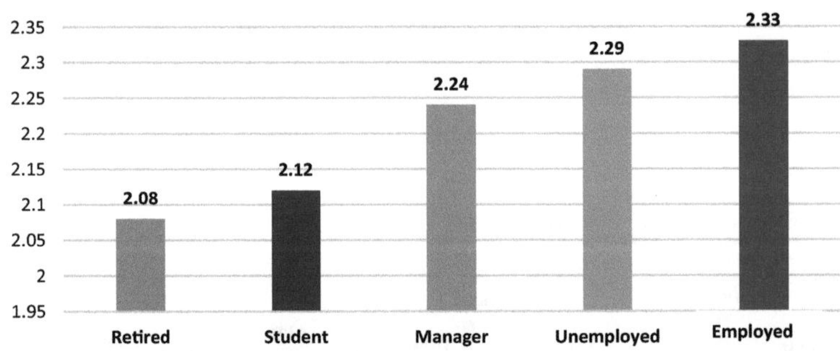

Fig. 6.44 Tax morale score by professional status. (Note: Tax morale scores range from 1 – the most active (ethical) attitude to 5 – the most passive (unethical) attitude toward cheating taxes)

6.2.2.2.5 Tax Morale and Education

This section intends to find answers to our research question RQ2.5: *How does tax morale depend on education?*

In Tables 6.1 and 6.2 from the Sect. 6.2.1, we find that the level of tax morale doesn't significantly differ by education. Figures 6.45, 6.46, 6.47, and 6.48 provide additional information. The results show that the highest percentage (86%) of active attitudes (always or usually receiving receipts) is found among people with doctoral studies, followed by people that graduate from high school or less, and master's

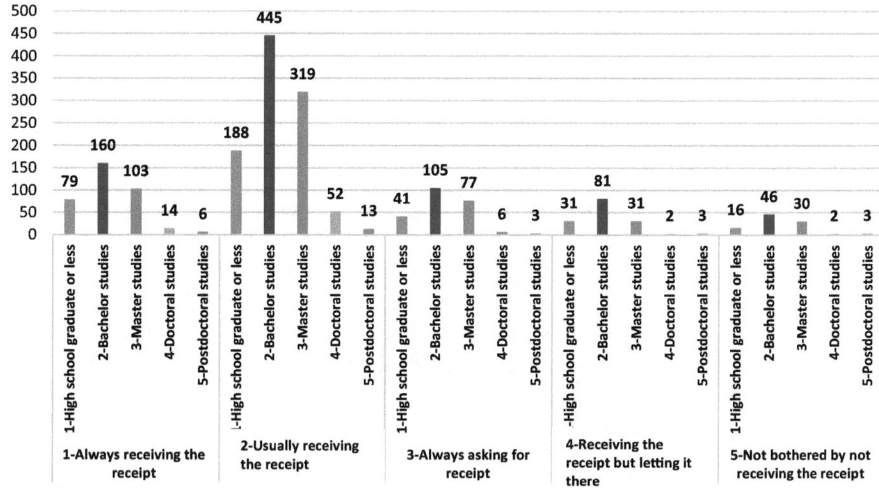

Fig. 6.45 Tax morale by education* (as number). (*Note: The results are obtained by responding to question 2 (Q2): "Upon receiving goods and services from the shops, restaurants, hotels, salons, etc., please choose one or more of the following, that fit you better…")

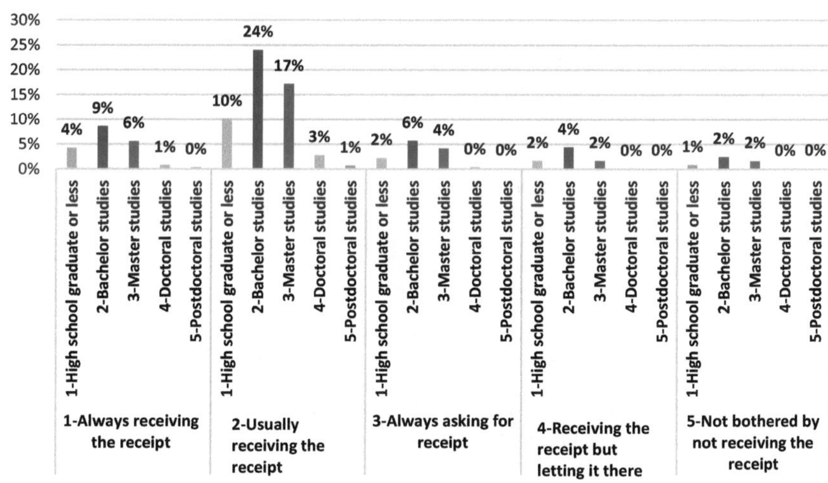

Fig. 6.46 Tax morale by education* (as % in the grand total). (*Note: The results are obtained by responding to question 2 (Q2): "Upon receiving goods and services from the shops, restaurants, hotels, salons, etc., please choose one or more of the following, that fit you better…")

studies (75%). The highest proactive attitude is found among respondents with master's studies (14%) followed by people with bachelor's studies (13%) and high school or less (12%). Then, it is interesting to learn that the highest passive attitude is found among respondents with postdoctoral studies (22%) while the lowest percent is found for respondents with doctoral studies (6%).

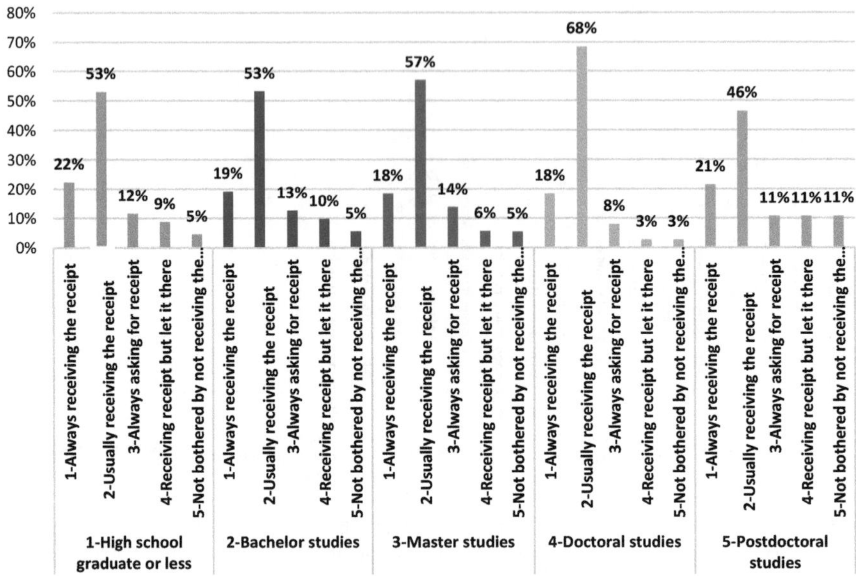

Fig. 6.47 Tax morale by education* (as % of the total). (*Note: The results are obtained by responding to question 2 (Q2): "Upon receiving goods and services from the shops, restaurants, hotels, salons, etc., please choose one or more of the following, that fit you better…")

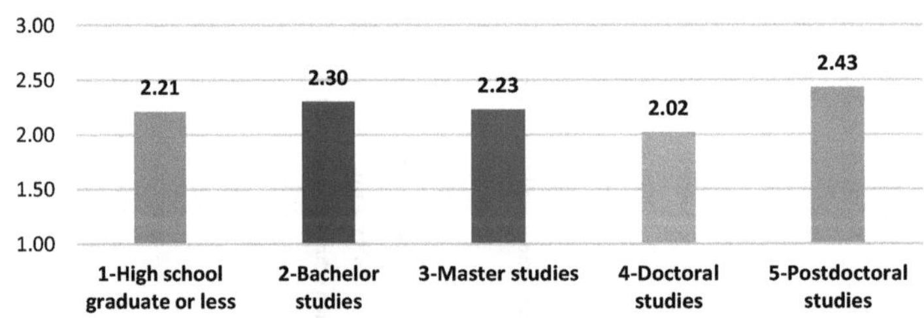

Fig. 6.48 Tax morale score by education. (Note: Tax morale scores range from 1 – the most active (ethical) attitude to 5 – -the most passive (unethical) attitude toward cheating taxes)

All in all, after calculating a tax morale score as it is presented in Fig. 6.45, we may conclude that the most active (ethical) attitude is met by respondents with doctoral studies (a score of 2.02) while postdoctoral studies are correlated with the passive (unethical) attitude (2.43). As the level of education increases toward bachelor's or master's degree, the level of unethical attitudes is reduced. Further, getting a doctoral degree means getting more complex knowledge, which permits the holder to understand the role of regulations and to better comply with them. Thus, at this level of education the extent of passive attitudes is reduced to a minimum. However, postdoctoral studies are correlated with the highest level of unethical attitudes (the score is maximum).

6.2.2.2.6 Concluding Remarks

Our findings show that the level of tax morale is significantly impacted by the demographic variables of age, professional status, and region at the 1% significance level. Although we find an impact of gender and education on tax morale, the impact is not significant.

Tax Morale by Age
Our results show that the higher the age is, the more increasingly active (ethical) attitude toward cheating taxes there is. Indeed, starting with 26 year olds, the higher the age is, the higher the ethical attitude toward cheating on taxes. The most ethical attitude toward cheating on taxes is found for the eldest respondents (over 65).

Tax Morale by Gender
We find that males have a significantly higher unethical attitude toward cheating on taxes than females. Thus, males are more inclined to accept cheating on taxes than females.

Tax Morale by Region
The most ethical respondents in terms of attitude toward cheating on taxes are found in Maramures followed by Muntenia, Oltenia, and Bucovina. At the opposite end of the spectrum, the most unethical regions in terms of accepting cheating on taxes are Crisana followed by Moldova and Banat.

Tax Morale by Professional Status
Related to professional status, we find that employees have the lowest level of ethical attitudes in regarding the acceptance of cheating on taxes, followed by the unemployed. At the opposed pole, with the highest ethical attitude in relation to accepting cheating on taxes, are the retirees and students.

Tax Morale by Education
Our study shows that master's and doctoral studies confer the proper level of knowledge to understand the role of regulations and to better comply with them. Thus, at this level of education, the degree of passive attitude is reduced to a minimum and people become aware of how the tax system functions. However, the highest level of education, such as postdoctoral studies, is correlated with the highest levels of unethical attitudes. We may explain this relationship by the fact that a better education ensures a better understanding of the functioning mechanisms of economic, financial, and information flows, and, in this way, they easily find openings for getting illicit benefits by breaking the law.

6.2.2.3 How Does the Perception of Corruption Depend on Age, Gender, Romanian Region, Professional Status, and Education?

The third set of research questions refers to checking how the perception of corruption level depends on age, gender, Romanian region, professional status, and education.

6.2.2.3.1 Perception of Corruption and Age

This section answers research question RQ3.1: *How does the perception of corruption depend on age?*

In Tables 6.1 and 6.2 from Sect. 6.2.1, we find that the level of perception of corruption significantly differs by age, at the 1% level. Figures 6.49, 6.50, 6.51, and 6.52 provide additional information. The results show that respondents aged between 26 and 35 had the highest level of perception of corruption among all the age groups, followed by the group of 16–25 and 36–45 year olds (Fig. 6.51). Seventy percent (70%) of the respondents aged between 26 and 35 perceived corruption in Romania as being high or very high, followed by respondents aged between 16 and 25 (69%) (Fig. 6.51). At the opposite end of the spectrum, the elder group of respondents aged over 65 had the lowest level of perception for corruption (with the lowest score of corruption perception, of 3.73) (Fig. 6.52).

Our findings show that the level of corruption perception is maximum for the 26–35 age group. Starting from 36 years old, the perception of corruption gets lower and lower as the age of respondents increases; people over 65 had the lowest level of perceived corruption.

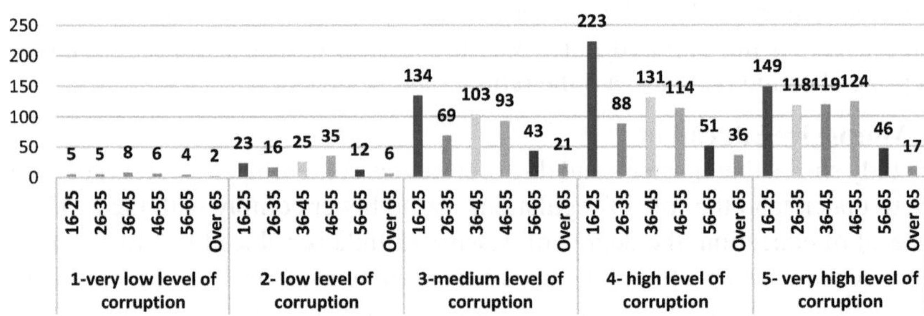

Fig. 6.49 Perception of corruption by age* (as number). (*Note: The results are obtained by responding to question 3(Q3): "How do you perceive the level of corruption in Romanian public institutions, on a scale range from 1 point (very low) to 5 points (very high)?)

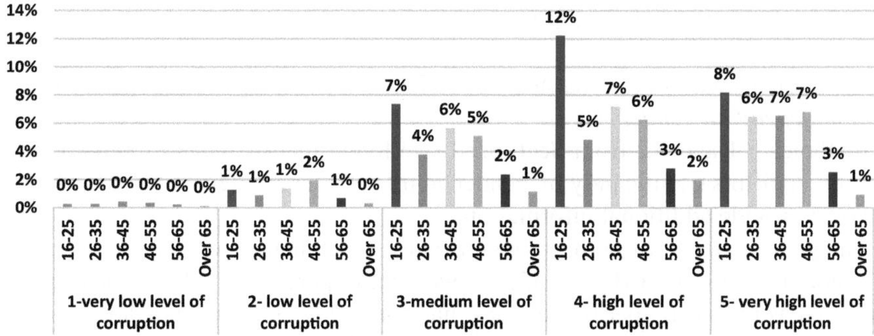

Fig. 6.50 Perception of corruption by age* (as % in the grand total). (*Note: The results are obtained by responding to question 3(Q3): "How do you perceive the level of corruption in Romanian public institutions, on a scale range from 1 point (very low) to 5 points (very high)?")

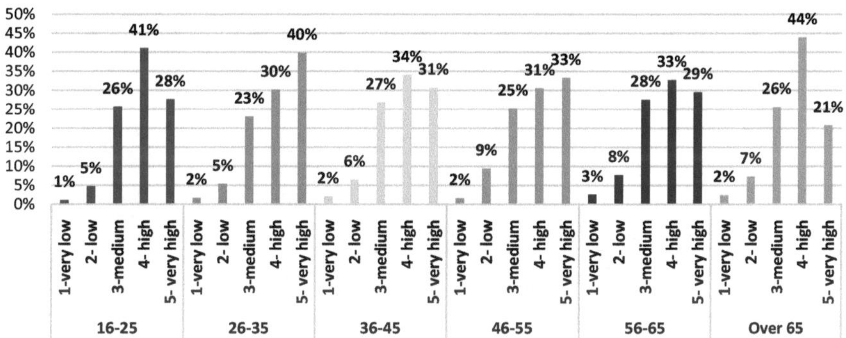

Fig. 6.51 Perception of corruption by age* (as % of the total). (*Note: The results are obtained by responding to question 3(Q3): "How do you perceive the level of corruption in Romanian public institutions, on a scale range from 1 point (very low) to 5 points (very high)?")

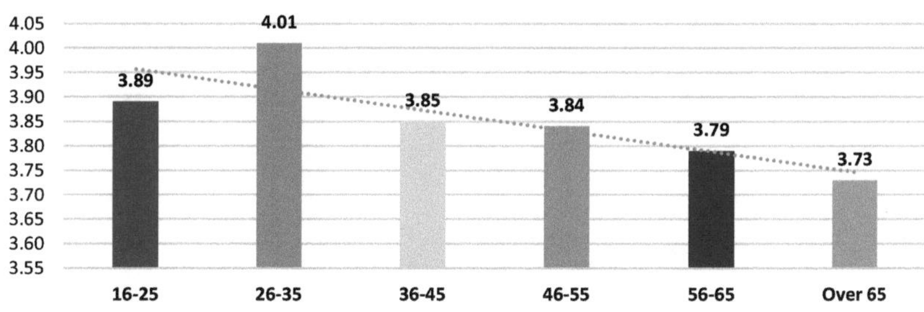

Fig. 6.52 Perception of corruption score by age. (Note: Perception of corruption scores range from 1 – the lowest level of corruption to 5 – the highest level of corruption)

6.2.2.3.2 Perception of Corruption and Gender

This section answers our research question RQ3.2: *How does the perception of corruption depend on gender?*

In Tables 6.1 and 6.2 from Sect. 6.2.1, we found that the level of perception of corruption differs significantly by gender, at the 10% level. Figures 6.53, 6.54, 6.55, and 6.56 provide additional information.

The great majority of both groups of males and females perceive corruption in Romania as being high (Fig. 6.55). However, the percent in which corruption is perceived as high is higher for females than for males (35% for females compared to 33% for males). Only 7% of females perceived corruption in Romania as being low or very low, compared to a higher percentage of 11% for males.

All in all, the corruption perception index calculated and presented in Fig. 6.56 shows that females perceive corruption in Romania at a quite higher level than males (the score of our corruption perception index for females is 3.91 compared with a lower score of 3.75 for males).

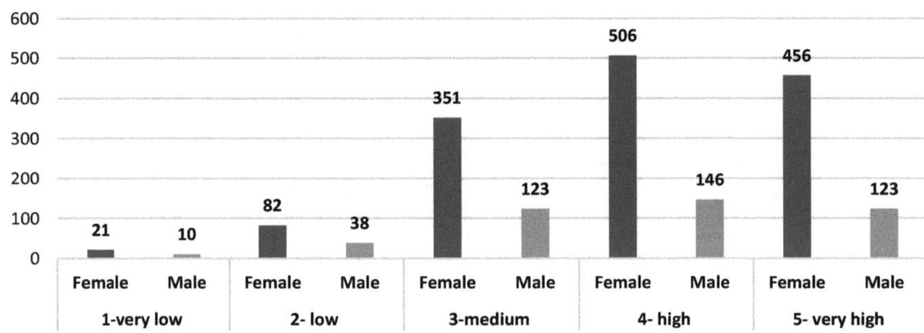

Fig. 6.53 Perception of corruption by gender* (as number). (**Note: The results are obtained by responding to question 3(Q3): "How do you perceive the level of corruption in Romanian public institutions, on a scale range from 1 point (very low) to 5 points (very high)?")

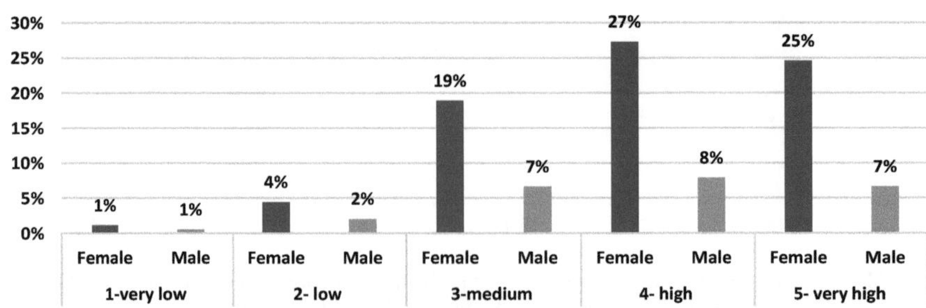

Fig. 6.54 Perception of corruption by gender * (as % in the grand total). (*Note: The results are obtained by responding to question 3(Q3): "How do you perceive the level of corruption in Romanian public institutions, on a scale range from 1 point (very low) to 5 points (very high)?)

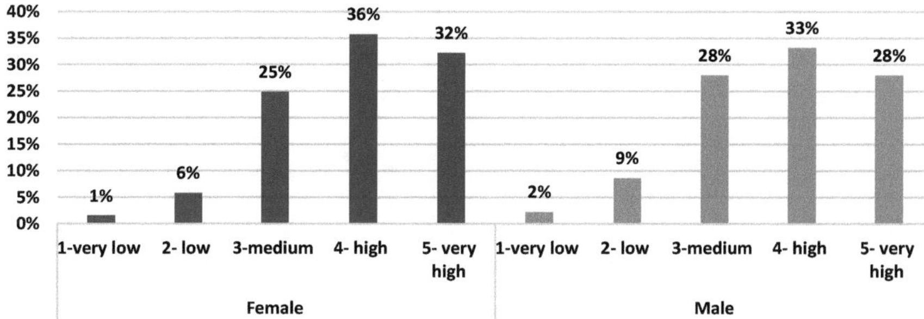

Fig. 6.55 Perception of corruption by gender * (as % of the total). (*Note: The results are obtained by responding to question 3(Q3): "How do you perceive the level of corruption in Romanian public institutions, on a scale range from 1 point (very low) to 5 points (very high)?")

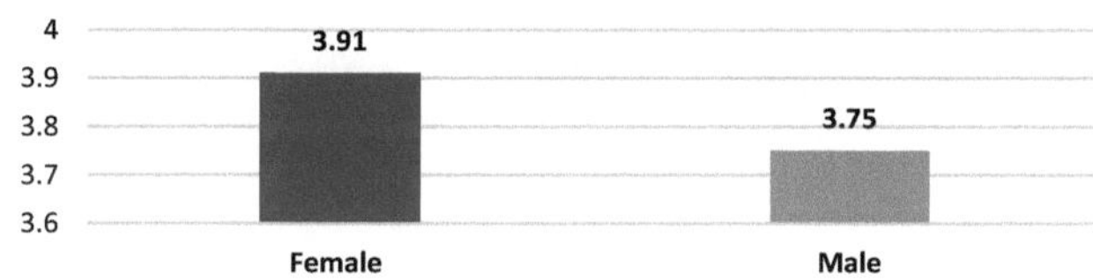

Fig. 6.56 Perception of corruption score by gender. (Note: Perception of corruption scores range from 1 – the lowest level of corruption to 5 – the highest level of corruption)

6.2.2.3.3 Perception of Corruption and Romanian Regions

This section answers research question RQ3.3: *How does the perception of corruption depend on Romanian region (Banat, Bucovina, Crisana, Dobrogea, Maramureş, Moldova, Muntenia, Oltenia, Transylvania)?*

In Tables 6.1 and 6.2 from the Sect. 6.2.1, we find that the level of perception of corruption does not differ significantly by region. The following Figs. 6.57, 6.58, 6.59, 6.60, and 6.61 provide additional information. The highest percentages in which the respondents assessed that the perceived corruption in Romania is high or very high are found in Dobrogea (79%) followed by Muntenia and Oltenia (with the same percentage of 70%). At the opposite end of the spectrum, the lowest percentage in which the respondents assessed perceived corruption to be high or very high are found in Banat, Transylvania, and Bucovina (with 63% for all these three regions).

All in all, the perception of corruption score, calculated for the Romanian regions, shows that Dobrogea, Muntenia, and Oltenia had the highest level of perceived corruption (scored 4.04, 3.95, and 3.94, respectively), while in Banat, Bucovina, Transylvania, and Crisana, the lowest levels of perceived corruption (scored 3.78, 3.83, and 3.84, respectively) were found (Fig. 6.60).

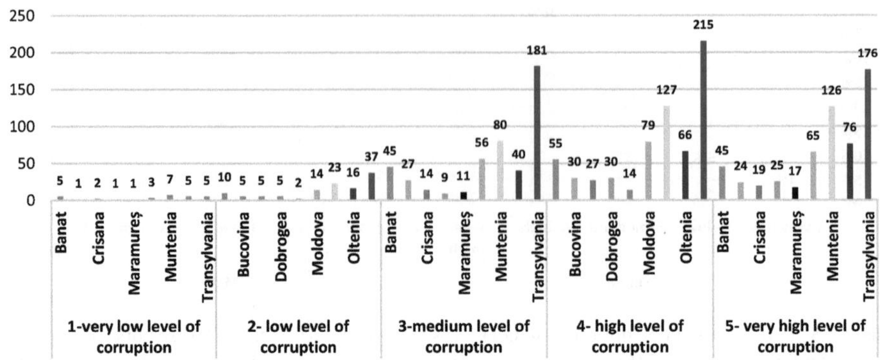

Fig. 6.57 Perception of corruption by Romanian region* (as number). (*Note: The results are obtained by responding to question 3(Q3): "How do you perceive the level of corruption in Romanian public institutions, on a scale range from 1 point (very low) to 5 points (very high)?")

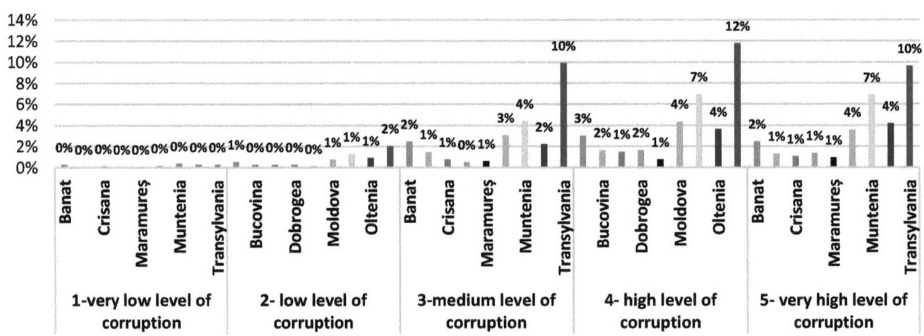

Fig. 6.58 Perception of corruption by Romanian regions* (as % of the grand total). (*Note: The results are obtained by responding to question 3(Q3): "How do you perceive the level of corruption in Romanian public institutions, on a scale range from 1 point (very low) to 5 points (very high)?)

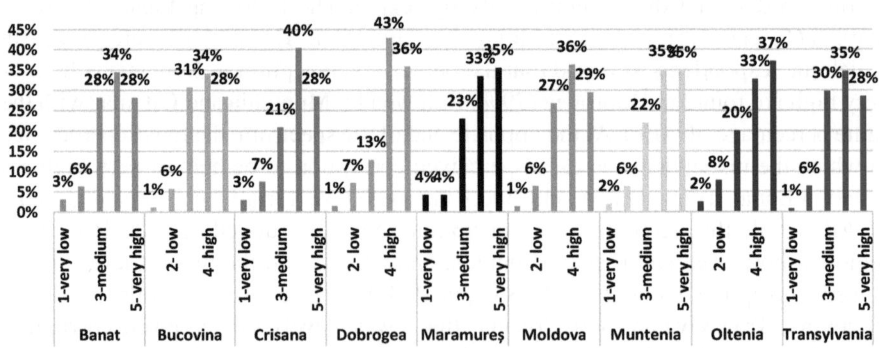

Fig. 6.59 Perception of corruption by Romanian region* (as % of the total). (*Note: The results are obtained by responding to question 3(Q3): "How do you perceive the level of corruption in Romanian public institutions, on a scale range from 1 point (very low) to 5 points (very high)?")

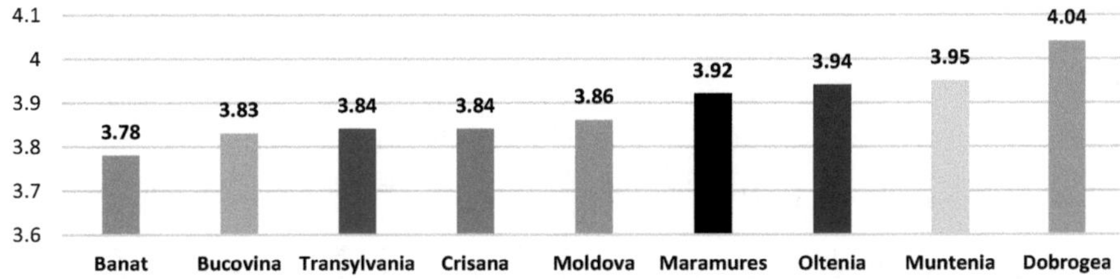

Fig. 6.60 Perception of corruption score by Romanian regions (bars). (Note: Perception of corruption scores range from 1 – the lowest level of corruption to 5 – the highest level of corruption)

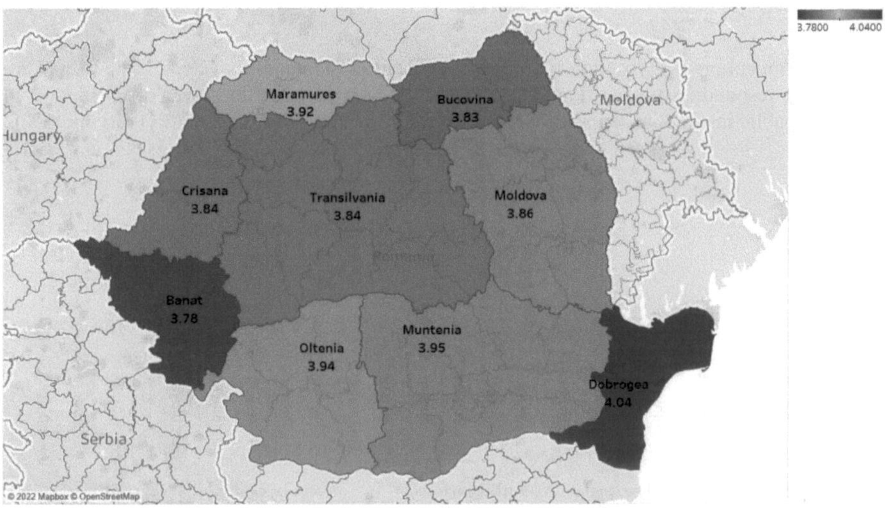

Fig. 6.61 Perception of corruption score by Romanian region (map). (Note: Perception of corruption scores range from 1 – the lowest level of corruption (colored in green) to 5 – the highest level of corruption (colored in red))

6.2.2.3.4 Perception of Corruption and Professional Status

This section answers research question RQ3.4: *How does the perception of corruption depend on professional status?*

In Tables 6.1 and 6.2 from Sect. 6.2.1, we find that the level of perception of corruption does not differ significantly by professional status. However, additional information is extracted after analyzing Figs. 6.62, 6.63, 6.64, and 6.65. Figure 6.64 shows that all the professional status groups predominantly appreciate the level of corruption in Romania to be high or very high. Corruption is perceived to be high or very high by unemployed people (86%), followed by managers (70%), employed people (66%), students (65%), and retired people (62%). All in all, accounting for

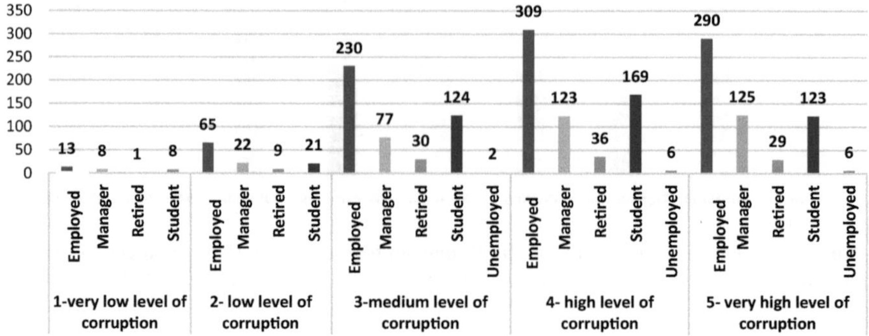

Fig. 6.62 Perception of corruption by professional status* (as number). (*Note: The results are obtained by responding to question 3(Q3): "How do you perceive the level of corruption in Romanian public institutions, on a scale range from 1 point (very low) to 5 points (very high)?")

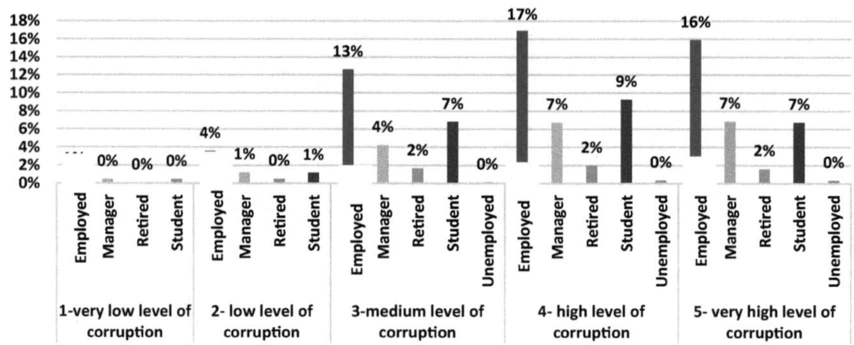

Fig. 6.63 Perception of corruption by professional status (as % in the grand total). (*Note: The results are obtained by responding to question 3(Q3): "How do you perceive the level of corruption in Romanian public institutions, on a scale range from 1 point (very low) to 5 points (very high)?")

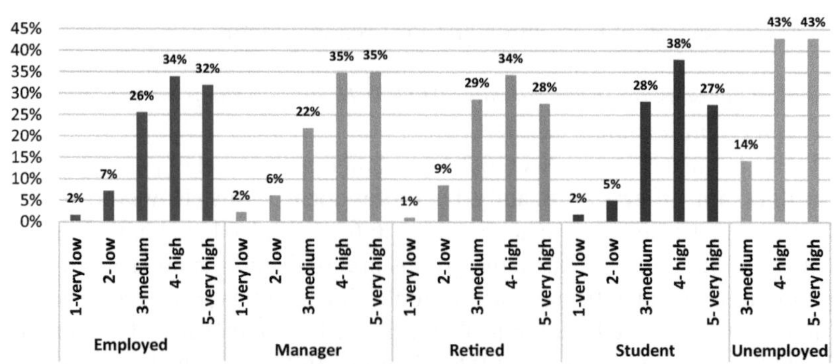

Fig. 6.64 Perception of corruption by professional status (as % of the total). (*Note: The results are obtained by responding to question 3(Q3): "How do you perceive the level of corruption in Romanian public institutions, on a scale range from 1 point (very low) to 5 points (very high)?")

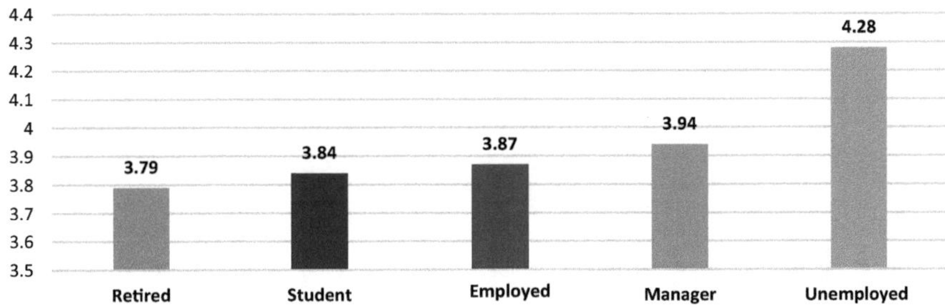

Fig. 6.65 Perception of corruption score by professional status. (Note: Perception of corruption scores range from 1 – the lowest level of corruption to 5 – the highest level of corruption)

the perception of corruption score, the highest level of corruption is perceived by unemployed (4.28) while the lowest level is perceived by the retired group (Fig. 6.65).

6.2.2.3.5 Perception of Corruption and Education

This section answers research question RQ3.5: *How does the perception of corruption depend on education?*

In Tables 6.1 and 6.2 from Sect. 6.2.1, we find that the level of perception of corruption differs significantly by level of education, at the 1% level. Additional information is extracted after analyzing Figs. 6.66, 6.67, 6.68, and 6.69. Figure 6.68 shows that people with high school diplomas or less have declared (73%) that the level of perceived corruption is high or very high. This category is followed by people with bachelor's studies (67%) and master's studies (66%) while the lowest percentages of 47% and 53% are found for people with doctoral and postdoctoral studies. In addition, the lowest percentage of respondents that declare the level of corruption to be low or very low were people with high school or less (4%), followed by bachelor's studies (8%) and master's studies (10%).

The percentages in which people with doctoral and postdoctoral studies declare the level of corruption to be low or very low are the highest among all the groups (15% and 18%, respectively). We may note that the highest percentages of respondents that consider corruption to be high or very high are found among less educated people. Similar conclusions are extracted from the calculated score of perceived corruption by education, which is presented in Fig. 6.69. The results show that higher levels of education are correlated with lower levels of perceived corruption while lower levels of education are correlated with higher levels of perceived corruption. Indeed, the highest level of perceived corruption is found for the lowest level of education (high school or less) while the lowest level of corruption is perceived by highly educated people (with doctoral or postdoctoral studies).

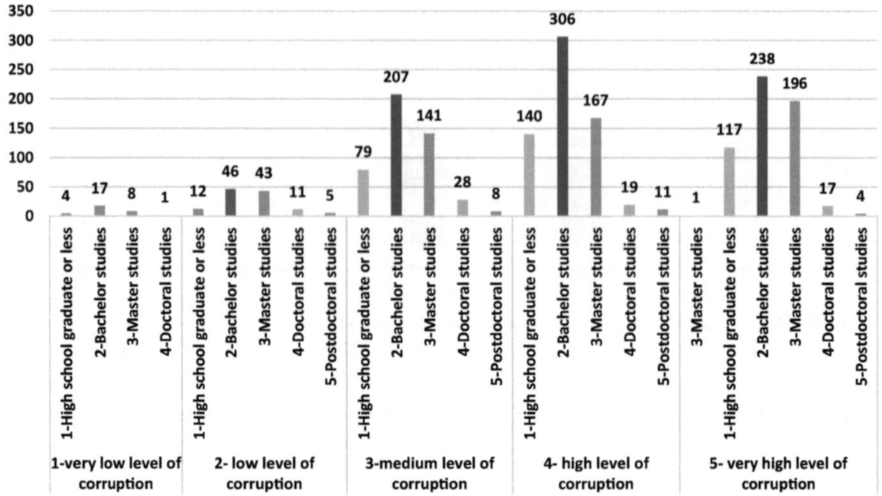

Fig. 6.66 Perception of corruption by education* (number). (*Note: The results are obtained by responding to question 3(Q3): "How do you perceive the level of corruption in Romanian public institutions, on a scale range from 1 point (very low) to 5 points (very high)?")

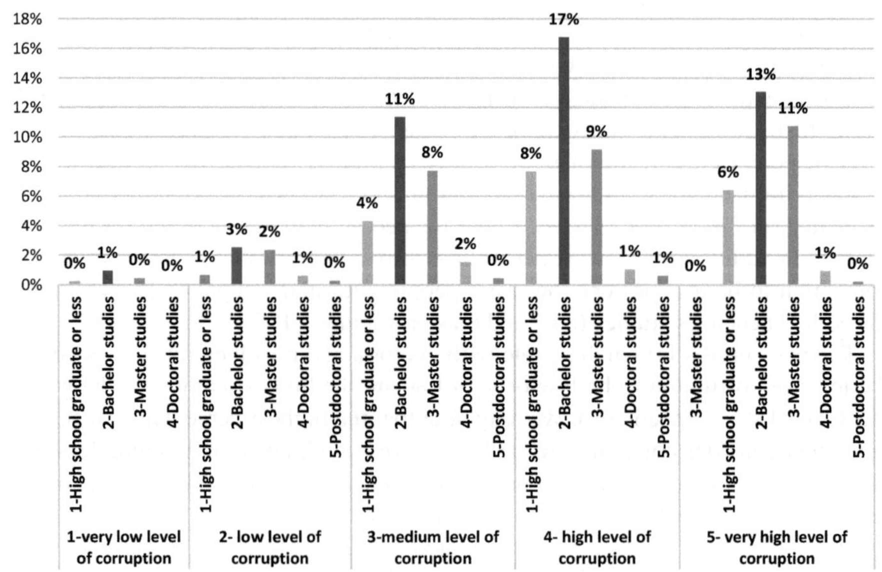

Fig. 6.67 Perception of corruption by education*(as % in the grand total). (*Note: The results are obtained by responding to question 3(Q3): "How do you perceive the level of corruption in Romanian public institutions, on a scale range from 1 point (very low) to 5 points (very high)?")

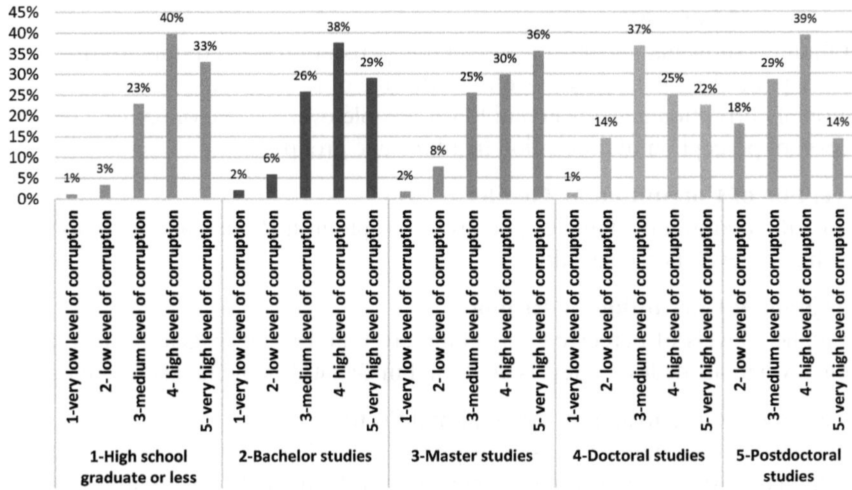

Fig. 6.68 Perception of corruption by education* (as % of the total). (*Note: The results are obtained by responding to question 3(Q3): "How do you perceive the level of corruption in Romanian public institutions, on a scale range from 1 point (very low) to 5 points (very high)?")

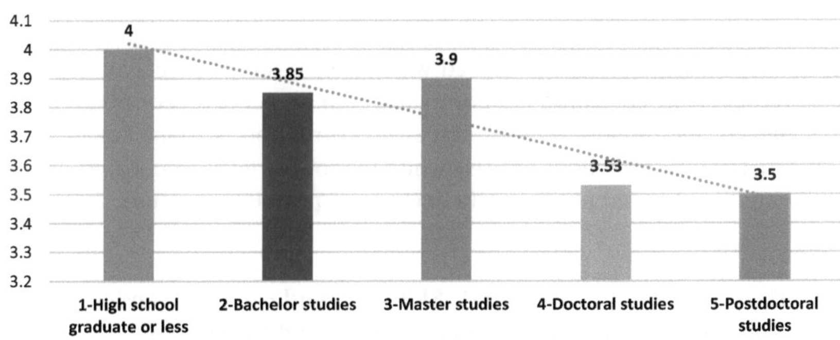

Fig. 6.69 Perception of corruption score by education. (Note: Perception of corruption scores range from 1 – the lowest level of corruption to 5 – the highest level of corruption)

6.2.2.3.6 Concluding Remarks

We find that the level of perceived corruption is significantly impacted by the demographic variables of age, gender, and education at the 1%, 5%, and 10% levels of significance. Still, there is some impact on professional status or region upon perceived corruption that are not significant.

Perception of Corruption by Age
Our findings show that the level of corruption perception is maximum for the 26–35 age group. Starting with 36 years old, as the age of respondents increases, the perception of corruption gets lower and lower. People over the age of 65 have the lowest level of perception of corruption in all the age groups.

Perception of Corruption by Gender
Among the two groups, females perceive corruption in Romanian institutions at a quite higher level than males do.

Perception of Corruption by Region
The highest levels of perceived corruption are found in Dobrogea, Muntenia, and Oltenia, whereas the lowest levels are found in Banat, Bucovina, and Transylvania.

Perception of Corruption by Professional Status
All the professional status groups greatly perceive the level of corruption in Romania to be high or very high. Corruption is perceived as being high or very high by unemployed people (86%), followed by managers (70%), employees (66%), students (65%), and retired people (62%). All in all, the highest level of corruption is perceived by unemployed (4.28), while the lowest level is perceived by retired people.

Perception of Corruption by Education
We find that the highest percentages of respondents that consider corruption to be high or very high are found among less educated people. The results show that higher levels of education are correlated with lower levels of perceived corruption while lower levels of education are correlated with higher levels of perceived corruption. Indeed, the highest level of perceived corruption is found for the lowest level of education (high school or less) while the lowest level of corruption is perceived by highly educated people (with doctoral or postdoctoral studies).

6.2.2.4 How Does the Level of AML Skills Depend on Age, Gender, Romanian Region, Professional Status, and Education?

The fourth set of research questions examines how the AML skills of citizens depend on age, gender, Romanian region, professional status, and education.

6.2.2.4.1 AML Skills and Age

This section answers question RQ4.1: *How does the level of AML skills depend on age?*

In Tables 6.1 and 6.2 from Sect. 6.2.1, we find that the level of perception of corruption differs significantly by level of education at the 1% level. Additional information is extracted after analyzing Figs. 6.70, 6.71, 6.72, and 6.73.

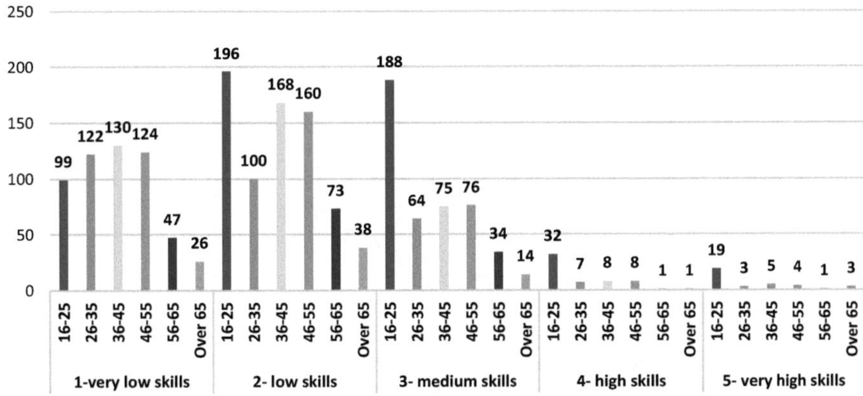

Fig. 6.70 AML skills depend on age* (as number). (*Note: The results are obtained by responding to question 4 (Q4): "Related to the risk of money laundering, do you think that people have suitable knowledge to be able to recognize a suspicious transaction in business?")

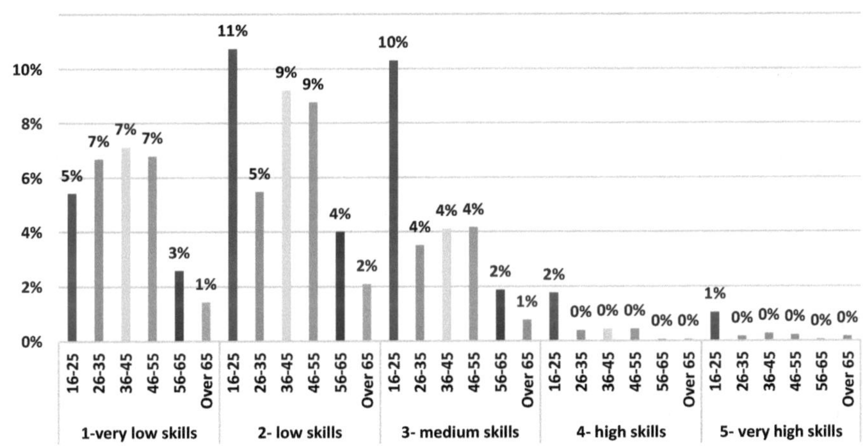

Fig. 6.71 AML skills depend on age* (as % in the grand total). (*Note: The results are obtained by responding to question 4 (Q4): "Related to the risk of money laundering, do you think that people have suitable knowledge to be able to recognize a suspicious transaction in business?")

The results show that for all age groups the majority of respondents had low or very low skills in detecting suspicious transactions. However, the lowest majority of respondents having low and very low AML skills were found for respondents aged 16–25 (46%), followed by those aged 26–35 (75%) and 46–55 (76%). On the other hand, the largest majority of respondents that have high or very high AML skills were found for the group aged 15–25 (10%), while the lowest majority of 5% were found for respondents over 65 (Fig. 6.72).

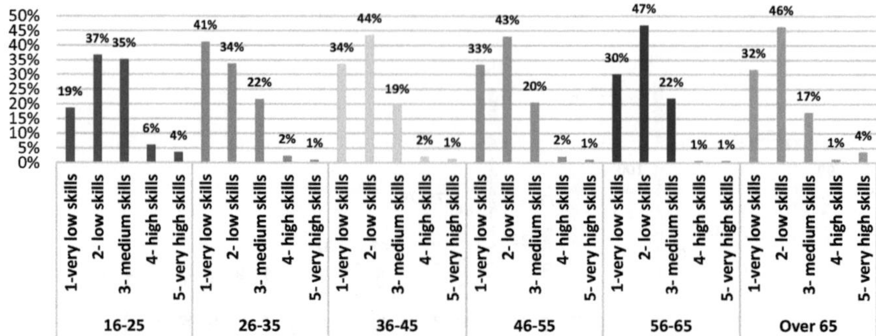

Fig. 6.72 AML skills depend on age* (as % of the total). (*Note: The results are obtained by responding to question 4 (Q4): "Related to the risk of money laundering, do you think that people have suitable knowledge to be able to recognize a suspicious transaction in business?")

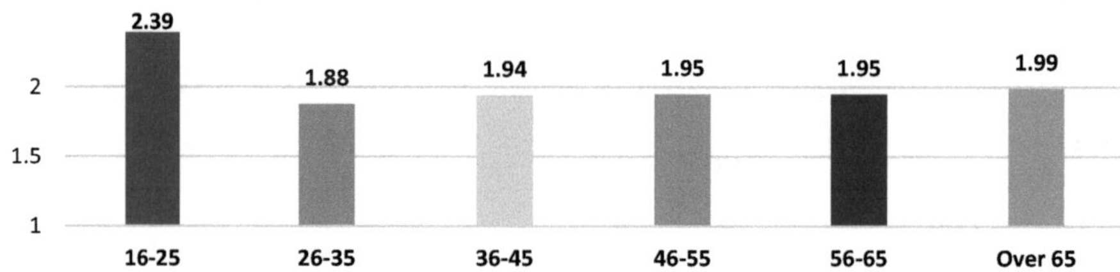

Fig. 6.73 AML skills scores by age. (Note: AML skills scores range from 1 – very low skills to 5 – very high skills)

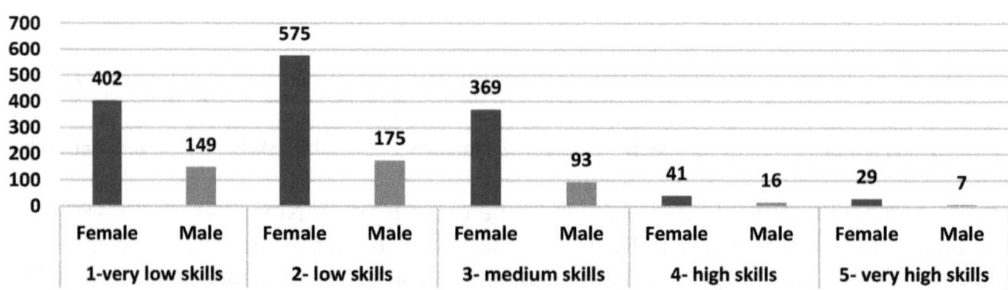

Fig. 6.74 AML skills depend on gender* (number). (*Note: The results are obtained by responding to question 4 (Q4): "Related to the risk of money laundering, do you think that people have suitable knowledge to be able to recognize a suspicious transaction in business?")

The calculated AML skills score is represented in Fig. 6.73. It shows that, with the exception of the 16–25 age group, there is an increase of AML skills as age increases (Figs. 6.74 and 6.75).

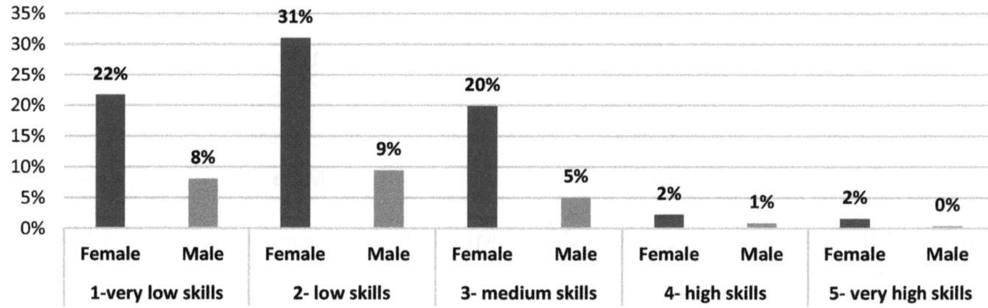

Fig. 6.75 AML skills depend on gender* (as % in the grand total). (*Note: The results are obtained by responding to question 4 (Q4): "Related to the risk of money laundering, do you think that people have suitable knowledge to be able to recognize a suspicious transaction in business?")

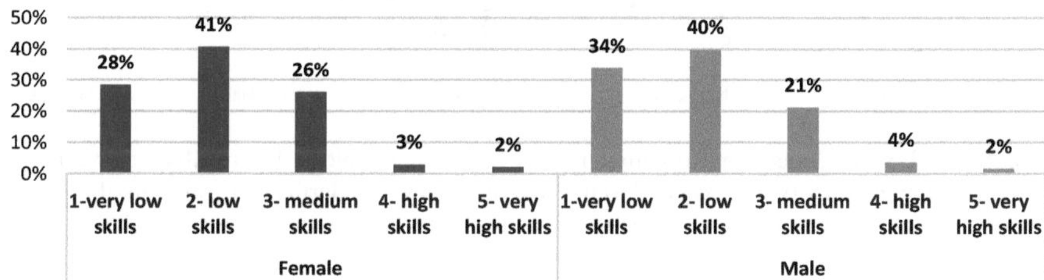

Fig. 6.76 AML skills depend on gender* (as % of the total). (*Note: The results are obtained by responding to question 4 (Q4): "Related to the risk of money laundering, do you think that people have suitable knowledge to be able to recognize a suspicious transaction in business?")

6.2.2.4.2 AML Skills and Gender

This section answers question RQ3.2: *How does the level of skills in AML depend on gender?*

In Tables 6.1 and 6.2 from the Sect. 6.2.1, our general results show that the level of AML skills does not differ significantly between males and females. However, additional analysis was conducted in order to extract analytical conclusions. We find from Fig. 6.76 that the majority of females (69%) have low or very low AML skills while this majority is even lower for males (64%). Five percent (5%) of females had high or very high skills, compared to 6% for males. About 26% of females have medium AML skills, while only 21% of males had medium AML skills (Fig. 6.76). All in all, the calculated AML skills score for the two groups of males and females showed no significant difference. However, for females the level of AML skills was slightly higher (the score of AML skills was 2.09 for females compared to 1.99 for males) (Fig. 6.77).

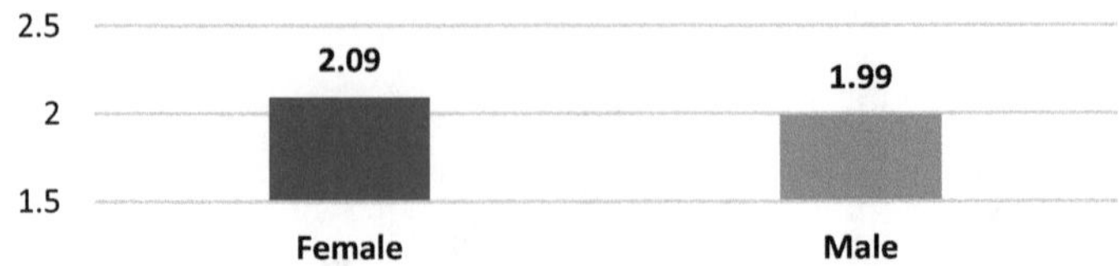

Fig. 6.77 AML skills scores by gender. (Note: AML skills scores range from 1 – very low skills to 5 – very high skills)

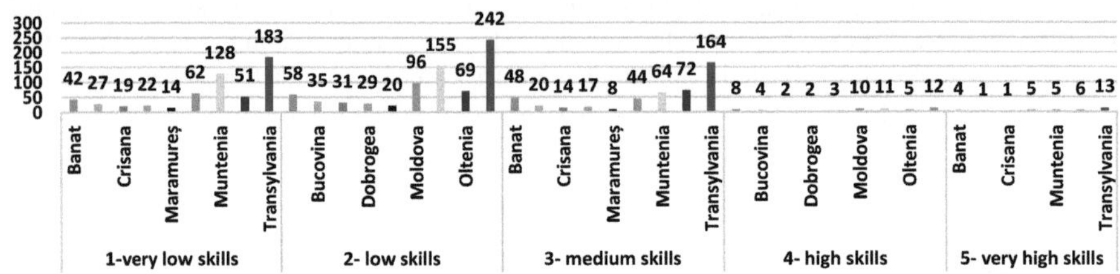

Fig. 6.78 AML skills depend on Romanian region* (number). (*Note: The results are obtained by responding to question 4 (Q4): "Related to the risk of money laundering, do you think that people have suitable knowledge to be able to recognize a suspicious transaction in business?")

6.2.2.4.3 AML Skills and Romanian Region

This section answers question RQ4.3: *How does the level of skills in AML depend on Romanian region (Banat, Bucovina, Crisana, Dobrogea, Maramureş, Moldova, Muntenia, Oltenia, Transylvania)?*

Tables 6.1 and 6.2 from Sect. 6.2.1 show that the level of AML skills differ significantly (at the 10% level) by Romanian region. Analyses are depicted in Figs. 6.78, 6.79, 6.80, and 6.81.

In all Romanian regions, the majority of respondents declared that they had low or very low AML skills (Fig. 6.80). However, the largest majority of people who had low or very low AML skills were found in Muntenia (78%), followed by Maramures (75%) and Crisana (74%). The highest percentage of people having high or very high AML skills were found in Banat (8%), followed by Maramures and Muntenia (each with 7%) (Fig. 6.80).

The score of AML skills by Romanian region is calculated and presented in Figs. 6.81 and 6.82. This score shows that the highest AML skills were possessed by respondents from Oltenia (2.24), Banat (2.21), and Moldova (2.09), while the lowest AML skills were found in Muntenia (1.92), Dobrogea (1.99), and Maramures (2.06).

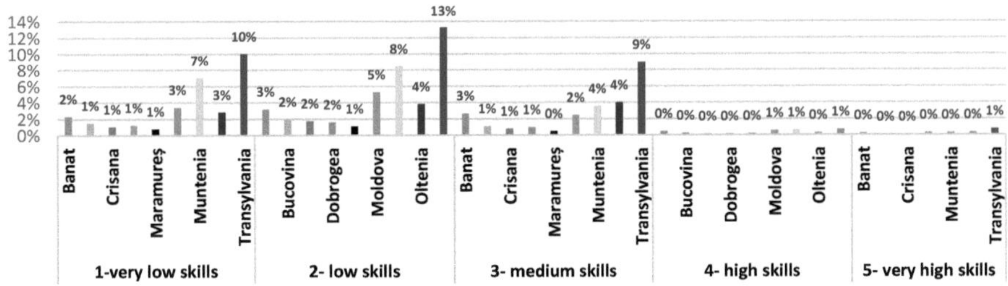

Fig. 6.79 AML skills depend on Romanian regions* (as % of the grand total). (*Note: The results are obtained by responding to question 4 (Q4): "Related to the risk of money laundering, do you think that people have suitable knowledge to be able to recognize a suspicious transaction in business?")

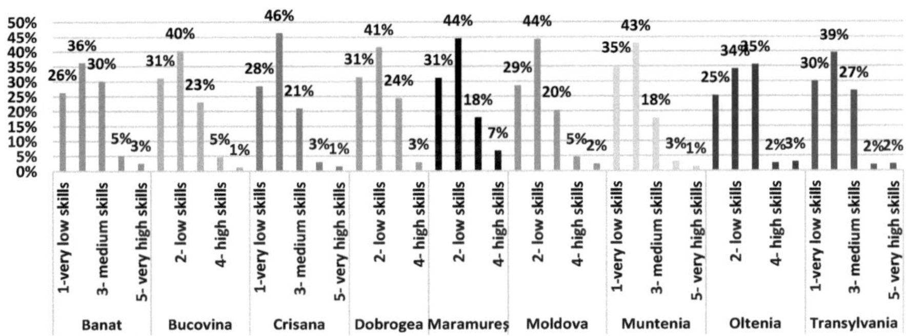

Fig. 6.80 AML skills depend on Romanian regions* (as % of the total). (*Note: The results are obtained by responding to question 4 (Q4): "Related to the risk of money laundering, do you think that people have suitable knowledge to be able to recognize a suspicious transaction in business?")

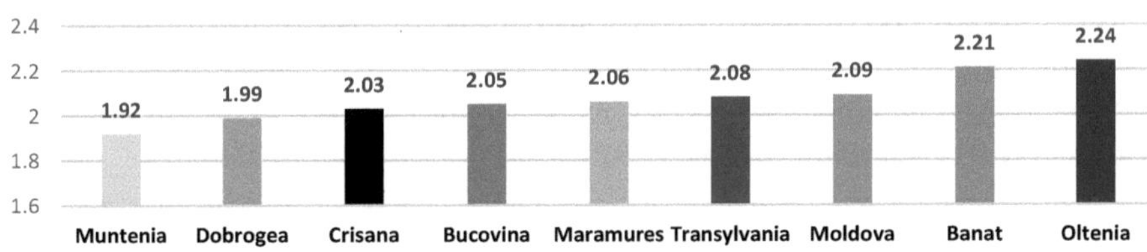

Fig. 6.81 AML skills scores by Romanian region (bars). (Note: AML skills scores range from 1 – very low skills to 5 – very high skills)

6.2.2.4.4 AML Skills and Professional Status

This section answers question RQ4.4: *How does the level of skills in AML depend on professional status?*

Tables 6.1 and 6.2 from Sect. 6.2.1 show that the level of AML skills differs significantly by professional status at the 1% level. Additional analyses were

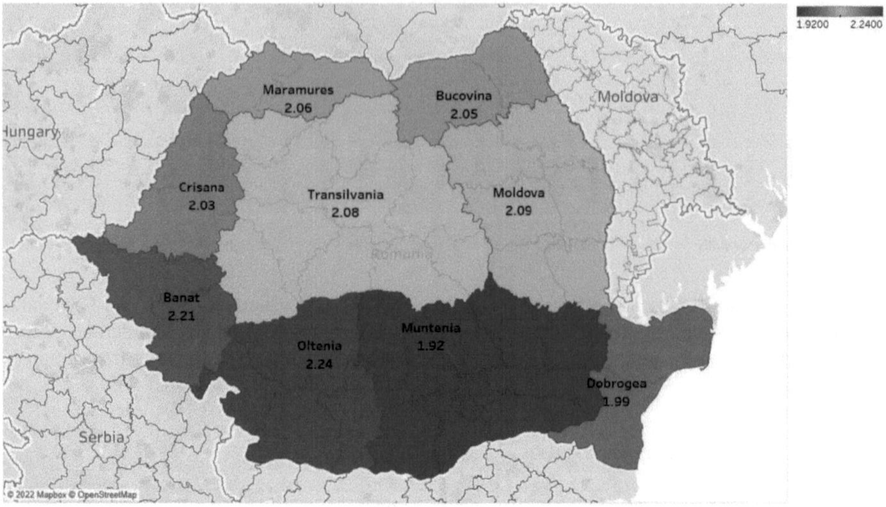

Fig. 6.82 AML skills scores by Romanian region (map). (Note: AML skills scores range from 1 – very low skills (colored in red) to 5 – very high skills (colored in green))

extracted from Figs. 6.83, 6.84, 6.85, and 6.86. In all groups of professional status the majority of respondents declared that they had low or very low AML skills (Fig. 6.85). However, the highest majority of people who had low or very low AML skills were found for retired people (80%), followed by managers and unemployed people (each group with 79%) and then employees (72%). Students had the lowest percentage, declaring low or very low AML skills. The highest percentage of respondents declaring high or very high skills was found for students (9%), followed by unemployed (7%) and employees (4%).

The score of AML skills by professional status is calculated and presented in Fig. 6.86. This score shows that the highest AML skills are possessed by students (2.35), followed by employees (2.01), while the lowest AML skills are found for managers (1.91) and retired people (1.92).

6.2.2.4.5 AML Skills and Education

This section answers question RQ4.5: *How does the level of skills in AML depend on education?*

Tables 6.1 and 6.2 from Sect. 6.2.1 show that the level of AML skills differs significantly by education at the 1% level. Additional analyses were extracted from Figs. 6.87, 6.88, 6.89, and 6.90. In all groups classified by education level the majority of respondents declared that they had low or very low AML skills (Fig. 6.89). However, the largest majority of respondents who declared that they had low or very low AML skills was found for people with doctoral studies (81%), followed by

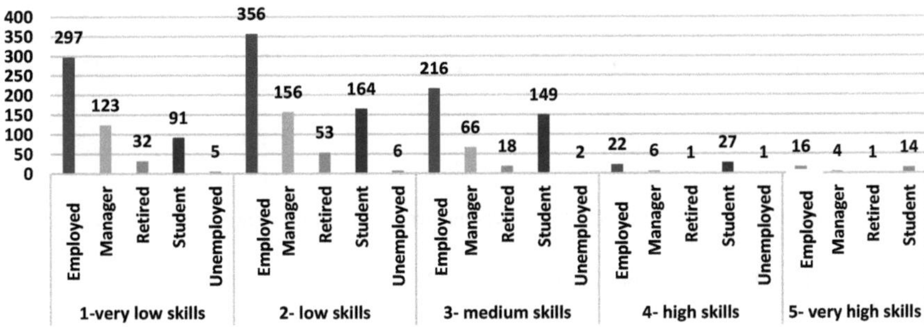

Fig. 6.83 AML skills depend on professional status* (number). (*Note: The results are obtained by responding to question 4 (Q4): "Related to the risk of money laundering, do you think that people have suitable knowledge to be able to recognize a suspicious transaction in business?")

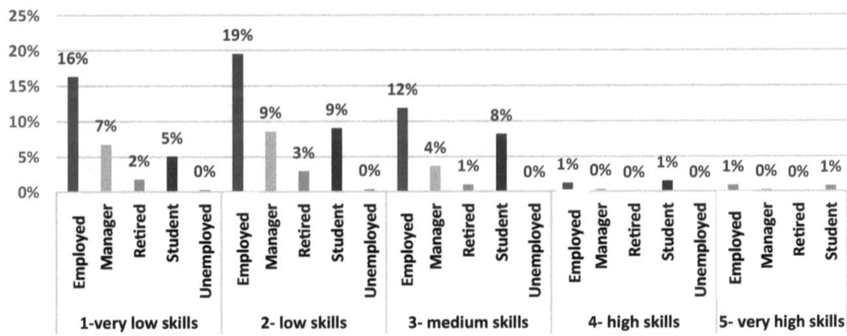

Fig. 6.84 AML skills depend on professional status* (as % of the grand total). (*Note: The results are obtained by responding to question 4 (Q4): "Related to the risk of money laundering, do you think that people have suitable knowledge to be able to recognize a suspicious transaction in business?")

Fig. 6.85 AML skills depend on professional status* (as % of the total). (*Note: The results are obtained by responding to question 4 (Q4): "Related to the risk of money laundering, do you think that people have suitable knowledge to be able to recognize a suspicious transaction in business")

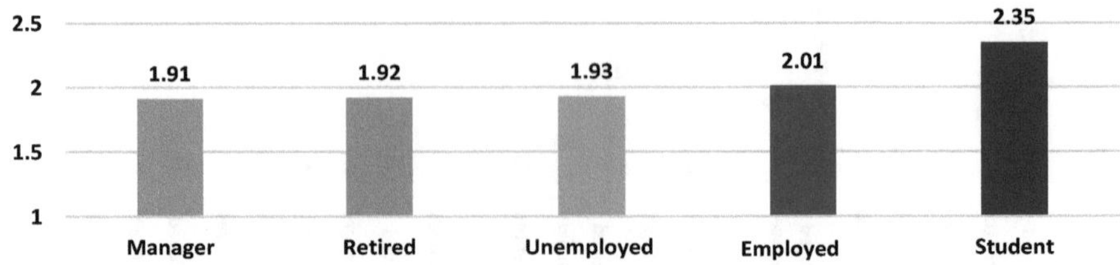

Fig. 6.86 AML skills score by professional status. (Note: AML skills scores range from 1 – very low skills to 5 – very high skills)

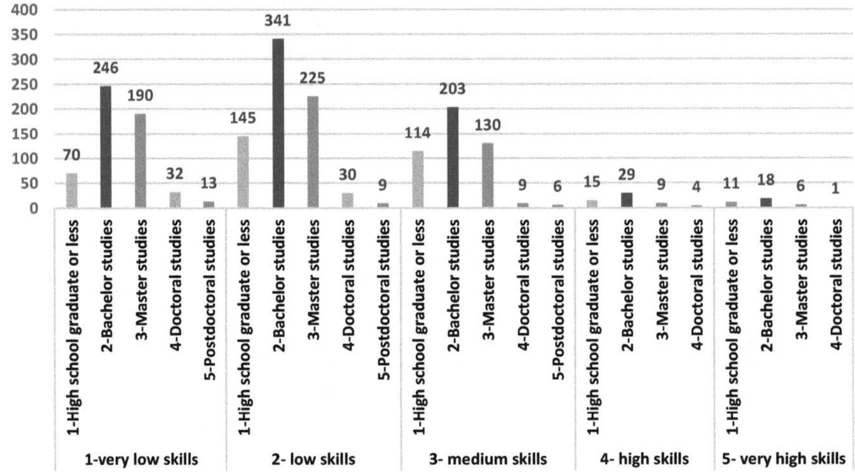

Fig. 6.87 AML skills depend on education * (as number). (*Note: The results are obtained by responding to question 4 (Q4): "Related to the risk of money laundering, do you think that people have suitable knowledge to be able to recognize a suspicious transaction in business?")

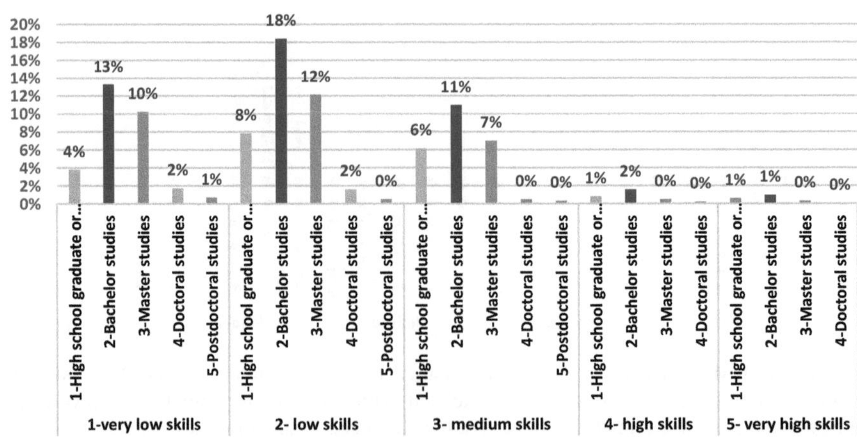

Fig. 6.88 AML skills depend on education* (as % of the grand total). (*Note: The results are obtained by responding to question 4 (Q4): "Related to the risk of money laundering, do you think that people have suitable knowledge to be able to recognize a suspicious transaction in business?")

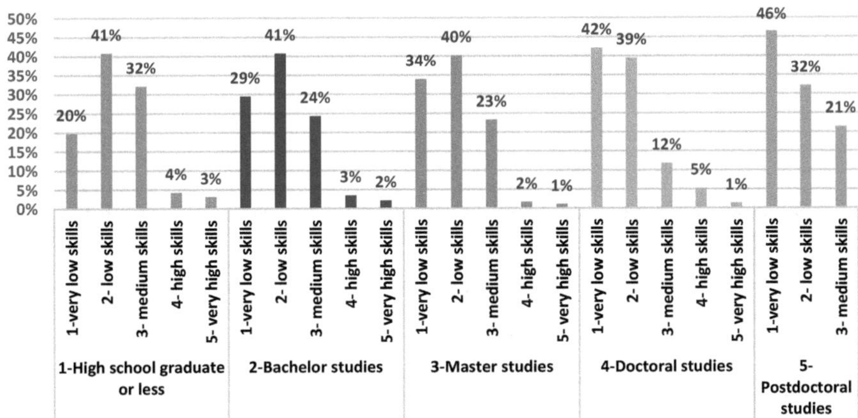

Fig. 6.89 AML skills depend on education* (as % of the total). (*Note: The results are obtained by responding to question 4 (Q4): "Related to the risk of money laundering, do you think that people have suitable knowledge to be able to recognize a suspicious transaction in business?")

postdoctoral studies (78%). The less educated respondents who had only a high school graduate diploma or less assessed themselves as having the lowest percentage of AML skills, i.e., low or very low (61%). The highest percentage of respondents declaring high or very high skills were also found for less educated people with only high school graduate diplomas or less (7%), followed by highly educated people with doctoral studies (6%), while 0% of those who had postdoctoral studies declared not to have high or very high AML skills at all.

The scores of AML skills by education level were calculated and presented in Fig. 6.90. It is interesting to find that the AML skills score was indirectly correlated with the level of education. This score shows the highest AML skills were possessed by respondents having high school diplomas or less (2.30), followed by those who had bachelor's studies (2.08), master's studies (1.96), doctoral studies (1.84), and postdoctoral studies (1.75).

6.2.2.4.6 Concluding Remarks

Our findings show that the level of AML skills was significantly impacted by all the demographic variables of age, gender, education, professional status, and region, at the 1%, 5%, and 10% levels of significance.

AML Skills by Age

Among all the age groups, the majority of respondents had low or very low skills in detecting suspicious transactions. However, the smallest majority of respondents having low or very low AML skills were found for respondents aged 16–25 (46%), followed by respondents aged 26–35 (75%) and 46–55 (76%). Starting with 26 years old, we found that as age increases, the level of AML skills increases as well.

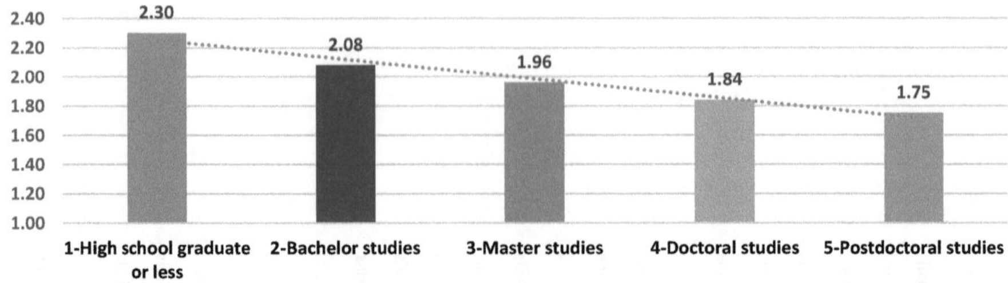

Fig. 6.90 AML skills scores by education. (Note: AML skills scores range from 1 – very low skills to 5 – very high skills)

AML Skills by Gender

We found that females had a slightly higher level of AML skills than males.

AML Skills by Region

The highest AML skills were represented by respondents from Oltenia, Banat, and Moldova, while the lowest AML skills were found in Muntenia, Dobrogea, and Maramures.

AML Skills by Professional Status

In all groups of professional status, the majority of respondents declared themselves as having low or very low AML skills. However, generally, the highest AML skills were possessed by students, followed by employees, while the lowest AML skills were found for managers and retirees.

AML Skills by Education

In all groups classified according to their education level, the majority of respondents declared that they had low or very low AML skills. However, the largest majority of respondents who declared that they had low or very low AML skills consisted of people with doctoral studies, followed by postdoctoral studies (78%). The less educated respondents who had only high school graduate diplomas or less declared the lowest percentages of having low or very low AML skills. All in all, we found that the perception of having a certain level of AML skills decreased as the level of education increased. Indeed, as we learn more, we may have the perception of knowing less. The less educated people may have the perception that they know all by not knowing anything.

6.2.2.5 How Does the Attitude Toward Know Your Clients (KYC) Procedures Depend on Age, Gender, Romanian Region, Professional Status, and Education?

The fifth set of research questions investigated how the attitude of citizens toward KYC procedures depends on age, gender, Romanian region, professional status, and education.

6.2.2.5.1 KYC Procedure Attitude and Age

This section answers question RQ4.1: *How does the attitude toward bank officers' job depend on age?*

Tables 6.1 and 6.2 from Sect. 6.2.1 show that the level of attitude toward *KYC procedures* differs significantly by age groups at the 1% level. Additional analyses were extracted from Figs. 6.91, 6.92, 6.93, and 6.94. The results showed that the majority (between 63% and 74%) of people had an open attitude toward the bank officers when they required a financial transaction (making a bank deposit, withdrawing cash from the account, etc.). However, this majority was quite higher for the people aged between 56 and 65 (77%), followed by the group aged above 65 (74%) and then by the group aged 46–55 (71%). The largest majority of those who refused to offer any details regarding KYC procedures belonged to the group aged 16–25 (15%), followed by the group aged 26–35 (10%) and these aged over 65 (5%) (Fig. 6.93).

All in all, after computing the KYC attitude scores, we found that the highest score of KYC attitude was found for the 16–25 age group (1.53), meaning the worst attitude toward the bank officers when they required a financial transaction. Then, as age increases, the level of KYC attitude scores systematically decreased and reached the minimum level for the 56–65 age group (1.26), meaning the best open attitude. However, people over 65 tend to be reluctant to provide the required information (Fig. 6.94).

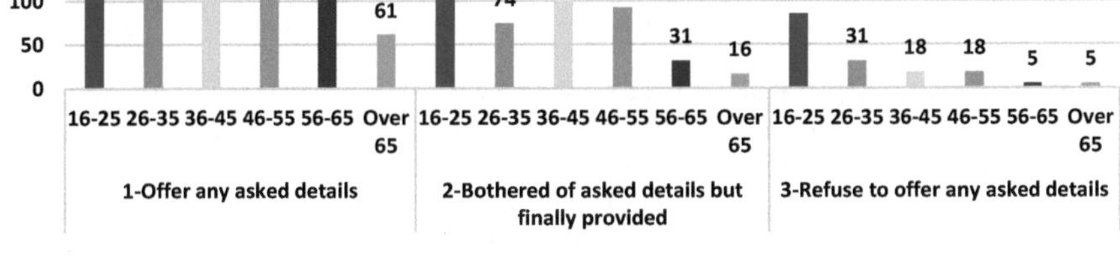

Fig. 6.91 Attitude toward KYC procedures depends on age* (as number). (*Note: The results are obtained by responding to question 5 (Q5): "When you or the people around you ask for bank transactions (making a bank deposit, withdrawing cash from the account, etc.), and the bank officer asks you to fill in some details regarding the provenience of the money, or where that amount goes, generally you or the people around you have different reactions")

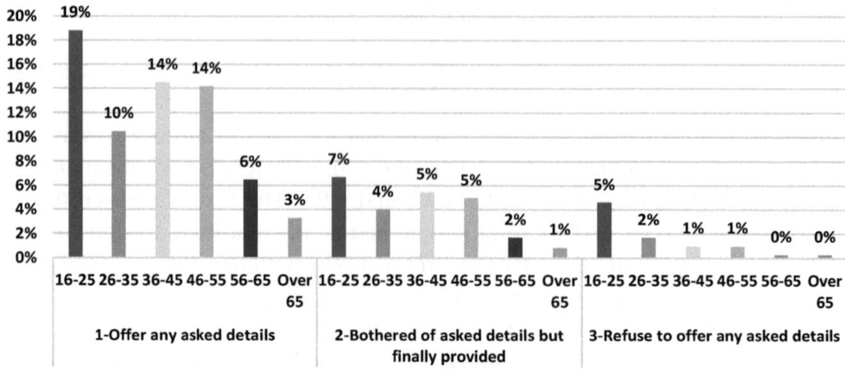

Fig. 6.92 Attitude toward KYC procedures depends on age * (as % of the grand total). (*Note: The results are obtained by responding to question 5 (Q5): "When you or the people around you ask for bank transactions (making a bank deposit, withdrawing cash from the account, etc.), and the bank officer asks you to fill in some details regarding the provenience of the money, or where that amount goes, generally you or the people around you have different reactions")

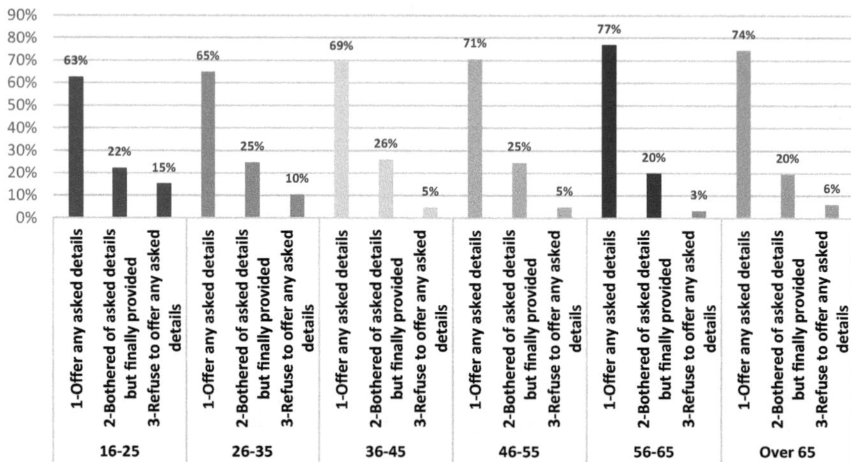

Fig. 6.93 Attitude toward KYC procedures by age * (as % of the total). (*Note: The results are obtained by responding to question 5 (Q5): "When you or the people around you ask for bank transactions (making a bank deposit, withdrawing cash from the account, etc.), and the bank officer asks you to fill in some details regarding the provenience of the money, or where that amount goes, generally you or the people around you have different reactions")

6.2.2.5.2 KYC Procedure Attitude and Gender

This section answers research question RQ4.2: *How does the attitude toward a bank officers' job depend on gender?*

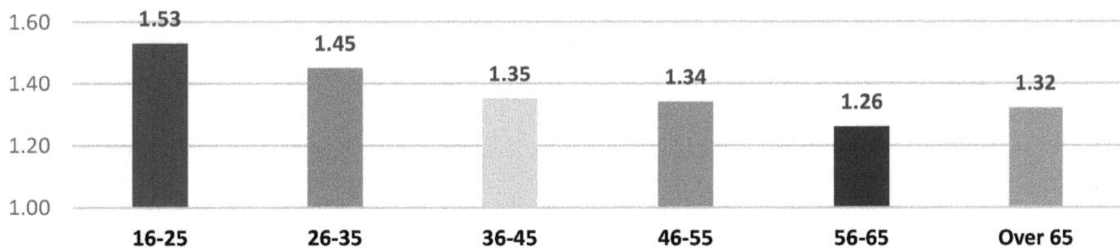

Fig. 6.94 KYC attitude scores by age. (Note: KYC attitude scores range from 1 – the best attitude to 3 – the worst attitude)

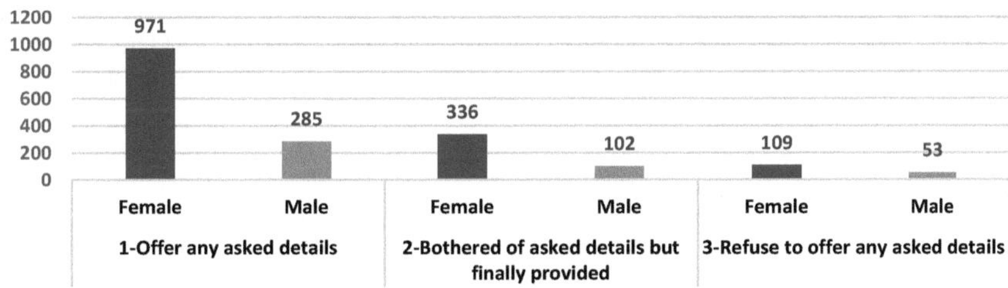

Fig. 6.95 Attitude toward KYC procedures by gender* (as number). (*Note: The results are obtained by responding to question 5 (Q5): "When you or the people around you ask about bank transactions (making a bank deposit, withdrawing cash from the account, etc.), and the bank officer asks you to fill in some details regarding the provenience of the money, or where that amount goes, generally you or the people around you have different reactions")

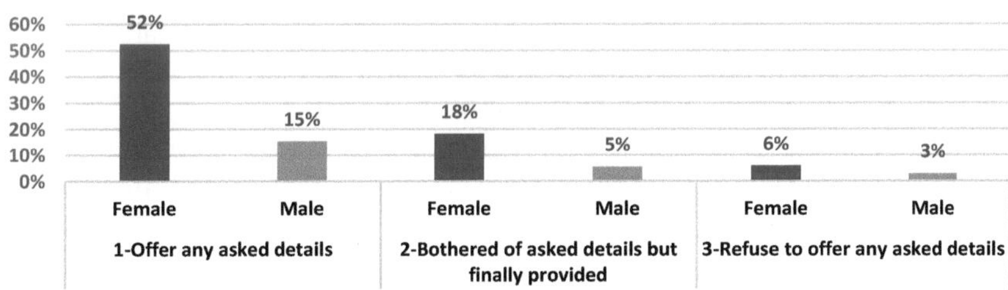

Fig. 6.96 Attitude toward KYC procedures by gender* (as % of the grand total). (*Note: The results are obtained by responding to question 5 (Q5): "When you or the people around you ask for bank transactions (making a bank deposit, withdrawing cash from the account, etc.), and the bank officer asks you to fill in some details regarding the provenience of the money, or where that amount goes, generally you or the people around you have different reactions")

Tables 6.1 and 6.2 from Sect. 6.2.1 show that the level of attitude toward KYC procedures does not differ significantly by gender. However, additional analyses were extracted from Figs. 6.95, 6.96, 6.97, and 6.98.

The results show that most of the time, (65–69%) males and females had an open attitude toward the bank officers when they ask for financial transactions (making a bank deposit, withdrawing cash from the account, etc.). However, this majority is quite larger for females than for males (69% for females compared to 65% for

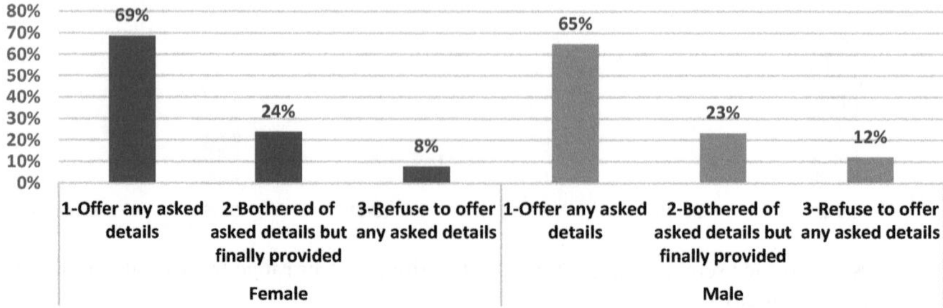

Fig. 6.97 Attitude toward KYC procedures by gender* (as % of the total). (*Note: The results are obtained by responding to question 5 (Q5): "When you or the people around you ask for bank transactions (making a bank deposit, withdrawing cash from the account, etc.), and the bank officer asks you to fill in some details regarding the provenience of the money, or where that amount goes, generally you or the people around you have different reactions")

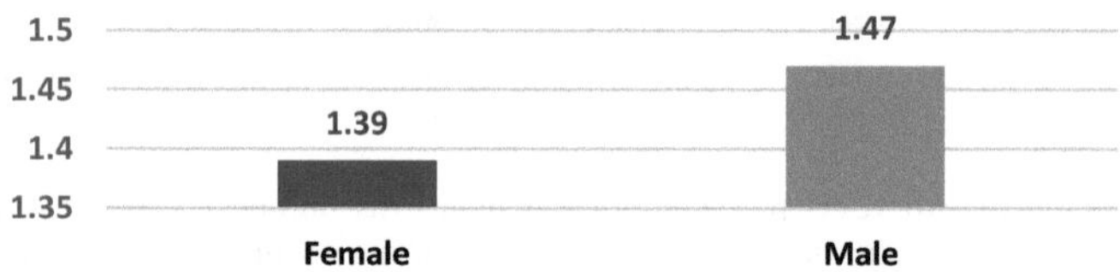

Fig. 6.98 KYC attitude scores by gender. (Note: KYC attitude scores range from 1 – the best attitude to 3 – the worst attitude)

males). In addition, males are keener to refuse to offer any asked details more than females do (the percentage of those males that refuse to offer details is 12% compared to lower percentages of 8% for females) (Fig. 6.97).

All in all, after the calculation of KYC attitude scores, we found that the highest score of KYC attitude was found for males (1.47), meaning the worst attitude toward bank officers when they ask for information about bank transactions compared to females (1.39). In other words, females were more open to offer details to the bank officers than males, meaning males were more reluctant.

6.2.2.5.3 KYC Procedure Attitude and Romanian Region

This section answers question RQ5.3: *How does the attitude toward bank officers' job depend on Romanian region (Banat, Bucovina, Crisana, Dobrogea, Maramureş, Moldova, Muntenia, Oltenia, Transylvania)?*

Tables 6.1 and 6.2 from Sect. 6.2.1 show that the attitude level toward KYC procedures does not differ significantly by Romanian region. However, additional analyses were extracted from Figs. 6.99, 6.100, 6.101, 6.102, and 6.103.

The results greatly showed that for all regions (64–75%) people had an open attitude toward the bank officers when they asked to conduct bank transactions

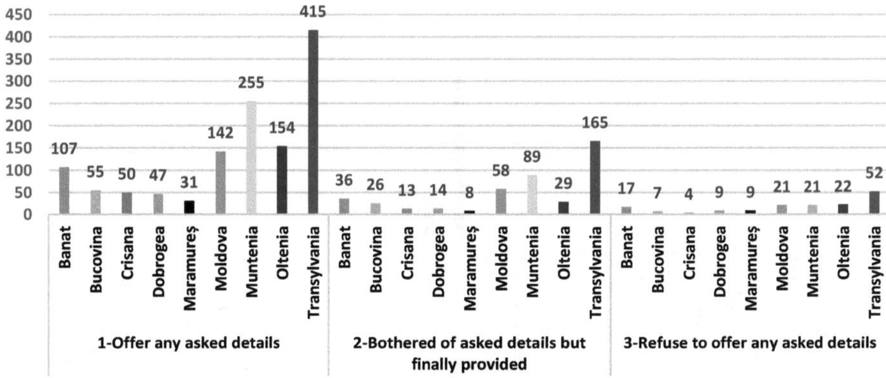

Fig. 6.99 Attitude toward KYC procedures by Romanian region * (as number). (*Note: The results are obtained by responding to question 5 (Q5): "When you or the people around you ask for bank transactions (making a bank deposit, withdrawing cash from the account, etc.), and the bank officer asks you to fill in some details regarding the provenience of the money, or where that amount goes, generally you or the people around you have different reactions")

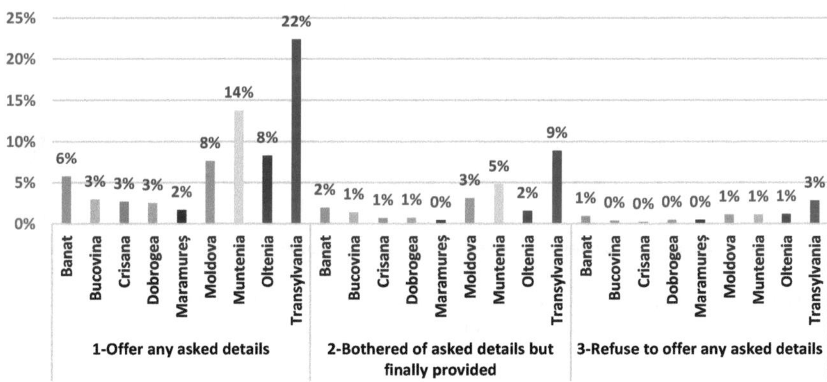

Fig. 6.100 Attitude toward KYC procedures by Romanian region* (as % of the grand total). (*Note: The results are obtained by responding to question 5 (Q5): "When you or the people around you ask for bank transactions (making a bank deposit, withdrawing cash from the account, etc.), and the bank officer asks you to fill in some details regarding the provenience of the money, or where that amount goes, generally you or the people around you have different reactions")

(making a bank deposit, withdrawing cash from the account, etc.). However, this majority of people having a good attitude toward bank officers was quite larger for Crisana and Oltenia (each with 75%), followed by Muntenia (70%) and Banat and Dobrogea (each with 67%). At the other end of the spectrum, with the most restrictive attitude, there were the people from Maramures and Dobrogea, where the percentage of people that refused to offer details to the bank officers were the highest (19% and 13%, respectively) (Fig. 6.101).

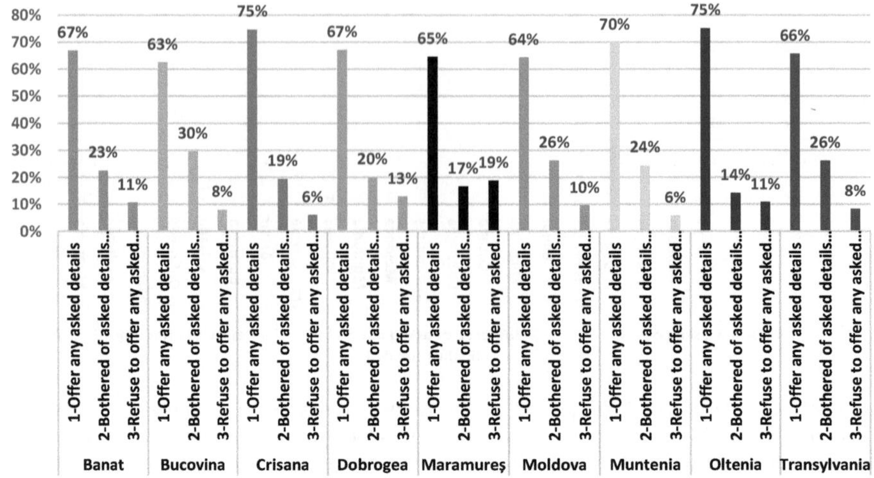

Fig. 6.101 Attitude toward KYC procedures by Romanian region* (as % of the total). (*Note: The results are obtained by responding to question 5 (Q5): "When you or the people around you ask for bank transactions (making a bank deposit, withdrawing cash from the account, etc.), and the bank officer asks you to fill in some details regarding the provenience of the money, or where that amount goes, generally you or the people around you have different reactions")

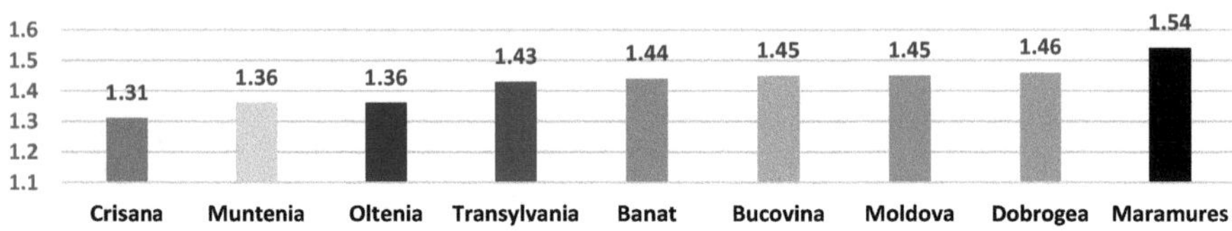

Fig. 6.102 KYC attitude scores by Romanian region (bars). (Note: KYC attitude scores range from 1 – the best attitude to 3 – the worst attitude)

All in all, after the calculation of the KYC attitude scores, we found that the highest score of KYC attitude, meaning the worst attitude, was found toward the respondents from Maramures (1.54), Dobrogea (1.46), and Moldova and Bucovina (both with a score of 1.45). At the other end were Crisana (1.31), Muntenia and Oltenia (each with a score of 1.36), with the lowest KYC attitude scores among all regions, meaning a tolerant attitude for the bank officers (Figs. 6.102 and 6.103).

6.2.2.5.4 KYC Procedure Attitude and Professional Status

This section answers question RQ5.4: *How does the attitude toward bank officers' job depend on professional status?*

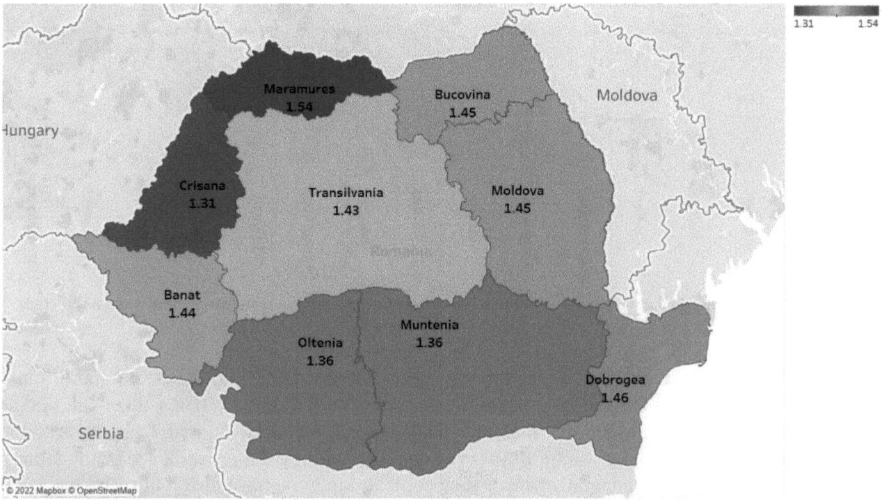

Fig. 6.103 KYC attitude score by Romanian region (map). (Note: KYC attitude scores range from 1 – the best attitude (colored in green) to 3 – the worst attitude (colored in red))

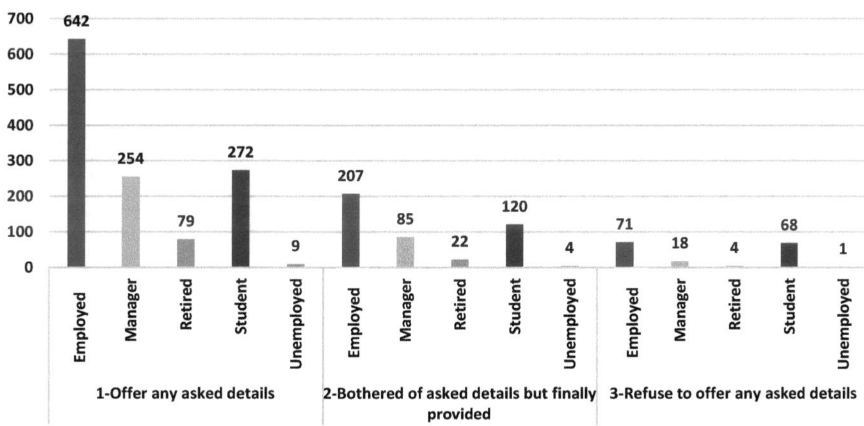

Fig. 6.104 Attitude toward KYC procedures by professional status* (as number). (*Note: The results are obtained by responding to question 5 (Q5): "When you or the people around you ask for bank transactions (making a bank deposit, withdrawing cash from the account, etc.), and the bank officer asks you to fill in some details regarding the provenience of the money, or where that amount goes, generally you or the people around you have different reactions")

Tables 6.1 and 6.2 from Sect. 6.2.1 show that the attitude level toward KYC procedures differs significantly by *professional status* at the 1% level. Additional analyses were extracted from Figs. 6.104, 6.105, 6.106, and 6.107.

The results show that for all the professional status groups (64–75%), people are tolerant with bank officers when they ask for information about bank transactions (making a bank deposit, withdrawing cash from the account, etc.). However, this

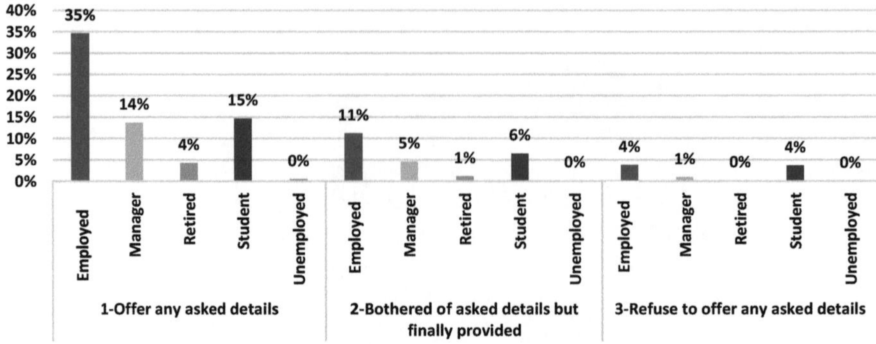

Fig. 6.105 Attitude toward KYC procedures by professional status* (as % of the grand total). (*Note: The results are obtained by responding to question 5 (Q5): "When you or the people around you ask for bank transactions (making a bank deposit, withdrawing cash from the account, etc.), and the bank officer asks you to fill in some details regarding the provenience of the money, or where that amount goes, generally you or the people around you have different reactions")

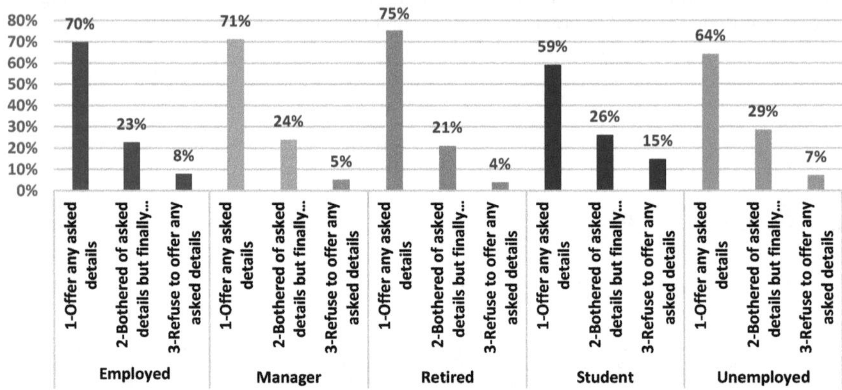

Fig. 6.106 Attitude toward KYC procedures by professional status* (as % of the total). (*Note: The results are obtained by responding to question 5 (Q5): "When you or the people around you ask for bank transactions (making a bank deposit, withdrawing cash from the account, etc.), and the bank officer asks you to fill in some details regarding the provenience of the money, or where that amount goes, generally you or the people around you have different reactions")

majority of people having a good attitude toward bank officers are the highest for retired people (75%) and the lowest for students (59%). In addition, retired people have the lowest percentage of refusal to offer details of all the groups (4%), while students have the highest percentage of refusal (15%) (Fig. 6.106).

All in all, after the calculation of KYC attitude scores, we found that the highest scores of KYC attitudes, meaning the worst attitude, were found for students (1.56), followed by unemployed people (1.43), while the most open attitudes were found for retired people (1.29) and managers (1.34) (Fig. 6.107).

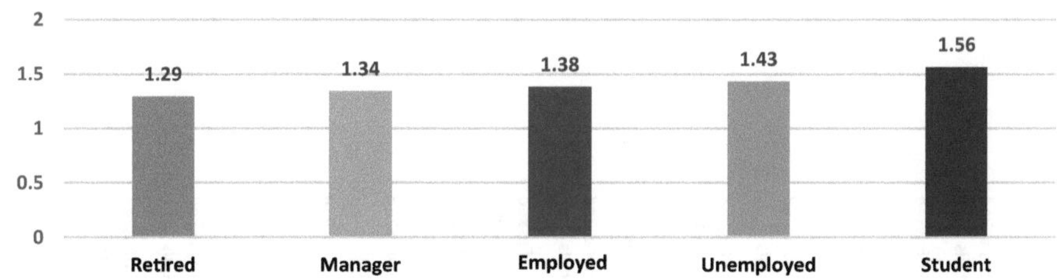

Fig. 6.107 KYC attitude scores by professional status. (Note: KYC attitude scores range from 1 – the best attitude to 3 – the worst attitude)

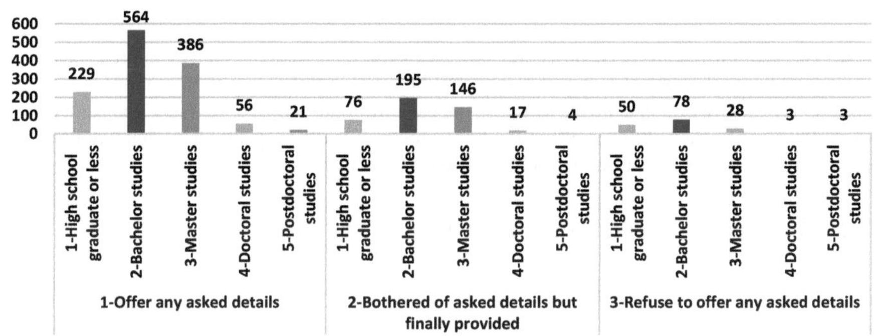

Fig. 6.108 Attitude toward KYC procedures by education* (as number). (*Note: The results are obtained by responding to question 5 (Q5): "When you or the people around you ask for bank transactions (making a bank deposit, withdrawing cash from the account, etc.), and the bank officer asks you to fill in some details regarding the provenience of the money, or where that amount goes, generally you or the people around you have different reactions")

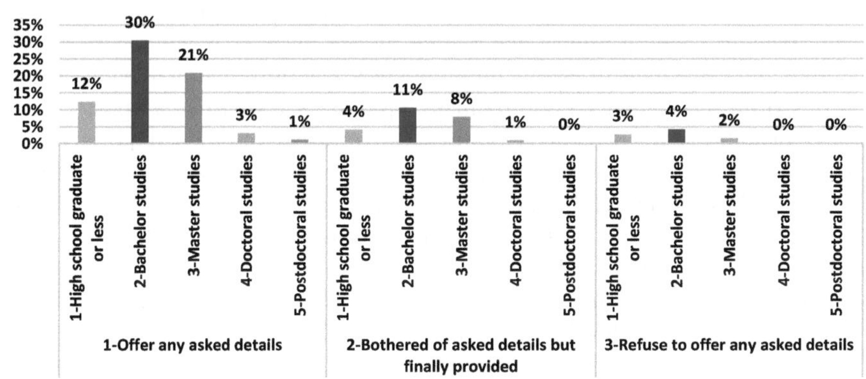

Fig. 6.109 Attitude toward KYC procedures by education * (as % of the grand total). (*Note: The results are obtained by responding to question 5 (Q5): "When you or the people around you ask for bank transactions (making a bank deposit, withdrawing cash from the account, etc.), and the bank officer asks you to fill in some details regarding the provenience of the money, or where that amount goes, generally you or the people around you have different reactions")

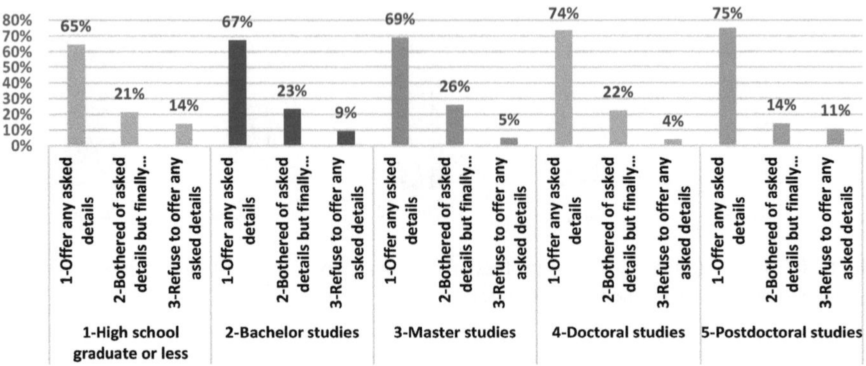

Fig. 6.110 Attitude toward KYC procedures by education * (as % of the total). (*Note: The results are obtained by responding to question 5 (Q5): "When you or the people around you ask for bank transactions (making a bank deposit, withdrawing cash from the account, etc.), and the bank officer asks you to fill in some details regarding the provenience of the money, or where that amount goes, generally you or the people around you have different reactions")

6.2.2.5.5 KYC Procedure Attitude and Education

This section answers question RQ5.5: *How does the attitude toward bank officers' job depend on education?*

Tables 6.1 and 6.2 from Sect. 6.2.1 show that the level of attitude toward KYC procedures differs significantly by *education* at the 1% significance level. Additional analyses were extracted from Figs. 6.108, 6.109, 6.110, and 6.111.

The results show that regardless of the education level, the majority (between 65% and 75%) of people are tolerant with bank officers when they ask for information about bank transactions (making a bank deposit, withdrawing cash from the account, etc.). However, this majority of people having a good attitude toward bank officers tend to become higher and higher as the level of education increases. Therefore, the percentage of people providing personal information to bank officers increases from 65% (high school graduate diploma or less) to 75% (postdoctoral studies). In addition, the percentage of those who refuse to offer any required details to bank officers decreases from 14% (high school graduate diploma or less) to 4% (doctoral studies). Thus, as the level of education increases up to getting doctoral degrees, the tendency to refuse to provide the information asked for declines. Thus, people become better informed as they become more educated. However, with post-doctoral studies the percentage of those who refuse to offer details is somehow larger compared to other levels of education (Fig. 6.110).

We found that the highest score of KYC attitudes, meaning the worst attitude, is found for high school graduates or less (1.5) and the lowest score is found for people with doctoral degrees (1.3). (Fig. 6.111).

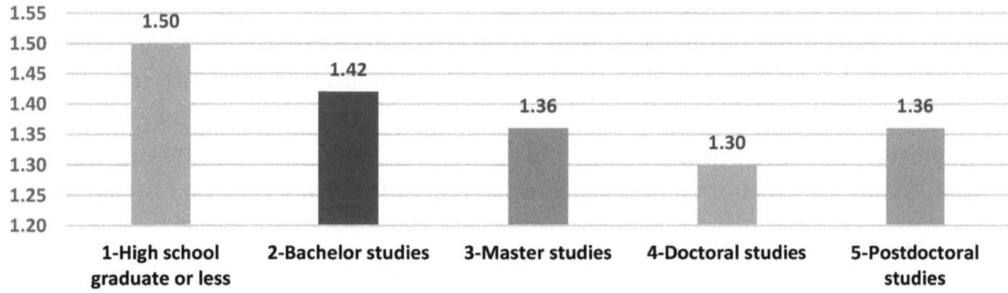

Fig. 6.111 KYC attitude scores by education. (Note: KYC attitude scores range from 1 – the best attitude to 3 – the worst attitude)

6.2.2.5.6 Concluding Remarks

Our findings show that the level of KYC procedures attitude is significantly impacted by the majority of demographic variables such as age, education, and professional status at the 1% level of significance. Regarding gender and region, their impact is hardly significant on KYC procedures.

KYC Procedures by Age

The results show that predominantly (between 63 and 74%) for all age groups, people have an open attitude toward bank officers when they ask for information about bank transactions (making a bank deposit, withdrawing cash from the account, etc.).

Moreover, the 16–25 age group has the worst attitude toward bank officers when they ask for information about a bank transaction. Then, as people grow older, up to the age of 65, the level of openness systematically increases. However, people over 65 tend to be quite reluctant to offer the required information.

KYC Procedures by Gender

The results show that the majority (65–69%) of males and females are tolerant with bank officers when they ask for information about bank transactions (making a bank deposit, withdrawing cash from the account, etc.). However, this majority is quite larger for females than for males (69% for females compared to 65% for males). In addition, males tend to refuse to offer any asked details more often than females (the percentage of those males that refuse to offer details is 12% compared to only 8% for females) (Fig. 6.97).

All in all, females are more open to offer details to bank officers and they have a better attitude toward KYC procedures than males, while males are more restrictive.

KYC Procedures by Regions

The results show that for most regions (64–75%), people are tolerant toward bank officers when they ask for information about bank transactions (making a bank deposit, withdrawing cash from the account, etc.). However, generally the worst attitude is found among respondents from Maramures, Dobrogea, Moldova, and Bucovina. The most open attitude toward bank officers was found for Crisana and Muntenia and Oltenia.

KYC Procedures by Professional Status

The results show that for all categories of professional status (64–75%), people are tolerant with bank officers when they ask for information about bank transactions (making a bank deposit, withdrawing cash from the account, etc.). However, among these groups, the worst attitude is found among students, followed by unemployed people, while the most open attitude was found for retired people and managers.

KYC Procedures by Education

The results show that no matter the education level, between 65 and 75% of people have an open attitude toward bank officers when they ask for information about bank transactions (making a bank deposit, withdrawing cash from the account, etc.).

We found that as the level of education increases up to getting doctoral degrees, the tendency to refuse to offer the required details declines. Thus, people become more aware about the importance of these asked details as they become more educated. However, for postdoctoral studies, the percentage of those who refuse to offer details is somehow larger compared to other levels of education. A very high level of education is associated with restrictions in offering details. Thus, the ethical behavior is compromised.

As our survey previously validates, high levels of education such as postdoctoral studies tend to be associated with lower levels of tax compliance (regarding the behavior in paying taxes) and tax morale (regarding behavior in tolerating cheating on taxes).

Monica Violeta Achim is full professor and doctoral supervisor in the field of finance at the Faculty of Economics and Business Administration, Babeş-Bolyai University, Cluj-Napoca, Romania. With over 24 years of experience in academia, she has authored and coauthored over 150 scientific articles and 25 books. Her most recent reference work is the book *Economic and Financial Crime: Corruption, Shadow Economy and Money Laundering*, published by Springer. In 2020 she received an Award for Excellence in Scientific Research at Babeş-Bolyai University, Faculty of Economics and Business Administration, Cluj-Napoca, Romania, in recognition of the results obtained in her research activity. She heads a big grant titled "Intelligent analysis and prediction of the economic and financial crime in a cyber-dominated and interconnected business world," conducted over the period 2021–2023, financed by the Romanian Ministry of Education and Research, CNCS – UEFISCDI, project number PN-III-P4-ID-PCE-2020-2174 (www.fincrime.net).

Sorin Nicolae Borlea is a professor and doctoral supervisor in the field of finance at the University of Oradea and Vasile Goldiş University, and an associate scientific researcher at the European Research Institute of Babeş-Bolyai University, Cluj-Napoca. He has over 16 years of experience in the academic field and 30 years in the business environment. He has authored over 90 scientific articles and 20 books. His most recent reference work is the coauthored book *Economic and Financial Crime: Corruption, Shadow Economy and Money Laundering*, published by Springer. In parallel with the academic field, he works in the business environment as financial auditor, accounting expert, tax consultant, and financial analyst, being strongly anchored in economic and financial crime issues in the files managed by the Court of Cluj-Napoca. He is well known in the business environment as a perfectionist, being ranked in the top10 accounting experts in Cluj County (2017). He is a member of the project titled "Intelligent analysis and prediction of the economic and financial crime in a cyber-dominated and interconnected business world," conducted over the period 2021–2023, financed by the Romanian Ministry of Education and Research, CNCS – UEFISCDI, project number PN-III-P4-ID-PCE-2020-2174 (www.fincrime.net).

Mihai Gaicu holds a BSc and an MSc in Business Engineering from Solvay Brussels School and a specialized master's in Data Science, Big Data from the Free University of Brussels. He acquired experience over two years in the banking sector and the IT industry, focusing on financial crime and artificial intelligence. He is a subject-matter expert in anti-money laundering (AML) and is working as Global Solution Advisor at SAS Institute. His role consists of collaborating with R&D and delivery teams to deploy industry best practices for AML solutions and helping financial institutions around the world to fight fraud and to meet regulatory compliance.

Codruța Mare is a professor at the Department of Statistics-Forecasts-Mathematics and PhD coordinator in the field of cybernetics and statistics, Faculty of Economics and Business Administration, and the Scientific Director of the Interdisciplinary Centre for Data Science, Babeș-Bolyai University, Cluj-Napoca, Romania. She teaches several types of statistics and econometrics methods, from descriptive statistics to economic forecasting and spatial econometrics. She has expertise in consultancy and research projects conducted both for public institutions (The World Bank, European Commission, Romanian Ministry of Structural Funds, Cluj-Napoca City Hall, etc.) and for private companies, along with delivering training both in data analysis and in visualization, in Romania and abroad. Results of her research were published in books and articles in prestigious international journals. She is a member of the project titled "Intelligent analysis and prediction of the economic and financial crime in a cyber-dominated and interconnected business world," conducted over the period 2021–2023, financed by the Romanian Ministry of Education and Research, CNCS – UEFISCDI, project number PN-III-P4-ID-PCE-2020-2174 (www.fincrime.net).

Robert W. McGee is a business professor at Fayetteville State University, USA. He holds 23 academic degrees, including 13 doctorates from universities in the USA and 4 European countries. He has authored more than 60 books, including several novels, and more than 1000 articles, book chapters, conference papers, and working papers. Various studies have ranked him No. 1 in the world for both accounting ethics and business ethics scholarship. He is an attorney and certified public accountant (CPA) (retired) and has worked or lectured in more than 30 countries. He drafted the accounting law for Armenia and Bosnia and reviewed the accounting law for Mozambique. He was in charge of assisting the Finance Ministries of Armenia and Bosnia convert their countries to International Financial Reporting Standards. He is also a world champion in taekwondo, karate, kung fu, and tai chi (both Yang and Sun styles) and has won more than 900 gold medals.

Gabriela-Mihaela Mureșan holds a PhD in Finance and works as lecturer at the Department of Finance, Faculty of Economics and Business Administration, Babeș-Bolyai University. She has authored more than 20 research papers, 2 international books, and 2 national books, and attended several international conferences. Her research interests are broadly focused in the field of insurance, financial analysis, and economic psychology. She is especially interested in human behavior, manipulation, money addiction, culture, happiness, ethics, corruption, fraud, corporate performance, bankruptcy, and creative accounting. She is a member of the project titled "Intelligent analysis and prediction of the economic and financial crime in a cyber-dominated and interconnected business world," conducted over the period 2021–2023, financed by the Romanian Ministry of Education and Research, CNCS – UEFISCDI, project number PN-III-P4-ID-PCE-2020-2174 (www.fincrime.net).

Mircea Constantin Șcheau is a PhD in Public Order and National Security with a topic of interest for economic and security fields, "Cybercrime on financial transfers," who received the "Victor

Slavescu Prize" awarded by the Romanian Academy. Author/co-author of three volumes, more than forty scientific articles on management, law enforcement, critical infrastructure, information technology, defense, lecturer at numerous international conferences and member, inter alia, of the "Policies and strategies in the European Union's single market" research group of the European Research Institute of Babeş-Bolyai University, Cluj-Napoca. He is a member of the project titled "Intelligent analysis and prediction of the economic and financial crime in a cyber-dominated and interconnected business world," conducted over the period 2021–2023, financed from the Romanian Ministry of Education and Research, CNCS - UEFISCDI, project number PN-III-P4-ID-PCE-2020-2174 (www.fincrime.net).

Viorela-Ligia Văidean is an associate professor in the field of finance at the Faculty of Economics and Business Administration, Babeş-Bolyai University, Cluj-Napoca. She holds a bachelor's degree in Finance and Banking from Babeş-Bolyai University (BBU), Cluj-Napoca, Romania in 2006, further graduating from a master's program in Corporate Finance and Insurances and another degree in Project Management and Evaluation. She successfully followed a full-time PhD program, obtaining her PhD in Finance, in 2010. In 2015 she graduated from a postdoctoral study program. She has worked as a teaching assistant and then a lecturer at the Finance Department within BBU, Cluj-Napoca. She has also worked as an expert for different EU-financed projects and grants. She has written more than 40 research papers and attended several international conferences. She has been the author or coauthor of ten books and international book chapters. Her research interests cover the areas of health economics, corporate finance, financial management, organized crime, and fiscal policies. She is a member of the project titled "Intelligent analysis and prediction of the economic and financial crime in a cyber-dominated and interconnected business world," conducted over the period 2021–2023, financed by the Romanian Ministry of Education and Research, CNCS – UEFISCDI, project number PN-III-P4-ID-PCE-2020-2174 (www.fincrime.net).

Chapter 7
Conclusions and Recommendations

Monica Violeta Achim, Sorin Nicolae Borlea, Mihai Gaicu, Robert W. McGee, Gabriela-Mihaela Mureşan, and Viorela-Ligia Văidean

Abstract This chapter discusses the conclusions and recommendations resulting from the study. A series of infographs is included to summarize the results of the study using a format that makes it easy for the reader to understand.

Keywords Financial crime · Romania · Survey results · Corruption · Tax compliance · Money laundering

7.1 General Conclusions

The aim of this study was to find the financial crime community pulse in Romania. For this purpose, a survey based on a questionnaire was conducted among 1856 respondents during May 27–June 6, 2022, time period.

The first objective of our study consisted in finding the main patterns that characterize the financial crime pulse in the Romanian community related to the level of tax compliance, attitude of citizens toward accepting cheating on taxes (tax morale), the perception of corruption levels in Romanian public institutions, the level of

M. V. Achim (✉) · G.-M. Mureşan · V.-L. Văidean
Faculty of Economics and Business Administration, Babeş-Bolyai University, Cluj-Napoca, Romania
e-mail: monica.achim@econ.ubbcluj.ro

S. N. Borlea
Faculty of Economics, University of Oradea, Oradea, Romania

Faculty of Economics, Computer Science and Engineering, "Vasile Goldiş" Western University of Arad, Arad, Romania

European Research Institute, Babeş-Bolyai University, Cluj-Napoca, Romania

M. Gaicu
SAS Institute, Brussels, Belgium

R. W. McGee
Fayetteville State University, Fayetteville, NC, USA

M. V. Achim, R. W. McGee (eds.), *Financial Crime in Romania*, SpringerBriefs in Finance, https://doi.org/10.1007/978-3-031-27883-9_7

skills possessed by citizens to detect the risk of money laundering (AML skills), and the attitude toward providing information to bank officers (KYC procedures attitude).

We find that the great majority (64%) of those interviewed had a good or very good level of tax compliance, meaning that they pay their taxes long before the deadline (for discount benefits or not). Regarding tax morale, we found that a majority of 74.3% of Romanian respondents had an active attitude *toward accepting cheating on taxes* (they usually or always receive the receipt and take it); about 13% of our respondents had a proactive attitude (they do not receive but ask for their receipt) while another 13% of our respondents had a passive attitude (if they receive or do not receive their receipt, it doesn't matter). When it comes to corruption, a majority of 66% of our surveyed Romanian citizens declared that they perceive the level of corruption in Romania as being high or very high. Additionally, our results show that a majority of 70% of respondents have low or very low skills to detect the risk of money laundering in business; about 25% had medium skills, while only about 5% had high or very high skills to detect suspicious transactions. Regarding the *attitude toward providng information to bank officers (KYC attitude),* a majority of about 68% had a good attitude toward being asked for personal information from bank officers while about 32% had a medium or bad attitude (refuse or hardly provide the required information to the bank officers).

The second objective of the study was to investigate how the demographic aspects considered in the survey (age, gender, region of living, professional status, and education) are associated with the considered financial crime community pulse (financial crime perception variables) represented by the level of tax compliance, tax morale expressed as the attitude of citizens toward accepting cheating on taxes, the perception of corruption levels in Romanian public institutions, the level of skills possessed by citizens in order to detect the risk of money laundering (AML skills), and the attitude toward being asked for information by bank officers (attitude toward KYC procedures).

Most of the time, demographic variables were a significant factor that affected the perception of financial crime. Age had the most significant effect on perception.

7.1.1 Age and Financial Crime Community Pulse

With respect to *age,* we found that in all cases, all types of financial crime perception variables were significantly dependent on the age of the respondent. Consequently, we may conclude that there are significant differences of financial crime perception among various age groups.

Regarding the level of tax compliance by age, we found an inverted U shape between these two variables. As age increases up to the age of 46–55, taxpayers tended to have a bad attitude toward tax duties (they pay taxes very close to the deadline or after the deadline). After this age, taxpayers become more and more aware about the payment of taxes on time and about the positive role of taxes for the economy. The best attitude toward paying taxes is found in the over 65 age group, who are the most conscientious taxpayers among all age groups.

Age was also found to be related to tax morale (ethical attitude toward cheating on taxes). Our results show that older people tend to be more ethical regarding cheating on taxes. Indeed, the most passive (unethical) attitude was found in the 26–35 age group. Over the age of 36, the higher the age, the higher the ethical attitude toward cheating on taxes. The most ethical attitude toward cheating on taxes was found for the oldest group of respondents (over 65).

The same relationship was found between age and the perception of corruption. Our findings show that the level of corruption perception is highest for the 26–35 age group and after 36 years old. Furthermore, the perception declines as the age of respondents increases, and finally, for people over 65, the level of perceived corruption was at the lowest level.

Regarding the relationship between age and AML skills, people between 26 and 35 had the lowest AML skills, while those over 36 tended to accumulate higher and higher knowledge regarding the level of AML skills, reaching the maximum level after the age of 65. The highest AML skills were in the youngest group (16–25).

The relationship between age and KYC attitude toward bank officers requesting information (making a bank deposit, withdrawing cash from the account, etc.) was a U-shape curve. As age increases, the attitude toward KYC becomes more and more open until one reaches the 56–65 age group. Those over age 65 tend to be quite restrained in providing the required information.

7.1.2 Gender and Financial Crime Community Pulse

Gender is significantly associated with tax compliance, corruption perception regarding public institutions in Romania, and the attitude toward banks asking for personal information. However, the contingency coefficients have very small values (0.07, 0.071, and 0.066). This shows that attitudinal and behavioral differences are much smaller between genders than between age groups. Males and females have similar characteristics for tax morale (attitudes toward cheating taxes) and capacity/skills to detect the money laundering risk.

Regarding tax compliance, in regard to gender, a small majority of 63% females pay taxes long before the deadline, compared to a percentage of 67% for males. In addition, a higher percentage of females (34%) pay taxes very close to the deadline compared with a lower percentage of 28% for males. Despite these differences, females are more inclined than males to respect the payment deadline, while a higher percentage of females of 97% pay taxes up to the deadline compare to a percentage of 95% of males. Overall, females have a slightly better attitude toward paying tax duties than males.

In addition, we find that males have a quite higher unethical attitude toward cheating on taxes than females, and are also more inclined to accept cheating on taxes compared to females. However, this difference in result was not statistically significant.

When we refer to the perception of corruption by gender, we find that among the two groups, females perceive corruption in Romanian institutions at a quite higher level than males, and this result is statistically significant at the 10% level.

When we analyze AML skills by age, we find a general equilibrium between AML skills scores for the two groups of males and females. However, for females, the level of AML skills is a little bit higher (the score of AML skills is 2.09 for females compared to a score of 1.99 for males).

In addition, females are more open to offer details to bank officers upon request and have a better attitude toward KYC procedures than males, while males are more restrictive.

7.1.3 The Romanian Regions and the Financial Crime Community Pulse

Regarding tax compliance, we find that the first three regions with the best attitude toward paying taxes are Oltenia, Crisana, and Bucovina, while the worst attitude toward paying taxes was found in the north: in Maramures and Moldova, respectively. The most ethical respondents in terms of attitude toward cheating on taxes were found in Maramures, followed by Muntenia, Oltenia, and Bucovina. The most unethical regions in terms of accepting cheating on taxes were Crisana, followed by Moldova and Banat. We may observe the region of Oltenia with the best practices both in the fields of tax compliance and tax morale, while Moldova was listed two times as the least ethical Romanian region.

Regarding the perception of corruption by regions, our results show that in Dobrogea, Muntenia, and Oltenia the highest levels of perceived corruption were found, while in Banat, Bucovina, and Transylvania the lowest levels of perceived corruption were assessed.

Again, Oltenia was in first place when we talk about AML skills by regions, followed by Banat and Moldova, while the lowest AML skills were found in Muntenia, Dobrogea, and Crişana.

Regarding KYC procedures by region, the worst attitudes were found in Maramures, Dobrogea, Moldova, and Bucovina. The most open attitudes toward bank officers were found in Crisana and Muntenia and Oltenia. All in all, Oltenia was seen as a model regarding financial crime attitude while at the opposite end were Moldova and Dobrogea.

7.1.4 Professional Status and the Financial Crime Community Pulse

Professional status also had significant differences, except for the case of corruption perception. This is quite an interesting result. While age, gender, and education were significant demographic variables, professional status was not. This means that all professional status groups had similar characteristics when corruption perception was assessed, employees registering the most, followed by managers and students. Once again, the highest impact was upon the issue of detecting money laundering situations, followed by tax morale.

Regarding tax compliance by professional status, we found that students, followed by unemployed people, had the best attitude toward paying taxes. Managers were the least inclined to pay taxes in advance; actually, they pay taxes very close to the deadline, covering the highest percentage of 42% among all professional categories.

When we talk about tax morale, we found that employees have the lowest level of ethical attitudes regarding accepting cheating on taxes, followed by unemployed people. At the opposite pole, with the highest ethical attitude in relation with accepting cheating on taxes, are retired people and students.

Regarding corruption, all the professional status groups greatly appreciate that the level of corruption in Romania is high or very high. All in all, the highest level of corruption was perceived by unemployed while the lowest level was perceived by retired people.

In addition, we found that in all groups of professional statuses the majority of respondents declared that they had low or very low AML skills. However, generally, the highest AML skills were possessed by students, followed by employees, while the lowest AML skills were found in managers and retired people.

Regarding the analysis of the relationship between KYC procedures related to professional status, the results show that generally, for all the professional status groups (64–75%), people had an open attitude toward bank officers when they ask for bank transactions information (making a bank deposit, withdrawing cash from the account, etc.). However, among these groups, students, followed by unemployed people, had the worst attitude, while retired people and managers were the most tolerant.

7.1.5 Education and the financial crime community pulse

Education was also a significant demographic variable, except for tax morale.

Regarding tax compliance by education level, we found that as people become more educated, they become more aware to pay taxes in time, trying to maximize some benefits in the form of discounts. However, the percentage of those who fail to meet deadlines increases as the level of education increases, reaching the maximum level of 7% for people with postdoctoral studies.

As the level of education increases at bachelor degree and master's studies, the level of compliance declines. Further, getting a doctoral degree means getting more complex knowledge that permits individuals to understand the role of regulations and to better comply with them. Thus, at this level of education, the degree of passive attitude declines. However, postdoctoral studies are correlated with the highest level of noncompliance.

Referring to the analysis of the relationship between tax morale and education, no significant relationship is found. Our survey provides evidence that master's and doctoral studies assure the proper level of knowledge to understand the role of regulations and better comply with them. Thus, at this level of education, the degree of passive attitudes declines to a minimum and people become aware of the way the tax system functions. However, the highest level of education, postdoctoral studies, is correlated to the highest level of unethical attitudes. We may explain this by the fact that a better education ensures a better understanding of the functioning mechanisms of the economic, financial, and information flows, and in this way, these highly educated people easily find ways to circumvent the system and break the law.

When we analyze the perception of corruption related to education, we find that the highest percentages of respondents that consider corruption as being high or very high are found among the less educated people. The results show that higher levels of education are correlated with lower levels of perceived corruption while lower levels of education are correlated with higher levels of perceived corruption. Therefore, the highest level of perceived corruption is found at the lowest level of education (high school or less) while the lowest level of corruption is perceived by highly educated people (with doctoral or postdoctoral studies).

Regarding AML skills by education, in all groups classified according to their education level, the majority of respondents declare that they have low or very low AML skills. In addition, we find that the perceptions of having a certain level of AML skills decrease as the levels of education increase. Thus, as we learn more, we may have the perception of knowing less. The less educated people may have the perception that they know all by not actually knowing anything at all.

Moving forward to analyzing the relationship between the attitude toward KYC procedures and education, the results show that regardless of the education level, between 65% and 75% of people have an open attitude toward bank officers when they ask information (making a bank deposit, withdrawing cash from the account, etc.). The relationship between education and KYC procedures looks like a U-shape curve with the minimum level reached for doctoral studies, meaning the best attitude. In other words, as the level of education increases until getting a doctoral degree, the tendency to refuse to offer the asked details declines; thus, people become more aware about the importance of these required details as they become more educated. However, the postdoctoral level of education is associated with restrictions in offering these details. Thus, ethical behavior is compromised.

Our results are important for Romanian policy makers in order to acknowledge the level at which Romanian citizens perceive the best practices in governance and are aware about the financial crime tendency, in order for them to adopt the best policies to reduce the level of financial crime in Romania.

The limits of our study are the result of the methodology we apply. Although our study is extremely complex, in the future we intend to apply cluster analysis techniques. We might also try to extend our study to include the central and eastern European countries, if not toward a wider sample of nations.

As recommendations, our study shows that granting discounts for the taxpayers who pay their taxes long before the deadline works: 36% of the taxpayers pay their taxes long before the deadline to benefit from discounts, compared to 28% of those who pay their taxes long before the deadline regardless of the discounts. Thus, the discount schemes work and may be further improved by policy makers. In addition, younger people are less moral regarding accepting cheating on taxes than older people. The results for possessing AML skills to detect suspicious transactions show that a 70% majority have low or very low such skills. This finding shows that there is a large gap that needs to be closed. Public governance should support education institutions and companies specialized in providing financial education and AML training, for providing specialized courses. Better educated people are always the key to success. A majority of about 66% from our interviewed citizens declare that they perceive the level of corruption in Romania as being high or very high. Thus, reducing the bureaucracy and the nepotism inside public institutions could be helpful for the health of our economy. Ultimately, the difference between regions regarding the level of tax compliance, tax morale, perception of corruption, AML skills, and attitude toward KYC procedures should be considered by the local policy makers in order to adopt specific policies AND courses of action. Romania can adopt good practices that are already being used in other countries. Increased economic prosperity, a more efficient fiscal system, and moral people would only improve Romania's situation.

7.2 Infograph Conclusions

The present subchapter presents brief infographs, which summarize the contents of this book.

7.2.1 Tax Compliance

The structure of respondents on tax compliance

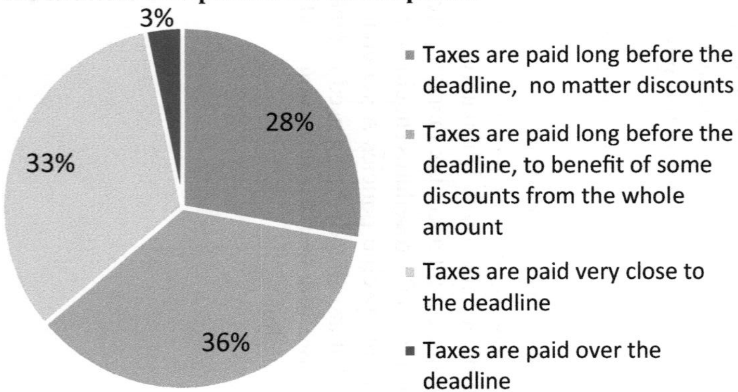

(Regarding paying your tax duties, which one of the following behavior is common for you?)

A majority of 64% of the citizens interviewed declare that they have a good or very good level of tax compliance, that is, they declare that they pay taxes well before the deadline (to obtain discounts or not). The remaining 36% of respondents declare that they pay their taxes very close to the deadline or after the deadline

<table>
<tr>
<td>Tax compliance score by age
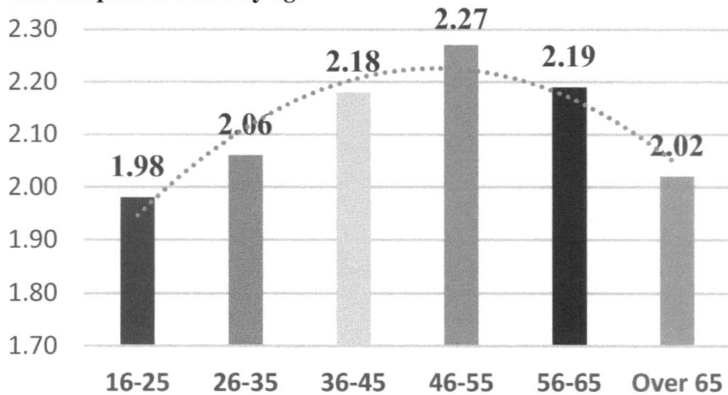

Note: Tax compliance scores range from 1 – the best attitude to 4 – the worst attitude toward paying tax duties.</td>
<td>As the age of our respondents increases up to the age of 55, taxpayers tend to have a more adverse attitude toward the payment of their taxes and fees (they pay their taxes very close to or even after the deadline).
After the age of 55, taxpayers become more aware of the need to pay their taxes and the beneficial role of taxes for the health of our economy.
Taxpayers over the age of 65 have the best attitude toward paying their taxes, being the most compliant taxpayers of all age groups.</td>
</tr>
<tr>
<td>Tax compliance score by gender
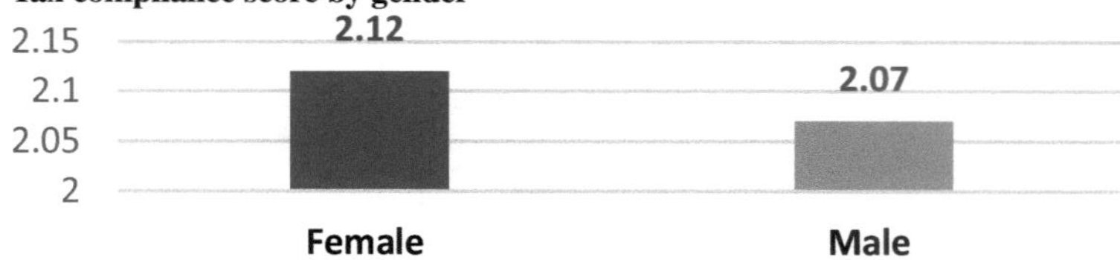

Note: Tax compliance scores range from 1 – the best attitude to 4 – the worst attitude toward paying tax duties.</td>
<td>Overall, women have a more unfavorable attitude toward paying taxes and fees than men. Practically, the percentage of women who pay their taxes ahead of the deadline is 63%, compared to a higher percentage of 67% for men.</td>
</tr>
</table>

Tax compliance score by Romanian regions

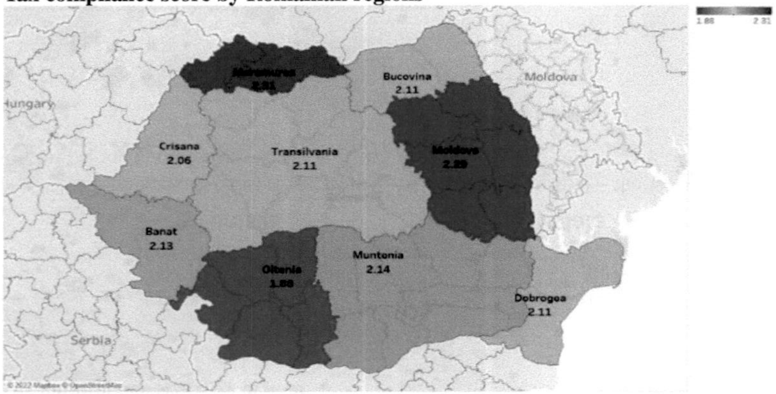

Note: Tax compliance scores range from 1 – the best attitude to 4 – the worst attitude toward paying tax duties.

From a regional point of view, the most tax compliant attitude is that of citizens from Oltenia, followed by Crişana, and the most reluctant attitude is that of taxpayers from Maramureş and Moldova.

7.2.2 *Tax Morale*

The structure of respondents on tax morale 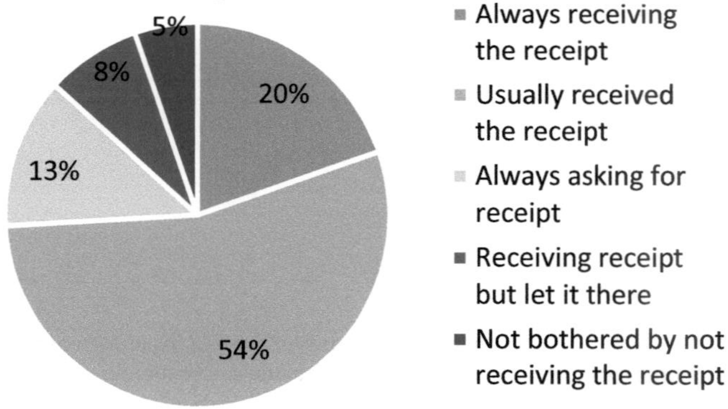 (When you receive goods and services from the shops, restaurants, hotels, salons, etc., please choose one of more of the following that fit better for you.)	**A majority of 74% of our respondents have an active attitude** toward accepting cheating taxes behaviors (they state that they "usually" or "always" receive their receipts for purchases made in shops, restaurants, etc.). About 13% of our respondents have a proactive attitude (they ask for their receipts). A similar percentage of about 13% of respondents have a passive attitude (they are not interested in whether they receive their receipts or not).

Tax morale score, by age

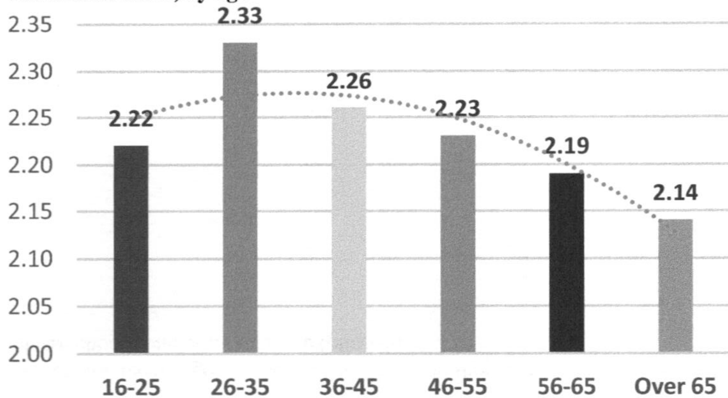

Note: Tax morale scores range from 1-the most active (ethical) attitude to 5-the most passive (unethical) attitude toward cheating on taxes.

As respondents get older, there is an **increasingly active (ethical) attitude toward tax evasion.**
The most ethical attitude toward cheating on taxes is held by our eldest respondents.

<table>
<tr>
<td>Tax morale score, by Romanian region
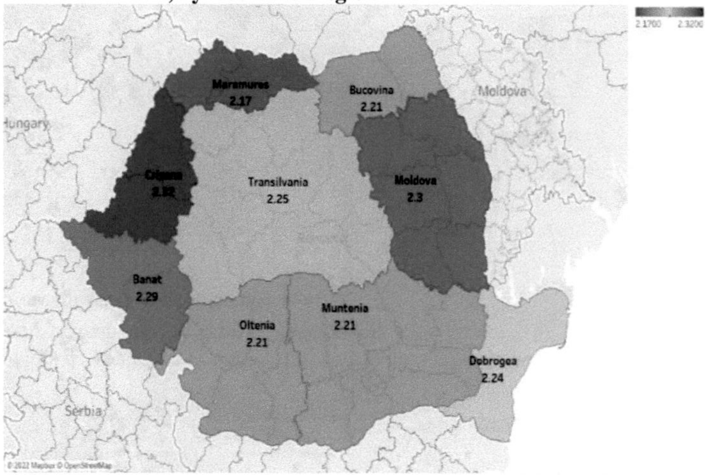

Note: Tax morale scores range from 1-the most active (ethical) attitude to 5-the most passive (unethical) attitude toward cheating on taxes.</td>
<td>From the regional analysis, the most ethical respondents from the point of view of their attitude toward cheating taxes are found in Maramureș, followed by Muntenia, Oltenia, and Bucovina.
On the other hand, the least ethical regions in terms of accepting tax evasion are Crișana, followed by Moldova and Banat.</td>
</tr>
</table>

7.2.3 *Corruption Perception Level*

The structure of respondents on corruption perception 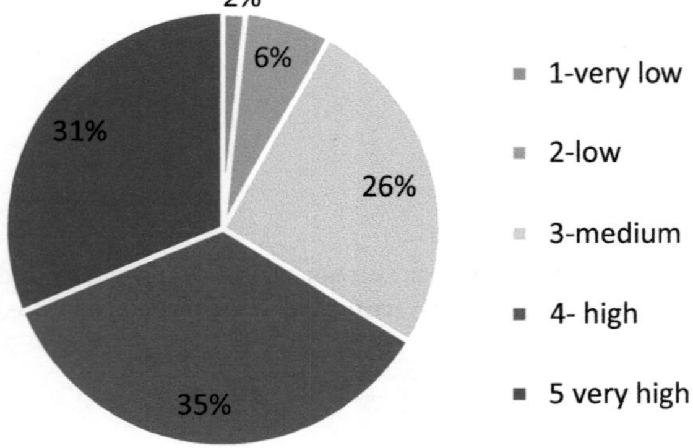 (How do you perceive the level of corruption in the Romanian public institutions, on a scale between 1 point-very low to 5 points-very high?).	**Two thirds** of our interviewed citizens state that they perceive the level of Romanian corruption to be **high or very high.**
Perception of corruption by age 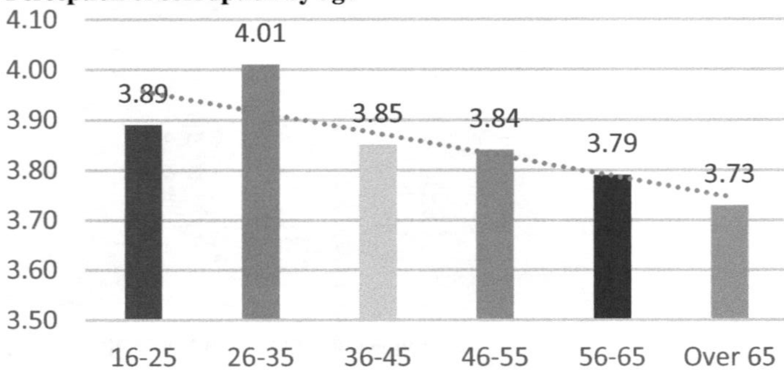 Note: Perception of corruption scores range from 1 – the lowest level of corruption to 5 – the highest level of corruption.	People aged 26–35 perceive corruption at the highest level; beyond this age group, the perception of Romanian corruption is attenuated, so that those above the age of 65 perceive Romanian corruption to be at its lowest level.

Perception of corruption by gender 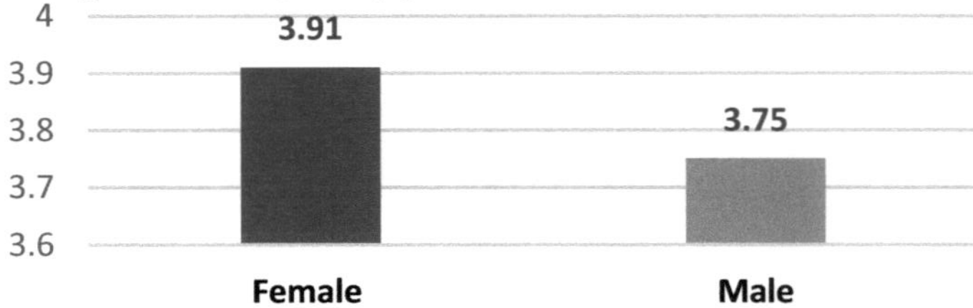 Note: Perception of corruption scores range from 1 – the lowest level of corruption to 5 – the highest level of corruption.	On average, women perceive corruption to be at a slightly higher level than men.
Perception of corruption by Romanian regions 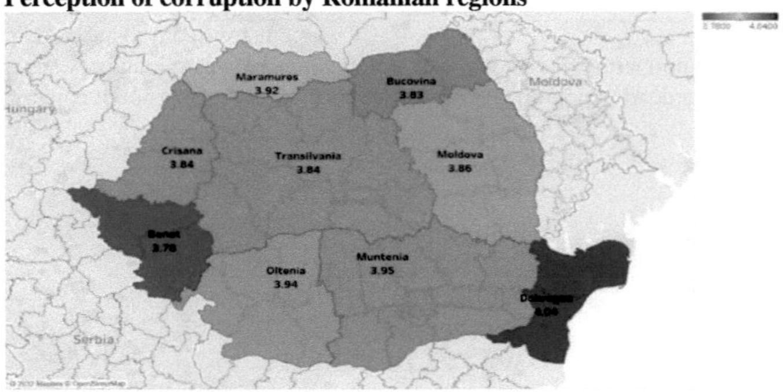 Note: Perception of corruption scores range from 1 – the lowest level of corruption to 5 – the highest level of corruption.	There also are perception differences between the regions of Romania that respondents come from. Thus, the highest level of assessed corruption is identified in Dobrogea, Muntenia, Oltenia, and Maramureş while in Banat, Bucovina, Transylvania, and Crişana the lowest levels of perceived corruption are assessed.

7.2.4 *Abilities to Detect the Risk of Money Laundering (AML Skills)*

<table>
<tr>
<td>The structure of respondents on AML skills
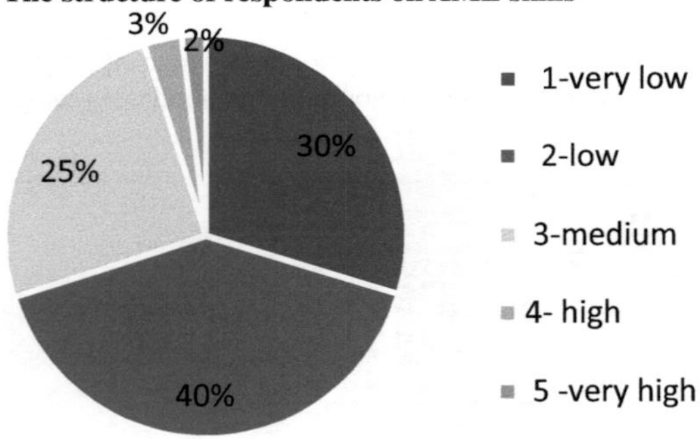
(Related to the risk of money laundering, do you think that people have suitable acknowledgments to be able to recognize a suspicious transaction in business? Please choose one of the following:)</td>
<td>A majority of 70% of our respondents have low or very low skills to detect the risk of money laundering through businesses; 25% of our respondents declare to have average skills; only 5% of our respondents have high or very high abilities to detect suspicious transactions.</td>
</tr>
<tr>
<td>Score AML skills, by age
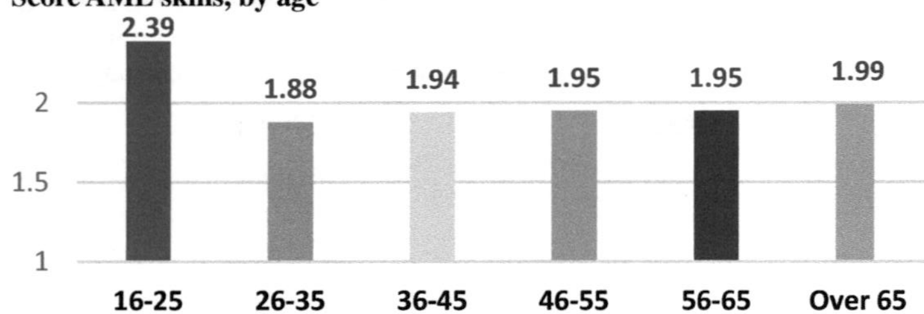
Note: AML skills scores range from 1 – very low skills (colored in red) to 5 – very high skills (colored in green).</td>
<td>Starting with the age of 26, we find that as the age increases, so does the level of AML skills of people.</td>
</tr>
</table>

Score AML skills, by gender  Note: AML skills scores range from 1 – very low skills (colored in red) to 5 – very high skills (colored in green).	Women seem to have a **slightly higher level of AML skills than men.**
Score AML skills, by Romanian region 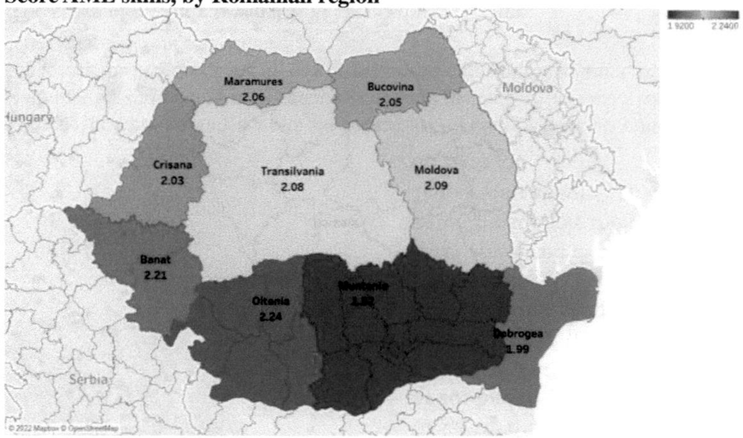 Note: AML skills scores range from 1 – very low skills (colored in red) to 5 – very high skills (colored in green).	From a regional point of view, the highest AML skills are held by respondents from Oltenia, Banat, and Moldova. The lowest AML skills are identified as belonging to the citizens of Muntenia, Dobrogea, and Maramureș.

7.2.5 *Atitude Toward "Know Your Clients" Procedures*

<table>
<tr>
<td>

The structure of respondents on attitude toward KYC procedures

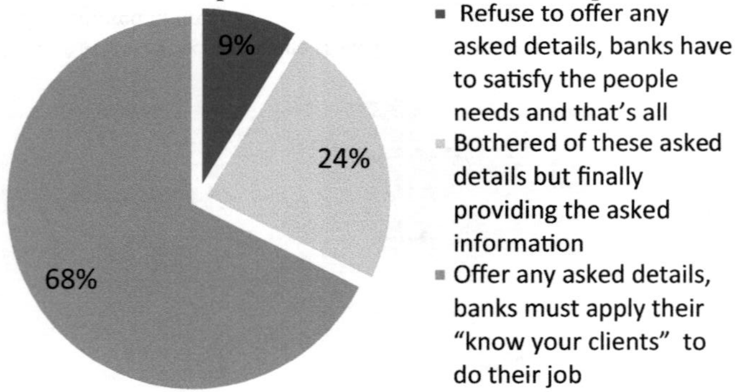

(Whenever banking transactions are performed (opening a bank account, making a deposit, withdrawing cash from one's account, etc.) and the bank officer asks for a set of details regarding the origins of the money or the destinations of the amount, respondents generally have very different reactions.

</td>
<td>

Our study shows that **a majority of 68% of people have a positive attitude** toward being requested to fill in some information from bank officials, while the remaining 32% have a negative attitude (refuse or hardly provide the information requested by the bank officers).

</td>
</tr>
<tr>
<td>

The score of attitude toward KYC procedures, by age

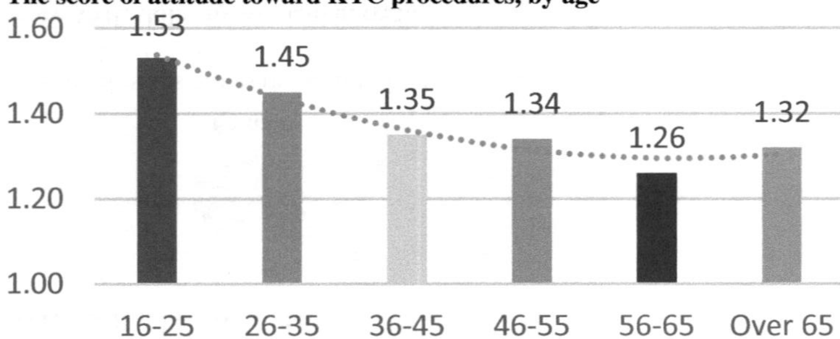

Note: KYC attitude scores range from 1 – the best attitude to 3 – the worst attitude.

</td>
<td>

The younger respondents tend to have a more restrictive attitude toward providing the requested details, compared to the older groups.

</td>
</tr>
</table>

The score of attitude toward KYC procedures, by gender 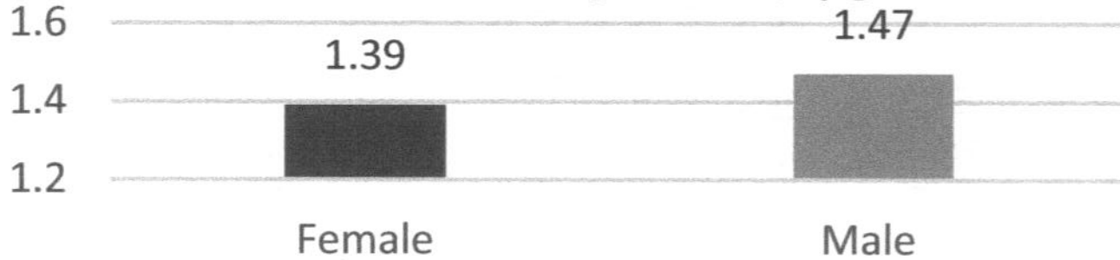 Note: KYC attitude scores range from 1 – the best attitude to 3 – the worst attitude.	**On average, women are more open** toward offering details to bank officials and have a more open attitude compared to men toward the Know Your Clients (KYC) procedures adopted by banks.
The score of attitude toward KYC procedures, by region 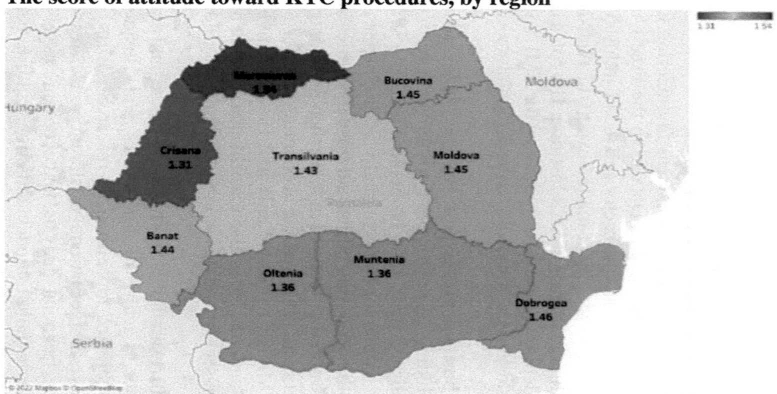 Note: KYC attitude scores range from 1 – the best attitude to 3 – the worst attitude.	The regional analysis highlights the fact that the most restrictive people in providing information to the banks are respondents from Maramures, Dobrogea, Moldova, and Bucovina while the most open respondents are those in Crişana, Muntenia, and Oltenia.

Monica Violeta Achim is full professor and doctoral supervisor in the field of Finance at the Faculty of Economics and Business Administration, Babeş-Bolyai University, Cluj-Napoca, Romania. With over 24 years of experience in academia, she has published, as author and co-author, over 150 scientific articles and 25 books. Her most recent reference work is the book *Economic and Financial Crime. Corruption, Shadow Economy and Money Laundering*, published by Springer. In 2020 she earned an Award for Excellence in Scientific Research at Babeş-Bolyai University, Faculty of Economics and Business Administration, Cluj-Napoca, Romania, in recognition of the results obtained in her research activity. She heads a big grant titled "Intelligent analysis and prediction of economic and financial crime in a cyber-dominated and interconnected business world," conducted over the period 2021-2023, financed from the Romanian Ministry of Education and Research, CNCS-UEFISCDI, project number PN-III-P4-ID-PCE-2020-2174 (www.fincrime.net).

Sorin Nicolae Borlea is professor and doctoral supervisor in the field of Finance at the University of Oradea and "Vasile Goldiş" Western University, and associate scientific researcher at the European Research Institute of Babeş-Bolyai University Cluj-Napoca. He has over 16 years of experience in the academic field and 30 years in the business environment. He has published over 90 scientific articles and 20 books. His most recent reference work is the co-authored book *Economic and Financial Crime: Corruption, Shadow Economy and Money Laundering*, published by Springer. In parallel with the academic field, he works in the business environment as financial auditor, accounting expert, tax consultant, and financial analyst, being strongly anchored in economic and financial crime issues in the files managed by the Court of Cluj-Napoca. He is well known in the business environment as a perfectionist, being ranked in the top 10 accounting experts in Cluj County (2017). He is a member of the project titled "Intelligent analysis and prediction of the economic and financial crime in a cyber-dominated and interconnected business world," conducted over the period 2021-2023, financed from the Romanian Ministry of Education and Research, CNCS-UEFISCDI, project number PN-III-P4-ID-PCE-2020-2174 (www.fincrime.net).

Mihai Gaicu holds a BSc and a MSc in Business Engineering from Solvay Brussels School and a specialized Master in Data Science, Big Data from the Free University of Brussels. He acquired experience over 2 years in the Banking sector and the IT industry, focusing on Financial Crime and Artificial Intelligence. He is a subject-matter expert in Anti-Money Laundering and currently working as a global solution advisor at SAS Institute. His role consists of collaborating with R&D and delivery teams to deploy industry best practices for AML solutions and helping financial institutions around the world to fight fraud and to meet regulatory compliance

Robert W. McGee is business professor at Fayetteville State University, USA. He has earned 23 academic degrees, including 13 doctorates from universities in the United States and 4 European countries. He has published more than 60 books, including several novels, and more than 1000 articles, book chapters, conference papers, and working papers. Various studies have ranked him #1 in the world for both accounting ethics and business ethics scholarship. He is an attorney and CPA (retired) and has worked or lectured in more than 30 countries. He drafted the accounting law for Armenia and Bosnia and reviewed the accounting law for Mozambique. He was in charge of assisting the Finance Ministries of Armenia and Bosnia convert their countries to International Financial Reporting Standards. He is also a world champion in taekwondo, karate, kung fu, and tai chi (both Yang and Sun styles) and has won more than 900 gold medals.

Gabriela-Mihaela Mureşan holds a PhD in Finance and currently works as lecturer at the Department of Finance, Faculty of Economics and Business Administration Babeş-Bolyai University. She has published more than 20 research papers, 2 international books, 2 national books, and attended several international conferences. Her research interests are broadly focused in the field of insurance, financial analysis, and economic psychology. She is especially interested in human behavior, manipulation, money addiction, culture, happiness, ethics, corruption, fraud, corporate performance, bankruptcy, and creative accounting. She is member of the project titled "Intelligent analysis and prediction of the economic and financial crime in a cyber-dominated and interconnected business world," conducted over the period 2021-2023, financed from the Romanian Ministry of Education and Research, CNCS-UEFISCDI, project number PN-III-P4-ID-PCE-2020-2174 (www.fincrime.net).

Viorela-Ligia Văidean is associate professor in the field of Finance at the Faculty of Economic Sciences and Business Administration, Babeş-Bolyai University, Cluj-Napoca. She obtained a Bachelor degree in Finance and Banking from Babeş-Bolyai University (BBU) Cluj-Napoca, Romania, in 2006, further graduating from a Master program in Corporate Finance and Insurances and another degree in Project Management and Evaluation. She successfully followed a full-time PhD program, obtaining her PhD in the Finance field, in 2010. In 2015 she graduated from a post-doctoral study program. She has worked as teaching assistant and then lecturer for the Finance Department within BBU Cluj-Napoca. She has also worked as an expert for different EU-financed projects and grants. She has published more than 40 research papers and attended several international conferences. She has been the author or co-author of 10 books and international book chapters. Her research interests cover the areas of Health Economics, Corporate Finance, Financial Management, Organized Crime, and Fiscal Policies. She is member of the project titled "Intelligent analysis and prediction of the economic and financial crime in a cyber-dominated and interconnected business world," conducted over the period 2021-2023, financed from the Romanian Ministry of Education and Research, CNCS-UEFISCDI, project number PN-III-P4-ID-PCE-2020-2174 (www.fincrime.net).

Appendix

Questionnaire

The Romanian FinCrime Community Pulse

Thank you for being part of the 2022 FinCrime community pulse. By answering the following ten questions, you will be helping the community better understand current sentiment, and plan future educational events. In return for your time, we will share with you our findings which will be published at the end of June, and a complimentary webinar on 7th July.

1. Let's start with how you feel about taxes. Regarding paying your tax duties, which one of the following behaviours is common for you and the people around you:
   (a) 1-Taxes are paid long before the deadline, regardless of the discounts
   (b) 2-Taxes are paid long before the deadline, to benefit from discounts from the entire amount
   (c) 3-Taxes are paid very close to the deadline
   (d) 4-Taxes are paid over the deadline.
2. When you buy goods and services from the shops, restaurants, hotels, salons etc., please choose one or more of the following that better fit you:
   (a) 1-Always receiving the receipt
   (b) 2-Usually receiving the receipt
   (c) 3-Always asking for the receipt
   (d) 4-Receiving the receipt but letting it there
   (e) 5-Not bothered by not receiving the receipt.
3. How do you perceive the level of corruption in Romanian public institutions, on a scale from 1 (very low) to 5 (very high)? Please choose one of the following:

M. V. Achim, R. W. McGee (eds.), *Financial Crime in Romania*, SpringerBriefs in Finance, https://doi.org/10.1007/978-3-031-27883-9

   (a) 1-Very low level of corruption
   (b) 2-Low level of corruption
   (c) 3-Medium level of corruption
   (d) 4-High level of corruption
   (e) 5-Very high level of corruption.

4. Regarding the risk of money laundering, do you think that people have suitable knowledge to be able to recognize a suspicious transaction in a business? Please choose one of the following:
   (a) 1-Very low skills to detect the risk of money laundering in a business
   (b) 2-Low skills to detect the risk of money laundering in a business
   (c) 3-Medium skills to detect the risk of money laundering in a business
   (d) 4-High skills to detect the risk of money laundering in a business
   (e) 5-Very high skills to detect the risk of money laundering in a business.
5. When you or the people around you ask for bank transactions (making a bank deposit, withdrawing cash from the account etc.), and the bank officer asks you to complete some details regarding the provenience of the money, or where the amount goes, then you or the people around you generally have different reactions. To help us analyse your responses, please indicate which of the following categories represents you best.
   (a) 1-You offer any required details; banks must apply their "know your clients" principle to do their job.
   (b) 2-You are bothered by the asked details but finally you provide the required information.
   (c) 3-You refuse to offer any asked details; banks have to satisfy the people's needs and that's all.
6. How old are you? Choose one of the following categories:
   (a) Between 16 and 25 years old.
   (b) Between 26 and 35 years old.
   (c) Between 36 and 45 years old.
   (d) Between 46 and 55 years old.
   (e) Between 56 and 65 years old.
   (f) Over 65 years old.
7. Which is your gender? Choose one of the following:
   (a) Male.
   (b) Female.
   (c) Other.
8. In which region of Romania do you live? Choose one of the following:
   (a) Banat.
   (b) Bucovina.
   (c) Crisana.

   (d) Dobrogea.
   (e) Maramures.
   (f) Moldova.
   (g) Muntenia.
   (h) Oltenia.
   (i) Transylvania.

9. Which is your professional status? Choose one or more of the following:

   (a) Student.
   (b) Employed.
   (c) Manager.
   (d) Unemployed.
   (e) Retired.

10. Which is your last level of acquired degree? Choose one of the following:

   (a) High school graduate diploma or less.
   (b) Bachelor studies.
   (c) Master studies.
   (d) Doctoral studies.
   (e) Postdoctoral studies.

Thank you for making it to the end of this short survey. If you wish to receive the report and/or invitation to our webinar, please provide your email address below. Your answers will remain anonymous.

My email address ______________________.

References

Achim, M. V., & Borlea, N. S. (2020). *Economic and financial crime. Corruption, shadow economy, and money laundering*. Springer Nature Switzerland AG. https://doi.org/10.1007/978-3-030-51780-9

Achim, M. V., Borlea, S. N., Găban, L. V., & Cuceu, I. C. (2018a). Rethinking the shadow economy in terms of happiness. Evidence for the European Union member states. *Technological and Economic Development of Economy, 24*(1), 199–228. https://doi.org/10.3846/20294913.2016.1209250

Achim, M. V., Borlea, S. N., & Anghelina, A. M. (2018b). The impact of fiscal policies on corruption: A panel analysis. *South African Journal of Economic and Management Sciences, 21*(1), a1970. https://doi.org/10.4102/sajems.v21i1.1970

Achim, M. V., Borlea, N. S., Gaban, L. V., & Mihaila, A. A. (2019). The shadow economy and culture: Evidence in European countries. *Eastern European Economics*. https://doi.org/10.1080/00128775.2019.1614461

Achim, M. V., Borlea, N. S., Văidean, V. L., Rus, A. I. D., & Dobre, F. (2020). The impact of intelligence on economic and financial crime: A cross-country study. *Singapore Economic Review*. https://doi.org/10.1142/S0217590820500782

Achim, M. V., Văidean, V. L., & Borlea, N. S. (2021). Does technology matter for combating economic and financial crime? A panel data study. *Technological and Economic Development of Economy, 27*(1), 223–261. https://doi.org/10.3846/tede.2021.13977

Achim, M. V., Mirza, N., & Văidean, V. L. (2022). The asymmetric impact of tax burden structures on the shadow economy: A panel analysis of old and new European Union countries. *Applied Economics Letters*. https://doi.org/10.1080/13504851.2022.2094876

Akdemir, T., & Yeşilyurt, S. (2023). Corruption and bribery in ottoman tax management: An evaluation of the period 1876–1909. In R. W. McGee & S. Benk (Eds.), *The ethics of bribery: Theoretical and empirical studies*. Springer, forthcoming.

Alm, J., & Torgler, B. (2006). Culture differences and tax morale in the United States and Europe. *Journal of Economic Psychology, 27*(2), 224–246.

Aniţei, N. C., & Lazăr, R. E. (2016). *Evaziunea fiscală între legalitate şi infracţiune* (Fiscal evasion between legality and crime). Universul Juridic Publishing House.

Armstrong, M. B., & Robison, J. (1998). Ethics in taxation. In R. W. McGee (Ed.), *The ethics of tax evasion* (pp. 330–348). The Dumont Institute for Public Policy Research. Summarized in McGee, R. W. The ethics of tax evasion: Summaries of 21 studies (March 12, 2022). https://doi.org/10.2139/ssrn.4056290

Association of Certified Fraud Examiners. (2020). *Report to the nations. Global study on occupational fraud and abuse*.

M. V. Achim, R. W. McGee (eds.), *Financial Crime in Romania*, SpringerBriefs in Finance, https://doi.org/10.1007/978-3-031-27883-9

Association of Certified Fraud Examiners. (2022). *Occupational fraud 2022: A report to the nations*.

Batrancea, L., Gómez, F. J. B., Nichita, A., & Dragolea, L.-L. (2023a). Crunching numbers in the quest for spotting bribery acts: A cross-cultural rundown. In R. W. McGee & S. Benk (Eds.), *The ethics of bribery: Theoretical and empirical studies*. Springer, forthcoming.

Batrancea, L., Nichita, A., Batrancea, I., & Dragolea, L. (2023b). Are we taxed in the same manner while making a purchase? A brief inquiry into taxation, gender equity and evasion. In R. W. McGee & S. Benk (Eds.), *The ethics of bribery, volume 2: Country studies*. Springer, forthcoming.

Bîzoi, A.-C., & Bîzoi, C.-G. (2023). Primum non-nocere: How to fight the 'pandemic' of healthcare corruption. In R. W. McGee & S. Benk (Eds.), *The ethics of bribery: Theoretical and empirical studies*. Springer, forthcoming.

Block, W. (1998). The justification for taxation in the economics literature. In R. W. McGee (Ed.), *The ethics of tax evasion* (pp. 36–88). The Dumont Institute for Public Policy Research. Summarized in McGee, R. W. The ethics of tax evasion: Summaries of 21 studies (March 12, 2022). https://doi.org/10.2139/ssrn.4056290

Borlea, S. N., Achim, M. V., & Rus, A. I. D. (2019). Behavioral determinants of corruption. A cross-country survey. *Studia Universitatis Vasile Goldiş Arad, Seria Ştiinţe Economice, 29*(1), 21–39.

Bose, S. (2012). Hindu ethical considerations in relation to tax evasion. In R. W. McGee (Ed.), *The ethics of tax evasion: Perspectives in theory and practice* (pp. 135–147). Springer. Summarized in McGee (2023d).

Brosio, G., Cassone, A., & Ricciuti, R. (2002). Tax evasion across Italy: Rational noncompliance or inadequate civic concern? *Public Choice, 112*(3–4), 259–273.

Chelliah, R. J. (1971). Trends in taxation in developing countries. *Staff Papers, International Monetary Fund, 18*, 254–0331.

Cohn, G. (2012). The traditional Jewish view of paying taxes. In R. W. McGee (Ed.), *The ethics of tax evasion: Perspectives in theory and practice* (pp. 149–158). Springer. Summarized in McGee (2023d).

Crowe, M. T. (1944). *The moral obligation of paying just taxes* (The Catholic University of America studies in sacred theology no. 84).

Cubillas, E., & Suárez, N. (2018). Bank market power and lending during the global financial crisis. *Journal of International Money and Finance, 89*, 1–22.

Çule, M., & Fulton, M. (2009). Business culture and tax evasion: Why corruption and the unofficial economy can persist. *Journal of Economic Behavior & Organization, 72*(3), 811–822.

DeMoville, W. (1998). The ethics of tax evasion: A Baha'i perspective. In R. W. McGee (Ed.), *The ethics of tax evasion* (pp. 230–240). The Dumont Institute for Public Policy Research. Summarized in McGee, R. W. The ethics of tax evasion: Summaries of 21 studies (March 12, 2022). https://doi.org/10.2139/ssrn.4056290

Devereux, M. P., & De Mooij, R. A. (2009). *Alternative systems of business tax in Europe: An applied analysis of ACE and CBIT reforms*. Study for the European Commission, DG Taxation and Customs Union.

Dikmen, S., & Cicek, H. G. (2023). Fighting against corruption and bribery in public procurements during the Covid-19 pandemic. In R. W. McGee & S. Benk (Eds.), *The ethics of bribery: Theoretical and empirical studies*. Springer, forthcoming.

Diodato, V. P., & Gellatly, P. (2013). *Dictionary of bibliometrics*.

Dreher, A., & Schneider, F. (2010). Corruption and the shadow economy. An empirical analysis. *Public Choice, 144*, 215–238.

Dreher, A., & Siemers, L. H. R. (2009). The nexus between corruption and capital account restrictions. *Public Choice, 140*, 245–265.

Englebrecht, T. D., Folami, B., Lee, C., & Masselli, J. J. (1998). The impact of ethics on tax compliance behavior: A multidimensional analysis. In R. W. McGee (Ed.), *The ethics of tax evasion* (pp. 372–402). The Dumont Institute for Public Policy Research. Summarized in McGee (2022).

Enste, D. H. (2010). Regulation and shadow economy: Empirical evidence for 25 OECD-countries. *Constitutional Political Economy, 21*(3), 231–248.
European Commission. (2012).
European Commission. (2013, February). *Project 'ECOLEF' the economic and legal effectiveness of anti-money laundering and combating terrorist financing policy*. Project funded by the European Commission DG home affairs JLS/2009/ISEC/AG/087.
European Payment Index (2014). Available at https://www.ansa.it/documents/1416338761618_2.pdf. Accesed on April 26th 2023.
Frey, B. S., & Stutzer, A. (2012). The use of happiness research for public policy. *Social Choice and Welfare, 38*(4), 659–674.
Gaspareniene, L., Remeikiene, R. R., & Navickas, V. (2016). The concept of digital shadow economy: Consumer's attitude. *Procedia Economics and Finance, 39*, 502–509.
Global Financial Integrity. (2020). *Trade-related illicit financial flows in 135 developing countries: 2008–2017*.
Global Initiative Against Transnational Organized Crime (2020, March). *Crime and contagion. The impact of a pandemic on organized crime*.
Gronbacher, G. M. A. (1998). Taxation: Catholic social thought and classical liberalism. In R. W. McGee (Ed.), *The ethics of tax evasion* (pp. 158–167). The Dumont Institute for Public Policy Research. Summarized in McGee, R. W. The ethics of tax evasion: Summaries of 21 studies (March 12, 2022). https://doi.org/10.2139/ssrn.4056290
Hackmageddon. (2020). Available at: https://www.hackmageddon.com/. Accessed 3 Mar 2022.
Halla, M. (2010). *The link between the intrinsic motivation to comply and compliance behavior: A critical appraisal of existing evidence* (IZA discussion paper).
Hassan, M., & Schneider, F. (2016). *Size and development of the shadow economies of 157 countries worldwide: Updated and new measures from 1999 to 2013*. Available at SSRN 2861026.
Head, K. (2003). *Gravity for beginner*. Mimeo, University of British Columbia.
Helliwell, J. F. (2000). *Language and trade, gravity modelling of trade flows and the role of language*. The Department of Canadian Heritage.
Jalili, A. R. (2012). The ethics of tax evasion: An Islamic perspective. In R. W. McGee (Ed.), *The ethics of tax evasion: Perspectives in theory and practice* (pp. 167–199). Springer. Summarized in McGee (2023d).
Johnson, S., Kaufmann, D., & Sleifer, A. (1997). The unofficial economy in transition. *Brooking Papers on Economic Activity, 1997*, 159–221.
Kelmson, B., Kirabaeva, K., Medina, L., Mircheva, B., & Weiss, J. (2019). *Explaining the shadow economy in Europe: Size, causes and policy options* (IMF working paper European Department, WP/19/278, pp. 1–29).
Kirchler, E. (2007). *The economic psychology of tax behavior*. Cambridge, UK.
Klapper, L., Lusardi, A., & Van Oudheusden, P. (2015). *Financial literacy around the world. World Bank*. World Bank.
Kogler, C., Bătrancea, L., Nichita, A., Pantya, J., & Belianin, A. (2013). Trust and power as determinants of tax compliance: Testing the assumptions of the slippery slope framework in Austria, Hungary, Romania and Russia. *Journal of Economic Psychology, 34*, 169–180.
Lagarde, C. (2017). *Addressing corruption with clarity*. Brookings Institution.
Leţia, A. A. (2014). *Investigation of business crime: Money laundering, corruption and tax fraud, theoretical and practical aspects*. Universal Juridic Publishing House.
Mara, S. (2021). Drivers of the shadow economy in European Union welfare states: A panel data analysis. *Economic Analysis and Policy, 72*, 309–325.
Masca, S. G., & Pitea, C. (2021, June 23). *Tax evasion within European Union – Trends and determinants*. https://ssrn.com/abstract=4153727
McGee, R. W. (1994). Is tax evasion unethical? *University of Kansas Law Review, 42*(2), 411–435.
McGee, R. W. (1997). *The ethics of tax evasion and trade protectionism from an Islamic perspective*. Available at SSRN 461397.

McGee, R. W. (1998a). The ethics of tax evasion in Islam. In R. W. McGee (Ed.), *The ethics of tax evasion* (pp. 214–219). The Dumont Institute for Public Policy Research. Summarized in McGee, R. W. The ethics of tax evasion: Summaries of 21 studies (March 12, 2022). https://doi.org/10.2139/ssrn.4056290

McGee, R. W. (1998b). When is tax evasion unethical? In R. W. McGee (Ed.), *The ethics of tax evasion* (pp. 5–35). The Dumont Institute for Public Policy Research. Summarized in McGee, R. W. The ethics of tax evasion: Summaries of 21 studies (March 12, 2022). https://doi.org/10.2139/ssrn.4056290

McGee, R. W. (1999). *Why people evade taxes in Armenia: A look at an ethical issue based on a summary of interviews*. https://ssrn.com/abstract=242568

McGee, R. W. (2006a). Three views on the ethics of tax evasion. *Journal of Business Ethics, 67*(1), 15–35.

McGee, R. W. (2006b). The ethics of tax evasion; a survey of Romanian business students and faculty. *The ICFAI Journal of Public Finance, 4*(2), 38–68. Summarized in McGee (2012k) at pp. 569–571.

McGee, R. W. (2006c). The ethics of tax evasion; a survey of Romanian business students and faculty. Reprinted in R. W. McGee & G. G. Preobragenskaya, *accounting and financial system reform in Eastern Europe and Asia* (pp. 299–334). Springer, 2006. Summarized in McGee (2012k) at pp. 569–571.

McGee, R. W. (Ed.). (2012a). *The ethics of tax evasion: Perspectives in theory and practice*. Springer. Summarized in McGee (2023d).

McGee, R. W. (2012b). Gender and the ethics of tax evasion; an empirical study of 82 countries. In R. W. McGee (Ed.), *The ethics of tax evasion: Perspectives in theory and practice* (pp. 415–439). Springer. Summarized in McGee (2023d).

McGee, R. W. (2012c). Age and the ethics of tax evasion. In R. W. McGee (Ed.), *The ethics of tax evasion: Perspectives in theory and practice* (pp. 441–449). Springer. Summarized in McGee (2023d).

McGee, R. W. (2012d). Education level and the ethics of tax evasion. In R. W. McGee (Ed.), *The ethics of tax evasion: Perspectives in theory and practice* (pp. 451–457). Springer. Summarized in McGee (2023d).

McGee, R. W. (2012e). Religious practice and the ethics of tax evasion. In R. W. McGee (Ed.), *The ethics of tax evasion: Perspectives in theory and practice* (pp. 459–469). Springer. Summarized in McGee (2023d).

McGee, R. W. (2012f). Religion and the ethics of tax evasion. In R. W. McGee (Ed.), *The ethics of tax evasion: Perspectives in theory and practice* (pp. 471–473). Springer. Summarized in McGee (2023d).

McGee, R. W. (2012g). Marital status and the ethics of tax evasion. In R. W. McGee (Ed.), *The ethics of tax evasion: Perspectives in theory and practice* (pp. 475–484). Springer. Summarized in McGee (2023d).

McGee, R. W. (2012h). The ethics of tax evasion in Islam: A comment. In R. W. McGee (Ed.), *The ethics of tax evasion: Perspectives in theory and practice* (pp. 159–165). Springer. Summarized in McGee (2023d).

McGee, R. W. (2012i). Christina views on the ethics of tax evasion. In R. W. McGee (Ed.), *The ethics of tax evasion: Perspectives in theory and practice* (pp. 201–210). Springer. Summarized in McGee (2023d).

McGee, R. W. (2012j). Income level and the ethics of tax evasion. In R. W. McGee (Ed.), *The ethics of tax evasion: Perspectives in theory and practice* (pp. 485–495). Springer. Summarized in McGee (2023d).

McGee, R. W. (2012k). Four views on the ethics of tax evasion. In R. W. McGee (Ed.), *The ethics of tax evasion: Perspectives in theory and practice* (pp. 3–33). Springer. Summarized in McGee (2023d).

McGee, R. W. (2012l). Annotated bibliography: 18 statement surveys. In R. W. McGee (Ed.), *The ethics of tax evasion: Perspectives in theory and practice* (pp. 499–598). Springer. An updated summary will appear in McGee & Shopovski (2023a).

McGee, R. W. (2012m). Christian views on the ethics of tax evasion. In R. W. McGee (Ed.), *The ethics of tax evasion: Perspectives in theory and practice* (pp. 201–210). Springer. Summarized in McGee (2023d).

McGee, R. W. (2022). *The ethics of tax evasion: Summaries of 21 studies* (Working paper). https://doi.org/10.13140/RG.2.2.12914.79049. Note: A slightly different version of this paper will appear in McGee, R. W., & Shopovski, J. (Eds.). (2023). *The ethics of tax evasion, volume 2: New perspectives in theory and practice*. Springer, forthcoming.

McGee, R. W. (2023a). The ethics of bribery: Summaries of 24 studies. In R. W. McGee & S. Benk (Eds.), *The ethics of bribery: Theoretical and empirical studies*. Springer, forthcoming.

McGee, R. W. (2023b). The ethics of bribery: Summaries of 28 studies. In R. W. McGee & S. Benk (Eds.), *The ethics of bribery: Theoretical and empirical studies*. Springer, forthcoming.

McGee, R. W. (2023c). The Rothbard-Block theory of bribery. In R. W. McGee & S. Benk (Eds.), *The ethics of bribery: Theoretical and empirical studies*. Springer, forthcoming.

McGee, R. W. (2023d). *The ethics of tax evasion: Summaries of 35 studies* (Working paper).

McGee, R. W., & Benk, S. (2023a). Confidence in government and attitudes toward bribery: Summaries of 15 studies. In R. W. McGee & S. Benk (Eds.), *The ethics of bribery: Theoretical and empirical studies*. Springer, forthcoming.

McGee, R. W., & Benk, S. (2023b). Confidence in the police and attitudes toward bribery: Summaries of 6 studies. In R. W. McGee & S. Benk (Eds.), *The ethics of bribery: Theoretical and empirical studies*. Springer, forthcoming.

McGee, R. W., & Benk, S. (2023c). Confidence in the justice system and attitudes toward bribery: Summaries of 15 studies. In R. W. McGee & S. Benk (Eds.), *The ethics of bribery: Theoretical and empirical studies*. Springer, forthcoming.

McGee, R. W., & Benk, S. (2023d). Political viewpoint and attitudes toward bribery: Summaries of 16 studies. In R. W. McGee & S. Benk (Eds.), *The ethics of bribery: Theoretical and empirical studies*. Springer, forthcoming.

McGee, R. W., & Benk, S. (Eds.). (2023e). *The ethics of bribery: Theoretical and empirical studies*. Springer.

McGee, R. W., & Benk, S. (Eds.). (2023f). *The ethics of bribery, Vol. 2: Country studies*. Springer.

McGee, R. W., & Benk, S. (2023g). Gender and attitudes toward bribery: Summaries of 31 studies. In R. W. McGee & S. Benk (Eds.), *The ethics of bribery: Theoretical and empirical studies*. Springer, forthcoming.

McGee, R. W., & Benk, S. (2023h). Age and attitudes toward bribery: Summaries of 26 studies. In R. W. McGee & S. Benk (Eds.), *The ethics of bribery: Theoretical and empirical studies*. Springer, forthcoming.

McGee, R. W., & Benk, S. (2023i). Education level and attitudes toward bribery: Summaries of 23 studies. In R. W. McGee & S. Benk (Eds.), *The ethics of bribery: Theoretical and empirical studies*. Springer, forthcoming.

McGee, R. W., & Benk, S. (2023j). Income level and attitudes toward bribery: Summaries of 18 studies. In R. W. McGee & S. Benk (Eds.), *The ethics of bribery: Theoretical and empirical studies*. Springer, forthcoming.

McGee, R. W., & Benk, S. (2023k). Social class and attitudes toward bribery: Summaries of 20 studies. In R. W. McGee & S. Benk (Eds.), *The ethics of bribery: Theoretical and empirical studies*. Springer, forthcoming.

McGee, R. W., & Benk, S. (2023l). Ethnicity and attitudes toward bribery: Summaries of 8 studies. In R. W. McGee & S. Benk (Eds.), *The ethics of bribery: Theoretical and empirical studies*. Springer, forthcoming.

McGee, R. W., & Benk, S. (2023m). Marital status and attitudes toward bribery: Summaries of 20 studies. In R. W. McGee & S. Benk (Eds.), *The ethics of bribery: Theoretical and empirical studies*. Springer, forthcoming.

McGee, R. W., & Benk, S. (2023n). Employment status and attitudes toward bribery: Summaries of 17 studies. In R. W. McGee & S. Benk (Eds.), *The ethics of bribery: Theoretical and empirical studies*. Springer, forthcoming.

McGee, R. W., & Benk, S. (2023o). Sector of employment and attitudes toward bribery: Summaries of 14 studies. In R. W. McGee & S. Benk (Eds.), *The ethics of bribery: Theoretical and empirical studies*. Springer, forthcoming.

McGee, R. W., & Benk, S. (2023p). Religious denomination and attitudes toward bribery: Summaries of 19 studies. In R. W. McGee & S. Benk (Eds.), *The ethics of bribery: Theoretical and empirical studies*. Springer, forthcoming.

McGee, R. W., & Benk, S. (2023q). Religiosity and attitudes toward bribery: Summaries of 12 studies. In R. W. McGee & S. Benk (Eds.), *The ethics of bribery: Theoretical and empirical studies*. Springer, forthcoming.

McGee, R. W., & Benk, S. (2023r). Happiness and attitudes toward bribery: Summaries of 19 studies. In R. W. McGee & S. Benk (Eds.), *The ethics of bribery: Theoretical and empirical studies*. Springer, forthcoming.

McGee, R. W., & Benk, S. (2023s). Health and attitudes toward bribery: Summaries of 11 studies. In R. W. McGee & S. Benk (Eds.), *The ethics of bribery: Theoretical and empirical studies*. Springer, forthcoming.

McGee, R. W., & Benk, S. (2023t). Size of town and attitudes toward bribery: Summaries of 10 studies. In R. W. McGee & S. Benk (Eds.), *The ethics of bribery: Theoretical and empirical studies*. Springer, forthcoming.

McGee, R. W., & Benk, S. (2023u). Gender and attitudes toward bribery. In R. W. McGee & S. Benk (Eds.), *The ethics of bribery: Theoretical and empirical studies*. Springer, forthcoming.

McGee, R. W., & Benk, S. (2023v). Age and attitudes toward bribery. In R. W. McGee & S. Benk (Eds.), *The ethics of bribery: Theoretical and empirical studies*. Springer, forthcoming.

McGee, R. W., & Benk, S. (2023w). Education level and attitudes toward bribery. In R. W. McGee & S. Benk (Eds.), *The ethics of bribery: Theoretical and empirical studies*. Springer, forthcoming.

McGee, R. W., & Benk, S. (2023x). Income level and attitudes toward bribery. In R. W. McGee & S. Benk (Eds.), *The ethics of bribery: Theoretical and empirical studies*. Springer, forthcoming.

McGee, R. W., & Benk, S. (2023y). Social class and attitudes toward bribery. In R. W. McGee & S. Benk (Eds.), *The ethics of bribery: Theoretical and empirical studies*. Springer, forthcoming.

McGee, R. W., & Block, W. E. (2023). Helping hand v. Greedy hand bribery. In R. W. McGee & S. Benk (Eds.), *The ethics of bribery: Theoretical and empirical studies*. Springer, forthcoming.

McGee, R. W., & Cohn, G. M. (2006, September). Jewish perspectives on the ethics of tax evasion (Andreas School of Business Working Paper). Barry University. https://doi.org/10.2139/ssrn.929027

McGee, R. W., & Cohn, G. M. (2008). Jewish perspectives on the ethics of tax evasion. *Journal of Legal, Ethical and Regulatory Issues, 11*(2), 1–32.

McGee, R. W., & Guadron, M. (2023). Do urban dwellers view bribery differently than rural dwellers? An empirical study of views in 76 countries. In R. W. McGee & S. Benk (Eds.), *The ethics of bribery: Theoretical and empirical studies*. Springer, forthcoming.

McGee, R. W., & Petrides, Y. (2023a). How risky is it to give or receive a bribe? A ranking of 56 countries. In R. W. McGee & S. Benk (Eds.), *The ethics of bribery: Theoretical and empirical studies*. Springer, forthcoming.

McGee, R. W., & Petrides, Y. (2023b). Are some forms of bribery more serious than others? In R. W. McGee & S. Benk (Eds.), *The ethics of bribery: Theoretical and empirical studies*. Springer, forthcoming.

McGee, R. W., & Ross, A. (2014). Education level and ethical attitude toward tax evasion: A six-country study. https://doi.org/10.2139/ssrn.2410582

McGee, R. W., & Rossi, M. J. (2006). The ethics of tax evasion: A survey of law and business students in Argentina. https://doi.org/10.2139/ssrn.875892

McGee, R. W., & Shopovski, J. (Eds.). (2023a). *The ethics of tax evasion, volume 2: New perspectives in theory and practice*. Springer, forthcoming.

McGee, R. W., & Shopovski, J. (Eds.). (2023b). *The ethics of tax evasion: Country studies*. Springer, forthcoming.

McGee, R. W., & Smith, S. R. (2012). Ethics, tax evasion, and religion: A survey of opinion of members of the Church of Jesus Christ of latter-day saints. In R. W. McGee (Ed.), *The ethics of tax evasion: Perspectives in theory and practice* (pp. 211–226). Springer. Summarized in McGee (2023d).

McGee, R. W., & Tyler, M. (2006). Tax evasion and ethics: A demographic study of 33 countries. https://doi.org/10.2139/ssrn.940505

McGee, R. W., & Zhou, E. (2023). How prevalent is bribery? A ranking of 52 countries. In R. W. McGee & S. Benk (Eds.), *The ethics of bribery: Theoretical and empirical studies*. Springer, forthcoming.

McGee, R. W., Nickerson, I., & Fees, W. (2006). German and American opinion on the ethics of tax evasion. In *Allied Academies international conference. Academy of legal, ethical and regulatory issues. Proceedings* (Vol. 10, no. 2, p. 31). https://doi.org/10.2139/ssrn.936743

McGee, R. W., Benk, S., & Budak, T. (2023a). Muslim attitudes toward bribery. In R. W. McGee & S. Benk (Eds.), *The ethics of bribery: Theoretical and empirical studies*. Springer, forthcoming.

McGee, R. W., Benk, S., & Pardisi, A. (2023b). Has the attitude toward bribery changed over time? A longitudinal study of 75 countries. In R. W. McGee & S. Benk (Eds.), *The ethics of bribery, volume 2: Country studies*. Springer, forthcoming.

McGee, R. W., Benk, S., & Yüzbaşı, B. (2023c). Religious attitudes toward bribery: A comparative study. In R. W. McGee & S. Benk (Eds.), *The ethics of bribery: Theoretical and empirical studies*. Springer, forthcoming.

McGee, R. W., Benk, S., & Yüzbaşı, B. (2023d). Atheist attitudes toward bribery. In R. W. McGee & S. Benk (Eds.), *The ethics of bribery: Theoretical and empirical studies*. Springer, forthcoming.

McGee, R. W., Benk, S., & Yüzbaşı, B. (2023e). Buddhist attitudes toward bribery. In R. W. McGee & S. Benk (Eds.), *The ethics of bribery: Theoretical and empirical studies*. Springer, forthcoming.

McGee, R. W., Benk, S., & Yüzbaşı, B. (2023f). Christian attitudes toward bribery. In R. W. McGee & S. Benk (Eds.), *The ethics of bribery: Theoretical and empirical studies*. Springer, forthcoming.

McGee, R. W., Benk, S., & Yüzbaşı, B. (2023g). Hindu attitudes toward bribery. In R. W. McGee & S. Benk (Eds.), *The ethics of bribery: Theoretical and empirical studies*. Springer, forthcoming.

McGee, R. W., Benk, S., & Yüzbaşı, B. (2023h). Jewish attitudes toward bribery. In R. W. McGee & S. Benk (Eds.), *The ethics of bribery: Theoretical and empirical studies*. Springer, forthcoming.

Medina, L., & Schneider, F. (2018). *Shadow economies around the world: What did we learn over the last 20 years?* (International Monetary Fund Working Paper, WP/18/17).

Medina, L., & Schneider, F. (2019). *Shedding light on the shadow economy: A global database and the interaction with the official one*. Available at SSRN 3502028.

Merton, R. K. (1968). *Social theory and social structure*. Free Press, Enlarged Ed edition.

Murtuza, A., & Ghazanfar, S. M. (1998). Taxation as a form of worship: Exploring the nature of zakat. In R. W. McGee (Ed.), *The ethics of tax evasion* (pp. 190–212). The Dumont Institute for Public Policy Research. Summarized in McGee, R. W. The ethics of tax evasion: Summaries of 21 studies (March 12, 2022). https://doi.org/10.2139/ssrn.4056290

Oliva, R. R. (1998). The schism between tax practitioners' ethical and legal obligations: Recommendations for the fusion of law and ethics. In R. W. McGee (Ed.), *The ethics of tax evasion* (pp. 350–371). The Dumont Institute for Public Policy Research. Summarized in McGee, R. W. The ethics of tax evasion: Summaries of 21 studies (March 12, 2022). https://doi.org/10.2139/ssrn.4056290

Pennock, R. T. (1998). Death and taxes: On the justice of conscientious war tax resistance. In R. W. McGee (Ed.), *The ethics of tax evasion* (pp. 124–142). The Dumont Institute for Public

Policy Research. Summarized in McGee, R. W. The ethics of tax evasion: Summaries of 21 studies (March 12, 2022). https://doi.org/10.2139/ssrn.4056290

Preobragenskaya, G. G., & McGee, R. W. (2016). A demographic study of Russian attitudes toward tax evasion. *Journal of Accounting, Ethics & Public Policy, 17*(1), 137–207 http://ssrn.com/abstract=2745666

Queloz, N. (2002). Criminalité économique et criminalité organisée. *L'Économie politique, 3*(15), 58–67.

Remeikiene, R., Gaspareniene, L., & Schneider, F. (2017). The definition of digital shadow economy. *Technological and Economic Development of Economy, 24*(2), 1–22.

Satalkina, L., & Steiner, G. (2020). Digital entrepreneurship and its role in innovation systems: A systematic literature review as a basis for future research avenues for sustainable transitions. *Sustainability, 12*(7), 2764.

Schansberg, D. E. (1998). The ethics of tax evasion within biblical Christianity: Are there limits to "rendering unto Caesar?" In R. W. McGee (Ed.), *The ethics of tax evasion* (pp. 144–157). The Dumont Institute for Public Policy Research. Summarized in McGee, R. W. The ethics of tax evasion: Summaries of 21 studies (March 12, 2022). https://doi.org/10.2139/ssrn.4056290

Scheau, M.C. (2018). Criminalitatea informatica privind transferurile financiare., Editura Economica Bucuresti.

Schneider, F., & Buehn, A. (2016). *Estimating the size of the shadow economy: Methods, problems and open questions* (IZA discussion paper no. 9820). IZA

Schneider, F. H., & Klinglmair, R. (2004). *Shadow economies around the world: What do we know?* (Working paper no. 0403) Universität Linz.

Smith, S. R., & Kimball, K. C. (1998). Tax evasion and ethics: A perspective from members of the Church of Jesus Christ of latter-day saints. In R. W. McGee (Ed.), *The ethics of tax evasion* (pp. 220–229). The Dumont Institute for Public Policy Research. Summarized in McGee, R. W. The ethics of tax evasion: Summaries of 21 studies (March 12, 2022). https://doi.org/10.2139/ssrn.4056290

Tamari, M. (1998). Ethical issues in tax evasion: A Jewish perspective. In R. W. McGee (Ed.), *The ethics of tax evasion* (pp. 168–178). The Dumont Institute for Public Policy Research. Summarized in McGee, R. W., The ethics of tax evasion: Summaries of 21 studies (March 12, 2022). https://doi.org/10.2139/ssrn.4056290

Torgler, B. (2002). *The economic analysis of 'creative' compliance* (WWZ-discussion paper). WWZ.

Torgler, B. (2004). Tax morale in Asian countries. *Journal of Asian Economics, 15*, 237–266.

Torgler, B., & Schneider, F. (2009). The impact of tax morale and institutional quality on the shadow economy. *Journal of Economic Psychology, 30*(3), 228–245.

Transparency International. (2021). *Corruption Perception Index 2021.*

Williams, C. C. (2020). Tackling informal entrepreneurship in East-Central Europe: From a deterrence to preventative approach. *Journal of Developmental Entrepreneurship, 25*(4), 1–20.

Williams, C. C., & Shahid, M. S. (2016). Informal entrepreneurship and institutional theory: Explaining the varying degrees of (in)formalization of entrepreneurs in Pakistan. *Entrepreneurship & Regional Development, 28*(1–2), 1–25.

Yew, B. K., Milanov, V. B., & McGee, R. W. (2015). An analysis of individual tax morale for Russia: Before and after flat tax reform. *International Business Research, 8*(1), 60–80. http://ssrn.com/abstract=2544702

MIX
Papier aus verantwortungsvollen Quellen
Paper from responsible sources
FSC® C105338

If you have any concerns about our products,
you can contact us on
ProductSafety@springernature.com

In case Publisher is established outside the EU,
the EU authorized representative is:
Springer Nature Customer Service Center GmbH
Europaplatz 3, 69115 Heidelberg, Germany

Printed by Libri Plureos GmbH
in Hamburg, Germany